NELLA LAST IN THE 1950s

'In this next volume of Nella's diary we gain further insight
into the life of this hard working, determinedly cheerful
woman, and the post war society that was changing around her'
Gilda O'Neill, author of *Secrets of the Heart*

'Nella Last's diaries give a fascinating and detailed account
of life in the early 1950s. The prose is such a delight to read
– lively, entertaining, observational and vividly realised'
Gervase Phinn, author of *Road to the Dales*

Robert Malcolmson is Professor Emeritus of history at Queen's
University, Kingston, Canada. **Patricia Malcolmson** is a
historian and a former executive in the Ontario public service.
They live in Cobourg, Ontario and Nelson, British Columbia.

The Mass Observation Archive at the University of Sussex
holds the papers of the British social research organisation
Mass Observation. The papers from the original phase cover
the years 1937 until the early 1950s and provide an especially
rich historical resource on civilian life during the Second World
War. New collections rel⸻   in
the 20th an⸻   l
collection si⸻   970.

ALSO AVAILABLE

NELLA LAST'S WAR:
The Second World War diaries of *Housewife, 49*
'I relished it ... her personality is so powerful ... There are so many things to admire about her' Margaret Forster

NELLA LAST'S PEACE:
The post-war diaries of *Housewife, 49*
'Tender, intimate, heartbreaking and witty – it grants us the privilege of knowing a stranger's heart' A. L. Kennedy

NELLA LAST IN THE 1950s

Further diaries of *Housewife, 49*

Edited by
PATRICIA AND ROBERT MALCOLMSON

P
PROFILE BOOKS

Published in Great Britain in 2010 by
PROFILE BOOKS LTD
3A Exmouth House
Pine Street
Exmouth Market
London EC1R 0JH
www.profilebooks.com

10 9 8 7 6 5 4 3 2 1

Typeset in Garamond 3 by MacGuru Ltd
info@macguru.org.uk
Printed and bound in Great Britain by
CPI Bookmarque Ltd, Croydon, Surrey

A CIP catalogue record for this book is available from the British Library.

ISBN 978 1 84668 350 3
eISBN 978 184765 286 7

Mixed Sources
Product group from well-managed
forests and other controlled sources
www.fsc.org Cert no. TT-COC-002227
© 1996 Forest Stewardship Council

This book is printed on FSC certified paper

CONTENTS

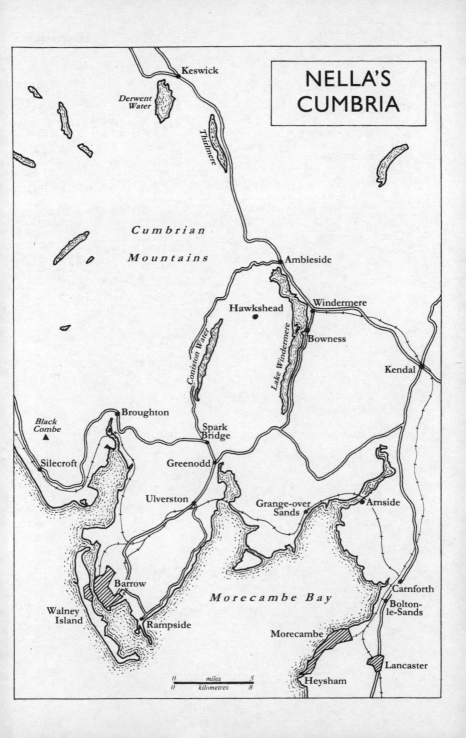

NELLA'S CUMBRIA

Keswick
Derwent Water
Thirlmere

Cumbrian Mountains

Ambleside
Windermere
Hawkshead
Bowness
Coniston Water
Lake Windermere
Kendal

Broughton
Black Combe
Spark Bridge
Silecroft
Greenodd
Ulverston
Grange-over-Sands
Arnside

Barrow
Walney Island
Rampside
Morecambe Bay
Carnforth
Bolton-le-Sands
Morecambe
Lancaster
Heysham

0   miles   5
0   kilometres   8

INTRODUCTION

'I can never understand how the scribbles of such an ordinary person, leading a shut-in, dull life, can possibly have value.'

Nella Last wrote the words above in her diary on 2 September 1949. Tens of thousands of people have now read and enjoyed some of her diaries, available in two edited books.* Many have also seen the television film inspired by her wartime diaries, *Housewife, 49*, starring Victoria Wood, which drew attention to the remarkable efforts of this previously largely unknown writer. Perhaps some day someone will be able to claim to have read all that she wrote for Mass Observation; we estimate it to be in the vicinity of ten million words – possibly more – which must make it one of the longest in the English language. And she didn't start it until she was forty-nine years old.

'When I was a girl at school and was asked what I wanted to be,' Nella Last wrote on 16 October 1952, 'I used to say "a writer" – but meant of books!' She was undeniably assiduous in her self-imposed task of writing, virtually daily, and often at great length – 1,000 words, 1,500 words, occasionally 2,000 words in a day – for over a quarter of a century. Without doubt, she was a tireless, dedicated writer, a lover of words. Usually, except on those rare occasions when she was away from home, she wrote at night, in bed (though some entries were written earlier in the

---

Nella Last's War: The Second World War Diaries of 'Housewife, 49' (Profile Books, 2006; first published 1981); and *Nella Last's Peace: The Post-War Diaries of 'Housewife, 49'* (Profile Books, 2008).

evening or even late afternoon) – she and her husband had separate bedrooms* – and her practice was to summarise the events
and routines of the day, starting with how she felt when she woke
up and concluding with how she was feeling or what she was
thinking as she was about to turn out her light. In some entries
she added commentary or ruminations or personal reminiscences
– in other words, she allowed her mind and pen to wander. She
stuck resolutely with her writing even though none of it was
published during her lifetime (except for a few passages from her
wartime diaries that were printed anonymously in Mass Observation's own books), and she only gave up writing shortly before
her death in 1968.

Nella admired creativity, even as she credited herself with pos-
sessing little of it. 'It must be grand to be gifted,' she wrote on
29 September 1950, 'to be able to create a picture or piece of
carving or sculpture, above all write a novel or play.' There was a
part of her that wanted to escape the mundane, the necessities of
life, the narrowness of routine and convention in rather out-of-
the-way Barrow-in-Furness, a shipyard town, population around
67,500, which was then in Lancashire and is now in Cumbria.**
And while in these years she never moved from Barrow physically
– though, since she did live close to the Lake District, day trips
there, usually to Coniston Water or Lake Windermere, were a

---

*'I've asked if he wouldn't feel happier if we slept together,' Nella wrote of her
husband on 10 June 1950, 'but he said he "liked to be free to toss and turn,
without disturbing you", and I didn't argue about it. To shut my bedroom door
sometimes and begin to write or read quietly *is* a privilege when things haven't
gone smoothly in the day.'
**Nella once remarked on the city's distinctive character. 'I think in Barrow, by
its isolation on the map, we tend to be neither North or South, just ourselves' (17
February 1949).

great tonic for her – her ability to write allowed her to give voice
to her experiences in Barrow and turn them and her thoughts
about living into often memorable prose. On a couple of occasions she seemed to think of this writing as the equivalent of
books. 'I feel sometimes', she wrote on 17 April 1951, 'I must
have written all the books I would have liked to write – if I'd been
clever enough – in the shape of letters and diaries for M-O.' Some
months later, on 16 October 1952, she said that 'I often wonder
how many long *long* novels in words I've written, the hundreds
of letters. Come to think of it, my diaries alone would count
up to a few books in the years since 1939.' (Her letters, none of
which is known to survive, were written mainly to her two sons,
Arthur and Cliff, born in 1913 and 1918 respectively, after they
left home in the 1930s.)

Nella and her husband, Will, who had his own small joinery
business, had moved into their semi-detached house on a new
estate 'on the outskirts of town' in 1936, and by the early 1950s
the population of Ilkley Road itself – the Lasts lived at number
9 – was (in Nella's eyes) ageing. 'Most of us are elderly or old
people,' she wrote, 'none given to standing talking at the front.
Our gossiping is always done over the back fence, when sweeping,
hanging out mats or clothes.' The locality was 'not the friendly
all-together type of district where anything communal goes on.
We pass the time of day or walk up from the bus with neighbours, and that's all' (6 June 1953). There were few children near
by, and those who make appearances in the diary are commonly
visiting or talked-about grandchildren.

The unifying force in a diary is usually the mind of the diarist
him- or herself; the period and occurrences written about may or
may not have noticeable unity. *Nella Last's War* is framed by the
realities of the Second World War. It starts when the war starts

and ends when it ends, and thus it benefits from this chrono-logical clarity. While *Nella Last's Peace* does not have this sort of obvious thematic coherence, it does convey a lot about the after-the-war atmosphere and common experiences of English life from the middle of 1945: transitions (many of them painful) from war to peace; comparisons between wartime and peacetime states of mind; letdowns and disappointments; the many different ways in which people hoped to move on (or feared moving on); and the drabness and austerity of post-war life in a nearly bankrupt nation. In *Nella Last in the 1950s* there is a kaleidoscope of subject matter and sentiment – anxiety about the possibility of another war, changes in popular culture, new technologies, 'modernising' trends – and this variety has informed the choices we have made in selecting what to print. Our selections represent around 10 per cent of the original diary for January 1950 to July 1952, though the percentage varies significantly from chapter to chapter (her writing from 1950, for example, is presented much more fully than her writing from 1952). While the central reality of Nella Last's diary is that it records a life unfolding in the ongoing present, without the wisdom of hindsight, it also testifies to changes in society – the intimate world of family and friends as well as the larger world of neighbourhood, city and nation.

Nella Last's diary is rich in detail and commentary – and decidedly unpredictable. It is full of surprises. As she regularly observed herself and others, new subjects kept cropping up, along with new perspectives, which arose from various circumstances and situations. Often she was at home, usually alone with her husband and cats; at other times she was out and about, notic-ing public incidents and participating in or overhearing conver-sations. Sometimes her writing is descriptive, at other times it is judgemental or reflective. Her mood was sometimes edgy or dark and brooding, at other times buoyant or at least intense – and this is the writing that our selections highlight. Her subject matter constantly changes, for her life and the lives of those she knew changed, and she frequently had novel observations to report, new stories to relate, fixed opinions to reconsider or expand on, endings or beginnings that she thought were worth writing about. In some sense her diary was, for her, a journey of everyday discovery and reflection; and her pen – which, when little was happening, might resort to recording the minutiae of meals, the weather, shopping, prices and bodily complaints – was always ready to find words for whatever was out of the ordinary, or perhaps ordinary but waiting to be described in an attractive, even captivating, way.

These are the literary and intellectual strengths that we have tried to highlight in this edition. Their presence (or absence) during any period of time is the main determinant of the fullness (or sparseness) of our selections. Some periods of her writing are richer than others, and some days in her life offered more in the way of incident and stimulus than others. Virtually no one who wrote at such length almost every day, whether the day was eventful or uneventful, lively or dreary, could produce prose of sustained high quality. The job of her editors, we believe, is (in part) to approach her diary as raw material from which an attractive book can be fashioned. The more technical aspects of our editorial practice, which are similar to those followed in *Nella Last's Peace*, are summarised in an appendix. The symbol † indicates a word defined or a proper name identified in the glossary (pp. 280–83).

NELLA LAST'S FAMILY, FRIENDS, NEIGHBOURS AND ASSOCIATES

Arthur	*Nella's elder son*
Arthur (Procter)	*A teacher; husband of Margaret*
Atkinson, Mr and Mrs	*Next-door neighbours*
Christopher	*Nella's younger grandson*
Cliff	*Nella's younger son; lives in Australia*
Dearie	*Nella herself (as she was known by family)*
Diss, Mrs	*Head of the local Women's Voluntary Services (WVS)*
Edith (Last)	*Arthur's wife*
Flo	*Sister of Nella's husband*
George (Holme)	*Neighbour; husband of Jessie*
Gilbert	*Apprentice in joinery shop*
Gran	*Deceased maternal grandmother; a Rawlinson*
Harry	*Brother of Nella's husband*
Helm, Mr and Mrs	*Neighbours in the house attached*
Higham, Mrs	*Friend*
Howson, Mrs	*Friend and neighbour*
Jessie	*Neighbour; wife of George*
Joe	*Cousin of Aunt Sarah; lives with her*
Jones, Mrs	*Neighbour; mentally ill*
Kath	*Daughter of George and Jessie*
Ken	*A nephew*

Leo	*Nephew of Mrs Howson; lives with her, his Aunt Mary and Mrs Stable, his grandmother*
Margaret	*The Atkinsons' younger daughter; now married*
Mary (Stable)	*Sister of Mrs Howson; lives with her*
Miller, Dr	*Family physician*
Mother	*Mother-in-law*
Murphy	*Cat*
Newall, Mrs	*Paid part-time secretary of the WVS*
Norah (Redhead)	*The Atkinsons' elder daughter*
Peter	*Nella's elder grandson*
Salisbury, Mrs	*Cleaning helper*
Sarah, Aunt	*Sister of Nella's late mother*
Shan We	*Siamese cat*
Sheila (Diss)	*Daughter-in-law of Mrs Diss*
Stable, Mrs	*Mother of Mrs Howson and Mary Stable; lives with them*
Steve	*Husband of Mrs Howson*
Wadsworth, Dr	*Psychiatrist*
Will	*Nella's husband*
Willan, Miss	*Associate in the WVS*

CHAPTER ONE

TROUBLES AND TRIALS

January–February 1950

'Such a heavy dull day,' Nella wrote on 31 December 1949, 'with the feeling in the air that the old year was actually dying. … Ever since I can remember I had a sadness on me on New Year's Eve. Cliff always teased me about my "Hogmanay Blues".' The next day, the first of the New Year, she and Will visited Aunt Sarah and Sarah's cousin Joe in Spark Bridge and then returned home to spend the evening alone.

Sunday, 1 January. The fire soon blazed when poked. I had banked† it with slack† and coal dust dampened, and I made tea, meat sandwiches (tinned), crushed pineapple and whipped cream, Xmas cakes and mince pies. I wished there had been someone in to share, as we sat by the fire and I stitched at my crazy patchwork. I felt the 'blues' I'd missed last night enfold me like a mist, helped no doubt by an article in an American magazine the Atkinsons sent in, speaking of war as *inevitable* after 1951, and hinting at atomic bombs being puerile when compared to the germ bombs Russia was concentrating on. All my fears and conjectures of before this last one rushed over me. I felt if I turned suddenly I'd see some of Arthur's friends' faces as they argued against such a thing as 'too inhuman' etc. I thought of the unrest of today, the state of affairs in Egypt, hoping if King Farouk did lose his throne for 'romance', it had as little effect as it had when it happened in England.* I felt, as I thought of one upset or worry, it brought its fellows along. I heard my husband ask me something and looked up to see him waiting for an answer. He was 'thinking how neglected we have let your parents' grave get – we will have to go up and clean the marble stone as soon as the weather gets better'. I felt it was the limit, and tuned in to *Palm Court*, which he had earlier refused as his head ached, and then we listened to the first instalment of *The Virginians* – sounds promising.

Tuesday, 3 January. Though it still rained heavily I persuaded my husband to go to the pictures to see *The Hasty Heart. Such* a well acted picture. It's a long time since we have enjoyed a picture so much. It had stopped raining, we walked home, and I soon had the fire blazing warmly, and did cheese and toast. Before we settled down, Mrs Howson and Steve came in, with the air of staying the evening. I *did* feel so glad. Then there was a ring, and an old school friend of Cliff's came in, one I'd never met when Cliff was at home. He is a 'fridge' engineer on a line of steamers that take frozen meat from Australia and America and bring it to England, and while in Adelaide had seen Cliff's exhibition posters the week after it had closed, and read the notices of the 'clever English sculptor', and tried to track Cliff down in Melbourne without success, so called for his address so as to find him next trip. We had a real merry party, laughing and joking. Steve and he soon got yarning. I opened a tin of Australian chopped ham, and there was rum butter, chocolate biscuits and Xmas cake, and

---

*She is referring to the abdication of the throne by Edward VIII in 1936 in order to marry Mrs Wallis Simpson. King Farouk of Egypt (b. 1920, king from 1936) was notably corrupt and incompetent, and was overthrown in 1952.

the table looked like a real party, and the cats were as delighted as I was – they *are* nice animals – to see them happily being 'one of us'. Their heads turning as if listening and enjoying everything was comical. Alan was so taken with Shan We, and I begged him to tell Cliff as much as he could of my little cats' funny ways. Shan We blinked understandingly and shared tit bits of chopped ham offered. Alan had to rush off to catch the last bus to take him to Walney but is coming again if he can before he rejoins his ship. Steve said, 'Well, we didn't think we were coming to a party when we came across. It *has* been a jolly evening.' I looked at my husband, sitting so quiet, who had refused even to sit at the supper table or eat anything in case it made him have a wakeful night, and sighed. But I *was* so grateful for my happy evening. I feel sometimes as if my face is ceasing to fit me properly, as if it creaks if I laugh. It's not good to get into a deep rut of passive acceptance of sickness of any kind, yet it is so difficult at times.

Wednesday, 4 January. Mrs Salisbury came earlier and didn't stay for lunch. Her eldest boy has started at the Co-op dairies, helping deliver milk – at 34s 6d a week! It's only a put-on till he can find somewhere to serve his time as a joiner or woodworker of some kind, but it means he is in mid-day and needs a hot meal. We worked busily, only stopping for a cup of tea and biscuits at 10.30, and I was glad really she wasn't staying for lunch, when the butcher didn't come before lunch, for we managed with a slice of chopped ham fried with an egg. I heated tinned tomato soup and added milk, cooked cabbage and potatoes and heated some raspberry blancmange left from yesterday for my husband. I had a cup of tea.

It was such a nice afternoon and we went out early and got as far as Bowness. Shafts of sunlight fell on fell and hill like magic fingers, making golden patches on the greyness when lighting up faded bracken. Little white-capped waves slapped on the shore, and there was a keenness in the air which hinted at snow on high ground. I got some locally made butter toffee, and met an old friend who lives at Greenodd, and she said she did all shopping in Bowness, registered there, and when the weather was bad got her groceries put on the bus. When I went in the front door I found my Co-op quarterly dividend cheque had come. Coal and milk, cat biscuits and compost maker are about all I get generally, making a total of about £6 I spend each quarter. Lately I've often had to count and recount my housekeeping, feeling sometimes I *must* have lost 10 shillings. There's been Allenburys Diet,[†] Sanatogen[†], Sloan's Liniment, Disprins[†], Frugoclone* bought every week, or when needed, and I've got into the habit of calling in the Co-op chemist's as it's on my way home from the Library. I felt 'No wonder I've felt so hard up at times' when I saw I'd spent over £13 this quarter, though that included extra milk – I always get two pints a day left lately.

I fixed some fillets of plaice and we had just finished tea when the phone rang, and it was long distance. It was Robert Haines, to say he would come this weekend if convenient – arrive off the mid-day train from Euston, which gets into Barrow about 6.40 – and leave for Leeds on Monday afternoon. I felt so happy he could come. I've only to change the beds – he can have mine and I'll make the small one up in the little front room. All is aired. I'll only need to bake on Friday and we plan to take him out to The Heanes for lunch Saturday if it is fine, and somewhere else on Sunday so he can get a glimpse of the Lakes. I put down the receiver and turned away, and then realised we wouldn't recognise

---

*We have not succeeded in identifying this (apparent) medication or tonic.

each other unless he sees some resemblance to Cliff – or in odd snaps! I've never even seen a photo with clear enough features; any I have had have been taken at a distance. As I sat down I thought suddenly and with amusement of the time I went to meet a girl Arthur knew – Agnes Schofield from Blackpool. Off my mind galloped on memory lane. I wonder where she is, if still a doctor's secretary at the dental clinic, still so dependent on advice from outsiders, always searching for someone 'to love me'. If we could only have as fair and sweet a day – or days – at the weekend as we have had today. Robert could have a nice look round, though I'd have really liked to give him an extra good time. If he doesn't have to return to Australia till March, he may possibly be able to come again. Train fares 'off his schedule', though, might be expensive. I wonder if his grant is a good one from the British Council of Arts.

Friday, 6 January. The train was only five minutes late, and I stood by the exit wondering which of the men walking alone from the train towards me would be Robert. From the end, as the crowd thinned, a slight, rather diffident looking man approached me and with a slight stammer said, 'I hope you have not been waiting long in the cold, Mrs Last', as if we had met before! Robert is 35 – odd how Cliff generally has friends about five years older. I wonder if it's the case of the difference in his and Arthur's age. Could be, I suppose. He is extremely likeable and walked round touching or looking at different things, saying, 'Cliff so often thinks of home and you. It's his deepest concern at times when he feels a bit down that he cannot pop in and see you, and talk things over. You know I think the chief attraction of Cliff is his love of discussing every and anything. He is so interested in life from every angle.' I sighed as I thought, 'No one knows better than I do that attraction possessed by my two sons.' I'm thankful little Peter shows signs of that same interest. All this 'strong silent men' talk leaves me cold. Any I've met have been too dumb – or too short of interest in things – to be anything else.

During the weekend, Nella and Will showed Robert around the Lake District – Kendal, Windermere, Bowness, Ambleside, Hawkshead and Coniston Water. Late on Sunday afternoon they were back at 9 Ilkley Road.

Sunday, 8 January. Robert fits in so well he might be one of the family. He so loves to talk, as we discussed conscientious objectors, Russians, Americans – whom he seems to detest, saying most Australians do! – flying saucers, the Australian way of life, the possibility of him living in London, even washing socks to keep them from shrinking – and things like central heating crept in. The day seemed to fly. My husband said it was just like when Arthur used to come home weekends! We settled by the fire, looking over old photos of Cliff and Arthur and a pile of odd snaps and cuttings of the war I'd kept, though tonight I did have a clear-out, feeling many more are for scrapping. I gazed in wonder and a little sadness at some of the earlier war snaps of myself, feeling that these last ten years have drained vitality and humour. Each I handled seemed to bring a train of memories of different little incidents and events and people I'd worked so happily with. Robert had a few chuckles over snaps. He has a few leg pulls for Cliff on his return!

My husband went to bed and Robert and I drew up our chairs. Even for an Australian, he is naïve and boyish for 35, and I had a little sadness as he spoke of future plans as if he was only 18, with golden youth ahead instead of past. He spoke of his fear of the future, whether he should marry, have children in today's chaos when to thinking people so many problems and difficulties beset youth. As I pointed out, they always did to a varying degree. I pointed out the quiet leisured peace of *The Forsyte Saga*, which we had discussed as a little cameo of life earlier in the evening. I drew a word picture of the countryside as I'd known it, before motors and planes, and earlier still before trains when Gran was a young bride – earlier still in Rogue Herries'[†] pack horse and bridle path days. I said 'It was said trains, later motors, would poison the air'. Every generation has its bogey, and fears of the future, but we who have lived through found compensations somewhere, and did live through.

Friday, 13 January. Wherever I've been today there's been little remarks about the loss of the *Truculent*.[*] Barrow people always feel they own a bit of the ships and subs they make. George came in and he had been talking to someone who had grown old in submarine building and had said, 'If those lads were in reach of their equipment, they would be up and floating like ducks.' I shivered as I said to George, 'In the dark cold water, no ship near to pick them up, it would only prolong the agony.' Such a dreadful senseless accident, no combat, no 'they died gloriously', as much an accident as if crossing the street and been knocked down by a bus.

Tuesday, 17 January. I got the pantry and kitchenette cupboards cleaned out this morning, and it took me most of the morning.

---

*On the evening of 12 January, the patrol submarine *Truculent*, which had been built in Barrow and launched in 1942, collided with a Swedish ship in the Thames estuary and sank. Sixty-four men lost their lives. Building submarines was a speciality of Barrow's shipyard.

I had cold meat and macaroni pudding to do, and opened a tin of soup and added grated onion and a little Bovril, and cooked frozen peas and potatoes. My husband went down to the doctor's and saw Dr Miller, who is better after his operation. He told my husband the same thing – that his cure is in his own hands. It's what he thinks and does for himself, rather than drugs and potions, but added too he realised how difficult it was to conquer 'nerve' health when one got low.

Wednesday, 18 January. We set off at 1.30 to go to Windermere for the two prints Robert wanted for Cliff. It was lovely motoring along the glassy lake, where shadows met on the steel dark water, not even a boat or a bird to mar the smooth stillness. Farmers worked busily everywhere. Hedges that were not done earlier are being cut and trimmed, fields drained, and the queer machine that cuts a deep neat furrow for the draining pipes fascinates me – so much time saved. Lime, dung and phosphates were being spread, with a speed that hinted the workers smelled snow in the keen air, and snow ploughs were on corners of waste land all along the roads. If we don't get a severe frost soon, grain *will* be poor next harvest. It's far too 'proud',[†] as the old ones say. It needs to be 'backened'[†] or else there will be too much stalk. I love the little Lakeland towns in off season. The shops are so attractive, with expensive fruit, flowers and vegetables as in a city, things we don't see in such profusion in Barrow, and the cakes, fish, game and poultry are always a delight to a shopper with a long purse!

Thursday, 19 January. I shocked and offended Jessie a little. They had been talking about Priestley's broadcast, and though Jessie is a real Conservative, I could tell Priestley's kindly humble puppy philosophy had affected her.* She said, 'Don't you like him?' I said 'Ah yes, as a playwright and real kindly man, he has no peer, but he *does* see life through rosy spectacles, which, though cosy, is not realistic nowadays. We could do with lots more like him. They are a good leaven.' Jessie said, 'Sometimes you are very cynical. *I* either like people or I don't' and Mrs Atkinson agreed. Mrs Atkinson said a bit crankily, 'Now if Mr Last had only been interested in cards we could have played whist and I wouldn't have missed going to the whist drive so much tonight.' I said, 'And if he only had wings, he would be able to fly', and joined in the laugh, but thought of what a lot of things he didn't do or want to do!

Saturday, 21 January. It was bitterly cold, but the sun shone, and we went round Coniston Lake. The day had that newly washed crystalline light that Hugh Walpole so loved and described so lovingly of Derwent, Skiddaw and round Keswick. The hills seemed to drowse in veils of soft amethyst to deep sepia shadows. Swale† fires nursing under the whin† and dead bracken made long plumes of smoke that rose up into the still air like fantastic fir trees, higher than the hills in the background. Age-old grey walls were jewelled with emerald-topiary from little tufts of green moss, and orange-yellow lichen where the sun rays picked out the colour. Evergreens glistened as if every leaf had been washed and polished separately. Horses' coats shone like burnished metal, and the hill sheep's wool dried in the keen wind and made a little

---

*J. B. Priestley's 'The Labour Plan Works', one of a series of party political broadcasts, was published in *The Listener*, 19 January 1950, pp. 112–13. Priestley did, indeed, profess political humility and a common-sense outlook. His socialist thinking was not to Nella's taste.

shimmering nimbus round them as they cropped the grass, or
lay quietly resting. In sheltered fields fresh hurdles made folds
for the expected lambs, in the rude shepherds' huts. The glint of
straw could be seen stacked and piles of turnips under rough shelters were ready. I stood by the smooth quiet lake, thinking how
Robert would have loved to be with us today. Nothing stirred
or broke the perfect stillness. The sun sank lower and brought
fresh beauty as its light crimsoned the delicate tracery of birch
and beech, larch and oaks against the clear blue grey of the sky.
The nut trees looked strangely out of place, their fringe of catkins
giving them the look of trees in a Japanese print. On the east
and quiet side of Coniston Lake there's several well built, stone
summer bungalows. A year or two ago a garage was built by the
largest one, a telephone installed and a boat house built for a
little outboard boat. Today smoke curled out of the chimney and
the place had a generally lived-in look. I wondered what kind of
people lived in that lovely peaceful place – perhaps a writer who
wove the calm, serene beauty of Brown Howe and the fells into
writing, perhaps only a very tired person or persons. With a companion of one's own way of thinking, life could be very pleasant,
for books and the wireless could make up for other entertainment.

Thursday, 26 January. My husband decided to go to Ulverston on
the bus. He wanted some ironmongery ordering, and I felt Mrs
Higham's visit was going to be like an old time one. She was in
a humour I'd never seen her in before – a bitter 'What's the use?'
kind of way. I felt anger for her when she told me, and a realisation of what makes for strikes and frustrations. Mr Higham's
'Head', an old school friend of mine, began to be ill about the
time my husband did and his wife and I had been worried for
some time previously about their health. A Cost and Estimate

office has few but very experienced men, who each take different branches of ship building, and while Jimmy has been ill, his work was divided up between three of them, Mr Higham and two others, and as that meant more journeys to London, Sheffield and Rosyth, it meant hundreds of hours unpaid for the work *had* to be done. Now the doctor has given his verdict. Poor Jimmy is doomed – some kind of kidney trouble as well as a weak heart. Promotion has always been the result of such cases, with a fresh man at the bottom. In this instance a curt note to each to say someone is being sent from London to take charge – and no thanks for carrying on for so long – is the only result, and it's made them bewildered and angered, and a feeling gone of feeling part of all the effort Sir Charles Craven [*Chairman of Vickers-Armstrongs 1936–44*] built and fostered amongst the men he gathered round him. They knew if orders were to be had, he got them. Once a ship barely cleared expenses – report put profit at less than £2. If men slacked, his language was something to fear – he had been a Naval Commander. Since he died the Chief Directors may be clever, but they are singularly colourless. We talked of leadership, of understanding that was a mixture of wisdom, that had to be first born in a person, then polished by contact, tolerance and good feeling. We sat up to the fire like Cassandras as we wondered with sadness where all the laughter 'working together', that purpose that got things done, had gone, which we knew in the war years.

I began to get fidgety. If my husband said he was going to climb onto the roof I would welcome it – or *any* thing he wanted to do – as a sign he felt interest, but when I know how easily he is upset, I don't like him out long on his own, and he was about 1½ hours away. Mrs Higham could see I felt uneasy, but understood. Perhaps because she was so upset over her husband's being treated as he had been, little barriers went down. I know so well why my mother's family were called 'proud' Rawlinsons. It's not really the right word for the feeling we have. It's a mixture of distaste that people should come too close into things which, for loyalty, pity, even love, we consider intensely personal to us, and a feeling that, after all, everyone has their own troubles and worries and don't want ours, all mixed up with a queer Pagliecachi 'laugh, clown, laugh'.* Mrs Higham said in a gentle tone, 'You are more worried than you own, Lasty, aren't you?' The old wartime name, her kind voice, made tears roll down my cheeks and I nodded. I said, 'Um, um. It's a lane that has no ending, but we all come to one sooner or later, don't we?' We sat and looked in the fire, as if we expected to find a solution there. She said, 'You *will* have to get out more on your own. You know you are beginning to show strain.' I said, 'Well, aching bones don't make for peace of mind. It will be better when he gets his glasses and can read, and when spring comes, for if I go out and work in the garden, he will come and I'll have to make an effort to work with him and take no notice of his odd little ways.'

It wasn't that we had a real good talk as much as little wordless silences that, when people know each other well, mean so much. She wants me to join the Fellowship Circle, a weekly meeting at St Paul's Church. I said I'd think about it, feeling I shrank a little with memories of things I'd tried to join and interest him in, when either he had offended people with offhand keep-off ways

---

*Nella is almost certainly referring to *Pagliacci*, the 1892 opera by Ruggero Leoncavallo about a company of strolling players, including a clown. As one authoritative account of the opera remarks, 'It is the old and ever effective story of the buffoon who must laugh, and make others laugh, while his heart is breaking' (The Earl of Harewood, ed., *Kobbé's Complete Opera Book* [London: Bodley Head, 10th edn, 1987], p. 552).

and sat morose and alone, or walked out and never gone back. I made tea and we began, for Mrs Higham had a friend calling at her house at 6 o'clock. I'd baked some crusty rolls. We had them buttered and lots of honey on, laughing at each other's crunching and enjoyment.

My husband came in exhausted, but I didn't fuss, just helped him off with his overcoat and made him a cup of scalding hot tea by the fire, and then we began to ask him about Ulverston on market day. He had met a former girlfriend of Arthur's, never married, and invited her down. I nearly gasped aloud. He had been so against the friendship and gone the whole bundle in condemning Eileen for a 'flighty, tiresome, man chasing baggage' etc!

Friday, 27 January. Cliff sent me *Sons and Lovers* by D. H. Lawrence, and I'm deeply interested though not read much. I felt a bit nowty† as I got into the car to career along cold wintry roads with my husband in a black mood when to get him interested was like trying to strike a match on a patch of damp moss. I thought longingly of the fire and my book. We went up the Cumberland coast to Millom, today so bleak and windswept, the hills beyond in grey-black silhouette against the wintry grey sky, the Irish Sea so wild. The tide was going out, leaving a wide band of snowy foam, and the sands were left in glistening swathes where all had frozen as the last wave washed over. No wonder sea gulls seek food inshore, and sit on roofs and chimneys on the lookout for scraps. It's a nice run with switchback hills. It's a bit odd when both of us tend to nerviness that we love flying up and down hills! When we stopped at Millom we had a cup of hot tea before beginning to walk round, so though it was so cold, we didn't feel it as bad as we would have done. I bought a small whistling kettle for 2s 9d – sale price. I paid more for my other before the war, and grieved when I found my husband had taken it for the shop, for on the red hot stove it soon burned through. I plan to be a gypsy this summer if it's at all fine, taking both lunch and tea outdoors whenever possible, either to Walney when warm or to sheltered Coniston Lake. My husband doesn't worry or brood as much outdoors and the fresh air will do him good.

There's a queer semi-junk jeweller's in Millom and I've often seen nice oddments – cut glass, bits of Edwardian or Victorian jewellery, like cameos or carved ivory heads, etc. There was a string of cut crystals – maybe topaz – today, and by their clasp looked good. My husband said, 'They look just your type of jewellery. I'd like to buy them if they hadn't been so expensive.' We didn't bother to ask the price, knowing anything unmarked was high priced. The junk around was a guide to what would be asked for good things. As we walked back to the car I wondered why I'd ceased to long for – covet – lovely things as I used to do. Somehow in the war, I got things sorted out, and have never recaptured that 'I'd *love* that' feeling. Pity. It's an added spice to a woman's life if she can shop and think, 'I'd get *that* if I had money'. Maybe it's a sign of age!

We were back well within two hours. I built up a good fire and snatched half an hour with my book while my husband covered up the car, put in the lamp and put mats to the bottom of the garage door. He has made such a fuss of this car, with it being new perhaps. I made toast and scrambled eggs. There was cake, bread and butter and honey, and warmth to take ache out of bones. When my bones ache so badly I think of homeless people, especially displaced persons, with no hope. I read the paper but my husband wasn't interested in anything tonight after he had listened half-heartedly to [*radio personality*] Wilfred Pickles at 7 o'clock. I got out my sewing and just before 9 o'clock there was a ring, and it was Alan Boyd. What a friendly lovely lad he is. He was going to a nearby hotel for the Hospital Dance and had said he would drop some cutting of Cliff's through the letter box, but rang to let me see him in his uniform because his mother thought he looked better in it than civvy clothes! He does too, like all men and *no* women, unless they have clockstopping faces and extra good figures, and then it's figures that matter more than femininity. He sat and talked till I reminded him the dance would be well started. He made me laugh as he said a bit ruefully, 'Yes, and I'll *have* to have a drink to get me in the mood to meet my sister's friends and dance for the rest of the evening'. My husband said, 'Don't you like dancing, Alan?' and he said, 'Yes, it's alright, but nothing beats yarning and listening to folk talk'. I felt he was a kindred spirit.

Monday, 30 January. The wind howled over the chimneys. More snow is on the way. It's a dreadful kind of weather for elections to be held [*on 23 February*]. A bill was put in the door tonight to say we were having a Liberal candidate in Barrow – the first for many years. Mrs Howson and I talked of politicking in general. I said, 'I think I lean to Liberalism most, perhaps because though my father was a staunch Conservative he had only been so over the Free Trade-Tariff Reform Bill and all his people and most of mother's were Liberals.' We had not discussed our political views before, not taking any view of any beyond Labour-Toryism. I was surprised to hear her say, 'All mother's brothers and sister are Liberal. Some never voted at all when only Tories put up against Labour.' It set us wondering if it would be the passive Liberal vote coming out for one of their own candidates that would affect this election. I've had a little cynical feeling as I listened

to J. B. Priestley and Maurice Webb* that for many waverers
and Pollyanna-minded ones the *last* speaker, provided he or she
insists that 'Everything is ALRIGHT, the worst is over, all our
mistakes and spade work finished with, only trust US', will win.
No one realises there will be any bills to meet. I've yet to meet
anyone with more than a hazy idea that Marshall Aid† will cease,
or be paid back. 'America has all the gold. Why *shouldn't* she
shell out?' idea.

When I sit thinking, my mind often drifts back to 50, even
55, years, for I've a good memory for details. I'd not a very happy
childhood and knew pain and endurance from five years old to
about twelve – to be crippled by an accident those days meant
effort to walk straight again.** Partly through love for me, partly
because he had a horror of anything marred, my father spared
neither money nor effort. All my pleasures were quiet, and the
happiest days spent with Gran who in her busy life had little
time for sorting out ages. She had the curious attitude of lumping
people and animals. Her farm hands were equal to the Squire or
her children in some queer alchemy of her own. She never talked
down to a little intense girl, who was let see the seamy side of
rural life as well as the lighter side. I was always conscious of
troubles and strife, 'sins' in the way of unexpected babies, shortage of money, bad luck, and all the real life of the countryside.

---

*Maurice Webb was a political journalist and broadcaster, a Labour MP and
Chairman of the Parliamentary Labour Party. He had spoken on the radio two
nights before (published in *The Listener*, 2 February 1950, pp. 201–2), and Nella
had described his speech as 'a triumph of wishful thinking mixed with sincere
conviction. If things *could* be as rosy and serene as some of the Labour speakers
make out.'
**'I broke my pelvis and hip bone at 5, and for many years limped badly and
seemed to always have pain' (diary, 2 March 1953).

My father always talked and talked of everything. I've sat mouse quiet and forgotten while the questions and problems of that far-off day were discussed and 'settled'. I try and search faithfully so as to avoid that rosy distortion that time brings to people who are lonely and growing old. There was poverty, misery, drunkenness, wife beating, lads running off to sea, dirt, more sickness – or was there now? – little money, such a lot that needed 'evoluting'. BUT, there was kindliness in need, laughter, that joy in scraping and scrounging for holidays you don't seem to get from holidays with pay to go to a noisy Holiday Camp as there was from a week in the country 'keeping yourself', only paying for rooms and attendance. People moved slower. There was more time for family life and less outside distraction. We've got a Health Scheme [*the NHS*], and less time for doctors to find out what's wrong with you.

Mrs Howson and I meandered slowly amongst her memories – at 42, of course, she is a decade behind mine. She began this 'Where has all the —— gone?' by grieving about some sixth-form boys she knew who had been found playing for money in the Grammar School Prefects' room, and the Head had told them, 'He couldn't recommend them to the university as he intended'. We wondered exactly what he meant, and if that lack of recommendation would carry weight. She always holds Cliff up as a shining light, neither knowing or understanding the problems and worry I had over that Arab[†] of a lad. She said in answer to a remark of mine, 'Boys *had* to be boys' – 'Your Cliff would never have done such a thing.' I said, 'Oh yes he would, *and* any darn fool monkey shine going, if he had had time. But my two always seemed to have so much they liked to do they never got round to antics like that, and as girls as well as boys thronged the house, practising for plays, or talking their heads off on all subjects, girls were never that "mystery" that made for furtive conjectures and daft motives like Dennis Veal' – another headache for the Head when he found a passionate love letter Dennis had written to a girl of 15 – he is 17. We wondered if there was a deep underlying meaning about idle hands!

My husband sat back in his chair, never joining in. Mrs Howson said, 'How we gabble Mr Last. You must be tired of listening.' He said in a tone of self-pity, 'Ah, I like it. I wish Mrs Last would be as bright and gay with me.' I said, 'No monologue is as interesting as a duet. You have to have *some* response you know.' But he only looked at me blankly, in a way that gave me a little sick feeling deep down inside, as I thought how more and more he resembled poor Mother. I try in vain to find out what deep fears he has to cause such dreadful nightmares. I wish he could go to one of those clever psychiatrists seen on the screen who seem to easily bring such fears to the surface and make them lose their terror. Perhaps they only exist on the screen anyway! The trouble lies so deep it's been there since I ever knew him – when he was only 19. I thought his extreme shyness so attractive, so different. I'd never known what it meant to be shy or out of place. I was so gay and lively, so full of life and fun. That's what attracted him – and what to him was such an attraction – I could 'stand up anywhere and recite or tell jokes'. Odd he should so quickly think differently, should think I should keep all and any gaiety for him alone, to show such boredom and aversion to going amongst people as soon as we were married. If I'd not been so young and inexperienced I could have seen the danger signals. If I'd been stronger minded and made a firm stand, perhaps then he would have grown to like company.

Tuesday, 31 January. I feel so down tonight. My husband had a wild nightmare – huge men with long shining swords were chasing him along deserted streets where no one appeared from whom help could be expected, and he had 'run and run till I dropped'. He looked ghastly, and complained of feeling as if his head had been kicked. I tidied round quietly while he lay back in his chair, and then wrote two letters while he had a nap ... [*His doctor had advised him to retire.*] We sat and talked. I said, 'Are you worrying about Mother? Do you dread the big change if you really did retire? You know how against change of any kind you have always been. Could it be that?' I pointed out how, when I'd really got on my top note, Harry had begun to take more on as regards Mother, and made the two daughters do the same, and it had made a great change. I said, '*I'll* settle the business, and if I cannot, Arthur will come over and do it. Say the word and go to bed if you like for a week. We will see to all.' I keep Mother out of his way, feeling sometimes the poor dear has a real horror of her and her ways, as if he fears his loss of concentration and memory will worsen and he will grow like her in every way. I wondered if that could be his fear. I scolded gently and pointed out our money would last as long as we were likely to live, that he hadn't any fear I'd resent any decision. I talked gently and persuasively about the future, though I feel I won't coax him to give up entirely. It's a matter he must finally decide for himself. If I did persuade him and he one day wished he hadn't, I know so well how he would blame me, and there would be nothing could be done about it. I said jokingly, 'If I win that Irish Sweep I'd whisk you off on a long sea voyage', and he half smiled as he said, 'You could do whatever you liked. I'd not disagree.' ...

I felt desperate with worry as I saw how old and ill he was looking. The doctor has changed his medicine again, saying, 'You will have to have sounder sleep'. I sat in the fire light, my little Shan We on my lap, and felt so worried, so alone, and so utterly helpless. I made tea when he woke, feeling refreshed. I'd minced the last of the cold meat and we had mint jelly to it, and bread and butter, and there was honey and cake. I tried so desperately hard to talk things over, recalling the brooding shut-in look the boys had had sometimes when things went wrong with their world, how it cleared as little grievances were brought out and talked over, things I'd no 'touch' with, and was no help in whatsoever. I've heard them say, 'Things look different when you talk about them', as if the mere fact of putting things into words made them real enough to face – and fight. It's so difficult to reach my husband – so impossible. Any subject, person, problem, viewpoint, angle, etc. he feels upsets him and he says, 'Don't talk about *that*' or 'I don't want to see so and so' or they 'upset me'.

I begin thinking and when I go to bed all comes back to me. With the boys under the circumstances we could have made up the fire and drank tea and talked for hours, but we would have found a solution, whether only suffering a thing or clearing it completely away. I stitched and stitched as my mind whirled in a wild montage of ideas and plans. If he only had friends – but he told his brother his visits and phone calls upset him. Granted Harry wanted to talk over Mother and her affairs at the time, and Nellie is one of those feather heads who open their mouths and let every passing thought out – like 'Ah dear, you *do* look ill, and how like Mother you are growing', etc. etc. If he could be told by the doctor, 'You *must* have a holiday at a Convalescent Home, by yourself', or if he had ever been on such friendly terms with the boys as to make me feel he could go to Arthur's for a holiday – many men could find joy in little Peter, and *want* to see something of the pet – or if he would write to them and look forward to the postman coming. I felt 'If only winter was over and we could go out every day – if I could get him interested in the garden'. I had a vision of every day of winter, before warmer days came. Sometimes when things looked dim the boys and I had a kind of fairy story – an 'If I had £1,000 to spend' fantasy.

Wednesday, 1 February. My husband looked so white and strained and said he had slept badly. After lunch and I had washed up and we had settled by the fire, I really pitched into him. I began by asking him, 'What are you so afraid of? Your wild dreams show a deep hidden fear that is sapping your strength. *Try* and talk to me dear. I'm sure I could help you if you would let me. You know what I once told Arthur when I'd helped him out of what he thought a scrape and he had said, "You are a pal to understand". I shocked you when I said, "It's what mothers are for. And remember whatever you did it would be the same – if you killed anyone, I'd help bury him." You didn't see it was a joking remark that was one meant to turn aside Arthur's concern and make him laugh, but I meant it in truth. I'd do *anything* to help you.'

When he said, 'There's nothing I can tell you – I don't feel more worried than usual', I had that queer clear feeling in my head as I have when I get on my top note and feel facts that have puzzled me grow clear. I said, 'Well, I'll tell you, you have always been a man to so dread change. I couldn't move a picture, discard outdated oddments of furniture. You never liked a pair of curtains in my remembrance till they were nearly worn out, and look how you made things so unpleasant when I altered the table and settee. You realise even what interest you take in the business is too much, but you are so afraid of taking the plunge and selling up, and making the rest of the family responsible for Mother. Tell me, don't you think *that* could be your bogey?' He thought for a while and he had to admit it 'might be'. I said, 'Well, search your mind and find out – and then quit worrying. I bet I'd settle things in a week, and if *I* couldn't, Arthur would help, and you wouldn't have the slightest worry. And remember,' I said warningly, 'things will have to be settled if you don't stop having these nightmares. I don't need Dr Miller or anyone else to tell me.' He looked so piteously at me I could have wept. I went on, 'We have only ourselves to think of. Our money will last, and you know that I'm adaptable enough to take what comes, country cottage or anything else.' He nodded, and I changed the subject, and read him bits out of the paper. I felt I sighed as I looked for bits with no 'worry', what with elections, hydrogen bombs and 'snow and ice in most roads' and the like, there wasn't much cheerful …

I feel sure I've found his hidden terror that hounds him in nightmares, shocking his whole nervous system. I recalled when Arthur would be about 14 and Cliff 9 and he had a bad bout of sciatica and had to go to Buxton for treatment – nine weeks that time. We seemed to have such a run of bad luck. I'd not had any painting or papering done for some years. I longed to be able to do. We heard of a very clever woman paper hanger, and after we had talked over ways and means we decided *if* we could do it out of what bit of money I felt I dare spend, we would begin. Our house had never had one thing destroyed or its position moved. After spring cleaning, every picture and ornament had to go back in exactly the same position, for dear peace's sake. How we planned and schemed, lived on herrings, cheese, vegetables and porridge, never spent money on any amusement, selling piles of oddments we felt wouldn't fit in with our new décor, even clothes and some bits of jewellery. We painted every scrap ourselves. What paint was not renewed had a coat of flat varnish. The walls were plain cream – no doll-eyed frieze or 'panelling'. We walked round the house before my husband was coming home and felt in ecstasy.

I'd not then realised how deep rooted was his aversion to change, that it was so vital a part of his make-up. He got out of the taxi looking so fit and well. His tea was ready and we left the first remark to him. We had written every day and told him how busy we were, but I don't think he could picture such a change. He looked round the dining room in silence, went upstairs, and came down again, still without a word. I felt vexed to see the bright glow fade from my two boys' faces. They had worked so hard, planned and schemed and been so delighted with the result. We went to bed. My husband was restless and in the morning had a temperature. I sent word to the doctor he had come home, but wasn't so well, and I'd like him to call. When he did he asked if my husband had had a shock of any kind, and I said I didn't know. He had had little to say of his journey home. He was ill for about a week, and I began to see what the shock was, and though the doctor laughed and said 'Nonsense' I was convinced I was right. Beyond a distant 'You have altered my home so much I don't feel it *is* my home', he never referred to the change, and when friends came in and said, 'How busy you must have been – everything is lovely' or words to that effect, he never answered!

Thursday, 2 February. When my husband came in I felt very glad I'd talked to him yesterday. The accountant wanted to see him about 'fast drifting into liquidation if you have another year like this'. I've known that with one thing and another he wasn't paying his way, but I'd not realised quite the position. The accountant, a pleasant friendly man who has done the books of the shop and also Harry's chemist shop for years, advised him to make up his mind to 'lock the door on it all, pay off the men as soon as existing jobs are through and all worked up, and give all a miss for about a year'. Arthur advised the very same thing but

my husband dismissed such a wild impractical suggestion. Now
it looks as if he will decide to give up, not selling up till he feels
well enough to go into things. I felt things were rushing away
with me. I've so often pleaded with him. It took a real top note of
mine to get him into a reasonable enough frame of mind to agree
to the accountant's suggestion, and not make it a shock!

Friday, 3 February. We settled by the fire. I read all and any bits
to interest my husband, both in the papers and a *Woman's Weekly*
Mrs Howson left, and then at 7 o'clock I so gladly turned on
to Wilfred Pickles [on *Have a Go*, broadcast live from London
Zoo] – that man often feels a personal friend lately. I felt so very
strung up, so little would have shattered the calmness on which
my husband's very well being depends nowadays. I felt as if
nothing could have cheered me, my husband looked so despondent and down. Then the elephant keeper 'had a go', and in a
perfectly serious voice, answering Wilfred's 'Why do elephants
marching along a street hold on to each other's tails?' said, 'It
keeps them decent'! not pausing to realise he meant decent in the
Northern Irish idiom meaning 'tidy'. We laughed and laughed.
And the poor woman's account of the abscess on her tail end, and
her evacuation from a hospital in the blitz in a blanket, with a
'gas mask and some papers', struck us as funnier than the most
comic things we had heard for a long, long time. As I picked up
my sewing and feeling as if I'd had a big glass of champagne or
something, I thought 'Black bitter luck follow anyone who ever
alters *Have a Go* in the very least detail. It's got something to last
as long as the BBC does.' Wilfred Pickles has a 'spark' of something. Tommy Handley had it, and amongst the very few who
have it are Gladys Young, Freddie Grisewood – yes, and Stewart
Macpherson. In such widely different personalities, I wonder if

it's some very personal streak of their very own they give into the microphone. A few others have it in different, sometimes fleeting, degrees. It's a great asset.

Saturday, 4 February. The birds have got their mating notes very early. We used to say when I was a child, they began courting on the 14th of February. I didn't feel well. My wretched bones nearly got the mastery of me. I felt a bit better after breakfast, and decided to clean the insides of the windows. The clear sunshine made them look cloudy with smoke and steam from cooking. I was in the lounge and my eyes fell on a little carved coconut wood elephant. I felt chuckles begin in my throat and a vision of five or six elephants swinging down the Strand, with their ponderous yet 'mincing' tread, so smug and confident in their 'decent' appearance as trunks gripped tails! My husband put his head round the door and said, 'What are you laughing about?' and I said, 'Decent elephants' and he laughed too.

Sunday, 5 February. A wild night, with the 'hoo hoooo' note of snow in the wind. I was relieved to find a bright morning when I rose. I expected to see snow. I had a rest but got up before 11 o'clock. My husband was wandering round in a real black mood. I read him bits out of the *Sunday Express*.* He reminded me of years gone by when the boys were busy with Meccano, or Arthur with his everlasting model stage making and Cliff modelling, and I read aloud. I can recall some of the books – most of Dickens, *Vanity Fair*, most of John Buchan's and earlier still Gene Stratton

---

*Will, who was waiting for new glasses, had been unable to read and thus Nella found it necessary to read to him, taking pains to omit items in the news or fictional stories that might alarm him.

Porter's books as well as some of Kipling's I thought suitable. My husband listened and spoke today as if I'd grown too lazy to read books now to him. As I pointed out, he grew more difficult – few of the above books but had *some* 'violence', deaths, separation or a bit of a 'thrill'. If I read them to him nowadays he would complain of their upsetting him and making him have nightmares! There was good mutton soup – the meat ate nicely – and we had bread and butter and mint jelly to it, and I made a steamed egg custard to stewed apples.

I felt in that edgy way as if a skin had been peeled off me, and so very glad we could go out. We went round Grange, and over Cartmel Fell, and could see the Yorkshire hills as well as all Lakeland ones, white with snow. There must have been a heavy fall in the night for there was not even a sprinkle of snow on the hills yesterday. I felt cold. Not even my fur coat and rug – and my little Shan We curled on my lap – could make me feel warm, and we were both glad of the thermos flask of tea I'd taken. The sun shone, and there were more people out walking than I've seen this winter. It was a good day for quick walking, but those who loitered looked blue with cold.

I made up a good fire, and before tea pressed the top panel and flounce of my crazy patchwork, ready to put together with a piping. I made some cheese and tomato sandwiches and got out the Xmas cake, wishing I could cheer my husband. Now the first idea of giving up work is fading. He only sees difficulties ahead in every direction. I can see I'll have a trying time till all *is* settled. I read out of a magazine thinking to interest him, and he fell asleep, so I picked up my sewing. Just before 8 o'clock there was a ring and it was Alan Boyd, come to say goodbye. He has got a ship and sails for either Australia or New Zealand on Thursday. He leaves Barrow for London on Tuesday morning. He sat and talked a while – he *is* a nice fellow. It was so kind of him to come and say goodbye, and he hopes to see Cliff if he touches Australia. I had that sad 'always goodbye' feeling as we wished him all the luck in the world. Such a pity he isn't married. He would have made the silly girl who wouldn't wait for him very happy. I was thankful when bedtime came. It's so very unfortunate my husband's glasses had to be changed just now. It's one thing after another against him.

Monday, 6 February. On our way to Spark Bridge we called to see my butcher's baby, a dear little seven weeks old girl with lovely blue grey eyes, and such tiny hands and feet. She is so good except for waking and demanding to feed in the middle of the night. Her mother said, 'I've tried to make her do without it as they recommended in the Home, but it's no use'. I said, 'Common sense and understanding raised babies before Clinics. I think there's a tendency to regiment babies a bit too much. Rules were made for babies, not babies for rules.' We talked about whether babies should be nursed and sung to. I said '*Yes* – it gave them a feeling of security to know loving arms'. I can tell her husband's mother believes in being stern.

Aunt Sarah looked so pinched and cold. She and I were the odd ones out in a hardy 'stir-about-and-you-won't-feel-cold' family. Snowdrops were out in her little garden, and a wee posy ring of them were on the table. Her tiny figure was swathed with a woollen coatee over her dress, and then a Shetland shawl. I thought she must have been outdoors, but she said, 'No fire, clothes or hot drinks keep out this bitter cold, do they?' Poor old pet – I understand to a degree! Sheep in the fields sheltered on the leeward side of hedges, their wool washed by rain, flowing in a cream nimbus, making their black faces look odd. What hens *did* walk had ruffled feathers and were only searching and picking food before nightfall. In the distance all the hills gleamed white.

I got nice fillets of plaice for tea, my husband's favourite fish, and tea was soon ready. He looked a little brighter, but when I suggested taking my raffle tickets in to Mrs Atkinson's to sell a few, he said, '*I'll* buy two and you can see her tomorrow surely'. In his poor sick mind I often wonder what I stand for exactly – some kind of anchorage and security? In his wildest most terrifying dreams, he says, 'And then I heard your voice' or 'You reached down and caught hold of me with your firm warm hand' or even 'You smiled at the great big man and he put the huge sword back in its sheath with a loud rattle and we just walked away'. Once he made me laugh loudly and long as he told a long rigmarole of a fearsome beast with, presumably, more than its share of heads and legs. He said, 'You *were* so cross. You said, "The devil toast you. Why cannot you drink a saucer of milk when there's nothing else? Poor old Murphy likes milk."' And he went on, 'You patted the beast as if it *was* Shan We, and it followed you round a corner of the road'.

I got out my crazy patchwork. I thought it had been my own idea to stitch and stitch, after blending colours that in themselves were a pleasure. Tonight I felt the idea had been put into my mind as a little indirect answer to my ever repeated plea for 'All Lovely Things', as my Gran called patience and kindness, pity, courage, etc. Now as my mind clearly tells a little rosary, I find my prayer short and ever shorter – kindness and courage so much more important than anything else – and health of mind and body to keep on. I looked at the brightly burning fire and my little cats. I'd quarrel with anyone who said cats don't think. Mine do much more. They see into my sad and often so lonely mind and show *they* understand. Old Murphy will rear his big kind head out of the tight ball he has made of himself and with a queer highly pitched purr that is almost a word come to lie on my foot. My Shan We is my shadow, leaving the warmth of the fire any time to seek me if I go upstairs, his anxious face pressed against the window frame if I'm sweeping outside.

Monday, 13 February. Ulverston always seems as familiar as Barrow, which was really my home town. I'd gladly go and live in Greenodd or Davy Bridge, about three miles away, if we could find a cottage – it would have to be for sale. We were coming home and my husband said, 'You're miles away again. What *are* you thinking?' I said, 'The bungalow of Lakeland stone, with the room in the roof, the long living room with wide windows each end, central heating, the walls and paths of well laid stone, and so on and so on, that I'd plan and have built if I won the Irish Sweep.' He said, 'What about your plan for Australia – going there?' I fell into another train of thought. I've always such an aversion to meddle with the boys, or make them feel I would cling, or interfere, perhaps because I've always had someone wanting to change me, from the days I realised my dark brown hair and eyes and excessive vitality when small were contrasted always with the child of mother's first marriage – to my total disadvantage. She had been blue-eyed and lily fair, quiet and gentle always. I always felt too as I grew older I shared the place with my father in mother's mind and heart – somehow we were interlopers. Her life really ended before the honeymoon days were over, before she realised they *would* end. In the 10½ years since Cliff left home, he has grown and developed. I've grown so much older and so desperately tired. He, I know, pictures me as I used to be – ready for anything, grave or gay. I'd be a great disappointment to him now. I don't feel there would be a place in his gay vivid life for anyone who felt so depleted of all vitality. I shrugged off my thoughts impatiently. They impinged on the new philosophy in which I rigidly schooled myself – to take every day as it comes, and when things do get on top of me, count my many blessings again and again, like a rosary.

Thursday, 16 February. My husband was in a queer mood. He said, 'When you ever had your fortune told, did anyone tell you I'd have to retire early?' I said, 'No, I don't think so'. He said, 'Well, *try* and think. You have such a marvellous memory for conversations that took place years ago.' I said, 'Well, I cannot recall anything remotely like "retirement".' I added, 'Remember I was told I'd not end my days in the home I'd just moved into?' – looks as if that country cottage about which we talk may be a fact! He went on, 'As soon as the weather is better we will go to Morecambe – you must go and have your hand read'. I shook my head firmly as I said, 'NO. I put away all and any little "gift" of my own for fortune telling when it began to worry and upset me, and as for having my hand read, I say what I said last summer – "I don't want to look ahead – much better to take each day and each problem as it comes".' Then he wanted my 'honest opinion' of his health, his prospects of recovery, etc., as if I was a doctor and a specialist. I told him he was absurd if he thought I knew more than Dr Miller. Poor dear, he looked so sadly at me as he said, 'But you *do*. If I'd listened to half your advice and what I called "nagging", I'd never have gone on and on till I collapsed. I'd never have grown in on myself as I have done.' There seemed so little to say. I felt so limp and tired myself. I could only say quietly, 'We will feel brighter when the spring comes. I wish often we could pack up and go to Australia and end our days in sunshine.'

CHAPTER TWO

PUBLIC AND PRIVATE

February–April 1950

Saturday, 18 February. It was sunny. We went out in the car, first to contact the secretary of the master builder who is going to try to get Gilbert, the apprentice, somewhere to finish off his apprenticeship. Then we got as far as Bowness, for we had set off early. The election apathy seems general. I thought of pre-war years as we went past little villages and groups of cottages and saw little or no signs of posters – except biggest ones on hoardings or walls, with notices of meetings in school rooms or village halls. I smiled to recall the real feuds elections used to cause, when every window showed a rosette of Party colours on the curtains, if not a photo of the favoured candidate, when Liberal yellow and Conservative blue ribbons were worn by every woman and small ribbon rosettes were flaunted on every coat lapel by the men. I fell into a long train of thought, a montage of Boer War cum elections cum First [World] War recollections. I thought wryly, 'We all seem to have just so much vitality and enthusiasm. Once it's spent it's gone.' But I realised I spoke for only my own generation. It didn't explain the apathy of youth. We all march to the sound of different drummers and music alters from one generation to another, even heard on the wireless. Twenty years ago I knew a thinking old man who bemoaned, 'We are evoluting too fast and "soon ripen, soon rot" you know'. I wondered what he would have thought of the ever increasing tempo of life and discovery today.

Sunday, 19 February. If I had been in reach of Cliff today, I'd have raised blisters on him with my tongue. *What* a day I've had. Yesterday some papers came, including an *Australian Digest.* In it was quite a good interview but it was very journalese. Cliff had warned us about the 'smoky Lancashire town' mentioned as the place where he was brought up. I felt annoyed myself at the way Cliff was referred to as having 'hard-working parents' who presumably had no patience with Cliff wanting to be a sculptor, and when it referred to my husband as a 'working man', with neither mentions he had been in the Navy in the First World War – and that was why we happened to be in the New Forest near Southampton – or the fact he was a businessman doing his own works *and* that Cliff had gone into it against every scrap of advice. I felt thoroughly annoyed with the slipshod, quite inaccurate write-up – whereby my father had been a wood carver on sailing ships! I thought of the quiet shy uncle, my accountant father's brother, whose murals and panels had decorated ships of the *Aquitania*'s age! My husband had evidently worked up a real upset to his nerves when he had gone to bed, and had one of his bad turns in the night and was shaky and ill till noon, and nothing I could say in excuse or explanation of 'anything to fill up' would calm him. He was quite bitter towards Cliff and his 'lies', as if Cliff would have been so misleading, and as I was daft and rash enough to say 'unless he has been a bit tight'. Then the band *did* play. I'd not felt too good myself when I rose, and his mood so upset me I was really ill, which pulled him together as nothing else would have done, when I felt faint and had to lie down, after having brandy. I pulled myself together and began to make lunch, knowing that however he felt my husband could eat, and needed, a good meal ...

Little remarks [*later that day*] showed how hurt and resentful he still felt. I said, 'You are taking it too seriously. Cliff was careless and the journalist wanted to make it a poor-English-boy-with-no-chance-at-home doing so remarkably well in Australia.' I thought of the discords there *had* been between him and Cliff, the years their opposite warring natures had nearly killed me, as I was first torn one way, then the other. I'll see before any newsprint from Australia is read aloud. I felt very little would have made me cry till I just couldn't cry. Little worries piled up like a snowball and bowled me over. Not even the real anger and annoyance I felt for Cliff's silly heedless way, and not seeing an interviewer had sensible facts on which to build, could spur me out of my weepy fit, by Gad, though if I could have had that lad alone for ten minutes I'd have felt better. It was one of the times that called for a top note, and I'd have flayed him with my tongue. My husband kept bursting out into remarks that showed how bitter he felt. He said after staring in the fire, 'Put the idea out of your head I'd ever go to Australia, even for a holiday. *I've* no notion to appear as "hard-working and non-understanding of a lad who wanted to be an artist", out of an industrial Lancashire town "where black smoke hid the blue skies" anyway. Where *is* such a town? Remember when Arthur was at Wigan and we used to go and see him. Remember the nice shops and the Standish Park.' Then there was a pause, and Palm Court music filled the room – the aerial has been partly repaired and reception's good at the moment.

Then another outburst. 'When I think of the way Cliff over-ruled and fought you when you were so ill after your last operation, when the doctors stressed you had to have no worry and your heart was so bad, and how he insisted on leaving the Grammar School and coming into my business. When I think of how quickly he saw his mistake and was so wildly discontented, when I think of how patient you always were – "no encouragement from the

working man, his father, who had no patience with boyish efforts
to carve and model"', and so on and so on, till I began to dread he
would have another bad attack of nerves. He said, 'The trouble
with you is that you always gave way to people, always tried to
see *their* point of view. You should have taken a stick to that lad
more.' As I pointed out, any slappings and correcting always *did*
come from me. A very little more and I felt I'd be telling him of
all his omissions as a father, as the boys grew up.

I shook with nerves, and butterflies fluttered so busily in
my tummy I began to feel deathly sick, and I went upstairs to
undress, thinking I'd get washed and come down in my dressing
gown to make supper. Instead I was so sick I had to crawl into
bed. I slept for nearly an hour and was wakened by my husband
with a beaker of milk food, and he said, 'I've fed the cats and laid
the breakfast table and there's nothing for you to go downstairs
for again'. He looked so scared as he sat on the side of the bed,
and he didn't say any more about that darned interview of Cliff's.
Earlier in the day I'd written a 6d airmail, read it and tore it up.
Then I wrote another, rather coldly mentioning that 'No doubt
your *Digest* article makes good reading – and publicity – for Australia, but people in Barrow reading it, knowing our families so
well, would no doubt wonder if *all* the article was a distortion,
and your efforts and success doubted. I prefer something a little
less journalese that I *can* proudly show round, and I understand
Daddy's feeling of resentment at being described as a "Lancashire
working man".' And I finished my letter in my usual gossipy way,
with none of the sharpness of the first letter, but knowing Cliff, I
know he would read between the lines!

Two days later Nella and Will were sunning themselves near the breakwater
in Walney, and she made 'a joking remark' about winning 'the Sweep' and

visiting Australia. This 'brought tight lips and a quiet sneer as he said, "We mustn't forget our clogs", which made me long intensely for the chance to tell Cliff just how deeply he had hurt and annoyed us by his cheap journalese interview.'

The Australian article that Nella and Will had read was Geoff Waye's, 'A Place in the Sun', *Life Digest* [Melbourne], January 1950, pp. 25–7. It was probably the following passage (p. 25) about Cliff that was most upsetting: 'He worked for his father, but should a piece of putty or a strip of wood come his way, his fingers fashioned it into little figures of grace and flowing lines. But the son of a working man was not intended for such time-wasting foolishness and his talents were not encouraged.' (Waye also wrote of the Last family living in 'Lancashire, where the smoke from the mills filled the skies', so it seems he was unaware that Barrow was not a mill town.) Some of the dismissive views on Cliff's English background that his parents disliked are reasserted in the introduction to Max Dimmack, *Clifford Last* (Melbourne: The Hawthorn Press, 1972). Cliff, according to this author, who had known him since his arrival in Australia in 1947, was 'frustrated by his well-intentioned but ill-informed parents who borrowed from the local public library books containing reproductions of the works of the old masters which they encouraged Last to try to copy in crayons and water-colours' (p. 6). Cliff was portrayed by both these commentators as misunderstood and unfulfilled in his early years. Nella's anger about the way in which Cliff, apparently, was portraying his family and upbringing resurfaces in her diary entry below for 29 December 1950.

Monday, 20 February. My husband went to the doctor's and came home very downcast. He said, 'The doctor doesn't think I'm improving as I should. He asked if I was a Mason or member of any club through which I could go to a Convalescent Home.' I felt tired and out of joint. I said snootily, 'Didn't you tell him that you thought paying into *any* kind of insurance for the future was a waste of money?'* I said 'You could go to Belfast. Edith asked us to go for a holiday when all is settled. You could even go to Australia if you only would. A sea voyage would perhaps set you up – as Mr Richardson set off on his own.' Perhaps because I felt tired I felt less patience. I thought of something I once read, 'In life there's no rewards, and no revenges, just consequences'…

We had our first canvassers tonight, one Labour, one Liberal. My husband went to the door for the first one and told the Labour canvasser 'As a business man, it's not policy to discuss elections'. I went the second time and recognised an acquaintance with whom I'd often talked of Liberalism (then almost extinct) versus Conservatism. He said, 'I'm sure *you* will give us a chance. Your views were more for us, even when you were Chair of Central Ward.' I said 'I'm anti-Socialist, putting my country before party politics, and regard Megan Lloyd's bid for power as traitorous.** Any Liberal who loves his country would vote Conservative – and I am not one you know, so cannot understand why you think I should vote that way.' My husband wasn't suited† because I'd 'spoken so plainly'. I said, 'Hell's blue light. I've walked too many miles and knocked at too many doors, canvassing at General Elections, not to prefer a straight answer to a shilly shally statement, and one that showed plainly enough where your vote *wouldn't* be given.'

Wednesday, 22 February. We settled down again, talking of past

---

*Later that week Mrs Higham was visiting, and she 'was really shocked when he went on to tell her he had "never believed in any kind of insurance", and she learned that I'd have *nothing* from any source if he died' (23 February 1950).
**Megan Lloyd George (1902–66), daughter of David Lloyd George and a Liberal MP from 1929 to 1951 – she later joined the Labour Party – championed radical causes in her party, whereas other Liberals were moving, or had already moved, to support Conservative positions, a trend that Nella approved of.

elections. Once a candidate was disqualified, for buying pies for all his helpers – the opponent built up a case against him – and tonight my husband said, 'Remember Mrs Marsh. She was the girl who started it all by a chance remark, and the result hung on her evidence. She had been the girl who carried the pies from the bake house.' I remember her as an old busybody till the day she died at 76! Odd how things lie quiet in your mind and then pop up like a Jack in the box. I began to tell of the first election I could remember, when I would be nearly six years old. I'd had the accident that was to make me lame for so long, and my father insisted we move from an outlying fishing village, where we had moved when I was only three months old, so I could have treatment. Nothing ever daunted my gay spirits when I was young, and I was a great novelty in a bamboo rickshaw affair of a go-cart, and older children would always take me along. Mother, so prim and proper, would inspect them and give them strict instructions and then off we would go, generally towards the docks where the ships were such an interest. I don't suppose my mother gave the election a thought, beyond voting,* though bands of children marched with placards, yelling slogans and singing words fitted to well known songs. I had a marvellous time, rattled over rough roads, my go-cart smothered in blue streamers and bunting. I've an idea children must only have had to ask to get red, white and blue rosettes, cockades, placards to carry at the ends of sticks, etc. I ate bits of food from paper bags and newspaper, sang till I was hoarse, bewildered and delighted by all the goings-on of town life, and really frightened when a policeman took me to the police station where mother and Aunt Eliza frantically welcomed me and my father came in looking relieved. I'd been 'officially lost,

---

*In fact, women did not at that time have the vote, except in some local elections.

a poor little crippled child, who knows what can have happened'
– for about eight hours. As my husband laughed at my first election and the little escapade, I thought with surprise, 'Why, that
was one of the happiest days I had. What a strange elusive thing
"happiness" is, to be sure.'

My final bet for the election result is pretty much how I
thought at first – a return of Labour with a small majority, with
Liberals and Conservatives in enough opposition if they combine
to curb them. Personally I hope it's like that. They *should* face consequences of all their 'leap before you look' actions, and though
at times a balanced Parliament would no doubt be a stalemate,
no fresh schemes of Nationalisation could be made, and existing
ones would be made to run more economically.

In the general election on 23 February, Labour won Barrow and retained an
overall parliamentary majority, though just barely.

Friday, 24 February. I've *blessed* the election turmoil of these two
days and when results began to come in and the local *Mail* was
delivered, my husband found even more interest.* We had cheese
and watercress, toasted raisin buns and chocolate sandwich and
then had the wireless on all evening. We once helped at a local
election where a fiercely contested seat had to have four recounts
before the winning candidate was announced, so we knew a little
of the feverish uncertainty that there would be in some places.
When I heard that at one time the Conservatives were even and
then more Labour victories came along, I thought of a prophecy
by Naylor the astrologer I'd read after the last election – that

---

*'This interest he has taken in the election has been a pleasure to both of us', she
wrote the next day. 'I wish something else would come along.'

Mr Churchill wasn't destined to lead the Conservatives back to power. He is the most wonderful, the most inspiring leader any country has known, but I've always a sneaking remembrance of Mrs Waite and her utter dominance at Hospital Supply. She towered above us all by her work in the First World War, and could see little good in any of us. Yet it was a *good* committee – each of us had 'something' – which, till the worms turned, was useless.* I couldn't help but wonder if there *were* strong men in the Conservative Party who, given their head, could lead. I wasn't surprised at Labour losing some seats and the Conservatives gaining, but not as much see-saw, or the Liberals losing so many deposits. What troubles me is that *no* one will do any good, and just when so much outside interest and endeavour is needed, bold ventures and ideas so essential, it looks as if it will be stalemate, the Socialists proposing and the rest saying NO. I wonder if there will be another election soon. One thing, there could never be any coalition. There's too wide a gulf now between Socialists and the rest. I listened to Mr Churchill's brave but broken voice with a pity so deep I began to cry bitterly. I don't cry easily, or often. My husband said, 'Now fancy you upsetting yourself so over so small a thing'. But somehow that brave gallant old voice got tangled up with my own worries and fears. I couldn't have separated them as I cried till I felt sick.

Monday, 27 February. Aunt Sarah *does* miss her little cat. It was such a clean, faithful little thing, and died as it had lived, at her bedside on its mat, peacefully and cleanly. She says she is too old

---

*Nella means that the somewhat meek and reticent committee members, who had been pushed around by the domineering Mrs Waite, retaliated by being active, assertive and effective.

to have another. I could see today she was upset because a picture had fallen from where it hung over her bedroom fireplace and broken two treasured old china figures. She said, 'Are *you* superstitious about pictures falling? Your mother and mine were, you know.' I said I'd never had any experience of falling pictures, but a magpie on the lawn made me feel really ill, though in the country I never bothered. She nodded as she looked in the fire. I felt sorry for her – till her next remark sent my lips twitching. She shook her head sadly and said, 'You know, Joe has never been *really* strong. That's why he never married and I promised his mother to always look after him.' (He is her cousin.) As Joe must be about 80 to her 85, I thought there was little fear of him being cut off in his prime! ...

Mrs Howson brought Cliff's papers across and stayed a while and her first words were 'Well, what did the doctor say today?' He began about the Convalescent Home proposal. Our eyes met. I knew she wondered, like I did, if he *would* go when the time came. He used to go to Buxton Hospital for six to nine weeks at a time, but under great protest. He hates things more nowadays that in any way upset his routine. Mrs Howson looked curiously at me and said, 'What will *you* do with yourself?' I had a passing idea I'd have had a little holiday in Belfast. I so long to see little Pete and feel a change would do me more good than a tonic. Then another thought had crossed my mind – of doing all the Spring cleaning, and having the back bedroom papered – the man said he would come soon after Xmas – and of having lazy afternoons after a busy morning, relaxed on the settee with a book, and no reading aloud. Luckily I didn't mention going to Ireland, for my husband said quickly, 'Ah, Nell can have a good rest. I'll soon be back and she will have to write *lots* of letters to me, like she used to do when I was at Buxton. She wrote every day and told me all she had been doing.' I sniffed as I said to Mrs Howson, 'So, if you see a cheap line in chastity girdles, let me know'. He wondered why we both set off laughing. He said, 'You've just got new corsets. What do you want another girdle for?' Which made Mrs Howson laugh till the tears ran down her face. She wiped them away, powdered her nose, and said, 'You *are* a pet Mr Last'.

Tuesday, 28 February. I've not felt well at all lately, just a low vitality feeling I get in February, and however I try to be bright – how I *hate* that word – I cannot rouse or interest him much. His moods were always difficult. I never in my life could cope easily with them. We listened to *Ray's a Laugh* and then to *Take It From Here*. I enjoyed them, but no smile came on my husband's face, and I suggested he would rather I read to him, but even then I couldn't interest him. When I talked I could see he wasn't hearing. It was one of the days when he was sure he wasn't going to get better. As I sat sewing, I suddenly realised I'd never once heard him say – or agree with – anything at all about his belief in the future life. I've always had a strong belief in life going on – not a Heaven where there's singing and walking by green pastures, but somewhere where we got the chances we threw away, or never had, to 'grow'. When the boys grew old enough to read fully, they developed more or less their own religion and way of thought, which always annoyed my husband. He is bigoted about any RC, Jew or Non-Conformist, yet never chose to go to church after we were young and it was the general custom. When most people get older they get their convictions clearer as a rule. It's odd to think anyone can know so little of their own husband's mind, beliefs, or convictions. If anyone ever talked seriously he would listen with wide eyes but would never be drawn into any discussion, and his irrelevant remarks after they had finished always showed he hadn't taken the interest I thought he was doing. It's so distressing when you cannot reach to a person, try and calm the fear in their mind, which you fully realise, looking back over the years, has *always* been full of fearing something. I can understand people who love life, who have achieved things, know they are needed to rear little children, or have a good time and enjoy life, looking forward to leaving it, but whether we go when the party is at its height or linger till the candles are guttering, we do have to go some time. I try to get him to talk when he has his black moods, but unsuccessfully. If he says anything, it's only 'I don't *want* to die'.

Wednesday, 1 March. I worked with Mrs Salisbury and cooked lunch – tinned mushroom soup, bacon and kidney, sprouts and potatoes and a steamed raisin pudding and custard. Mrs Salisbury feels quite well off now. Her boy of 15 is working, taking milk out for the Co-op, and when his round is over doing odd jobs at grocery and seed shop branches. He gets 37s 6d a week and it's a blow to his labourer father who, when insurance etc. is stopped out of his wage, hasn't £4 10s 0d a week! Last week I gave her a very good working overcoat. My brother bought it and it was too tight and he sent it for my husband, who didn't wear it much. She got it cleaned and says, 'It's just like new and I'm going to buy him a *real new* suit too. It will be the first suit he has ever had bought, for anything new before has been odd jackets and flannels.'

Saturday, 4 March. Soon the plumber and his boy mate came. [*The lavatory was blocked.*] I was a bit taken back to have a screw[†] of tea and sugar given and asked to make tea before they started. But then the plumber said, 'I've not had a drink of tea yet this morning – I've not a very good landlady and she sleeps in and

I've got some bread and jam, love', and he pulled out a repulsive-looking newspaper packet, soiled with being in his pocket. He was very tall with that sick monkey look that some people get through pain, and as he unpacked his kit mentioned casually he had duodenal trouble. *Any* stomach sufferer has my deepest sympathy. I asked him if he wouldn't sooner have milk and I heated him some and began to advise him to take slippery elm food [*a laxative*]. I neither hindered him, nor did he stop work, only to take a drink of milk and a mouthful of bread and jam. A bit dropped and separated and I could see no butter or marg was under the scrape of jam. I marvelled at any woman being so mean and greedy. When I went down my husband was holding forth to Mrs Howson, who had called, and was telling her all about my 'cooing over the plumber'. I pursed my lips and shook my head a little behind his back, meaning 'He isn't too well this morning – take no notice'. She had refused to sit down, saying she was in a hurry, but the kind little thing *did* sit down, and began a string of silly Canteen reminiscences in which to hear her talk I'd always gone 'starry eyed' over enough Merchant Navy men and very young sailors whose clothes looked too big for them. She got my husband laughing before she went. I blessed her visit …

The plumber's boy had interested me by saying he liked singing and he had been in two talent shows, and offered to sing the song for me he had then. I was in the kitchenette and heard the hiss of the upstairs cistern and thought they must have finished – till I was horrified at water pouring out from above the door leading into the garage. My husband had touched the handle as he got up off his knees, and with no pan fixed it had flooded the floor and found its own outlet. I hope none has lodged over my nicely enamelled kitchenette ceiling. When a pure passionless boy's voice rang out 'This is my lovely day', I felt I echoed the savage 'If you don't shut up I'll clout you' of the plumber! …

I became conscious [*at teatime*] my husband looked wild-eyed and distraught and before I could ask if he felt ill he burst out, 'I'm losing my senses, I know I am'. I felt startled, then dismayed, then really angry. It seems he had upset Billy's arrangements for the partnership* by telling Billy the man must be a real shark to want half of all profits, and had told Billy to ask his father to lend him the money to buy the stock and machinery – and offered to lend him £100 to 'work on'. I said, 'If you have as you say hinted that you would take the money for the stock etc. at several times, and on top of that offered to lend Billy £100 – with no security, no business sense, and a retarded development generally. How *are* you getting rid of your business worries? You are adding to them. What guarantee have you that Billy won't use up all stocks and then fail, before you have got the money for it, or your £100 back?' I was really angry, but his miserable bewildered face checked the tirade I felt I could have given him. He said, 'What *will* I do?' I said, 'You mean "What will *I* do?" I will see Billy and make the situation plain and I hope you haven't done too much damage by your crazy interference. If that man was backing Billy in every way he would naturally want some security of return, and all this talk you seem to have had about how the rates and bills for light are to be solved – darn and blast it, they're not your problems, dear – it's a matter for the Rates Office.'

---

*Negotiations were under way to sell the joinery shop to Billy Newington, who, according to Nella on 3 March, 'has been carrying on the business, more or less', during Will's struggles. But Billy had little cash – Nella was shocked at his and his wife's disinclination to save – and he had been offered a loan by an accountant, a relative, on condition that the lender be given half the profits of the business. 'Billy at 37 has less sense' than her own sons 'had at 17 at thinking for themselves', she wrote on 9 March.

Cross and angry as I was outwardly, in my heart was sick fright. I do try and take each day as it comes and not look ahead to the days ahead. I nerved myself to be really brutal as I drove a hard bargain. 'I'll get things all straightened out on one condition – that in future you won't talk business unless I am there. You are tired and ill and cannot think things out properly. *I'll* have to do it, and get Arthur if I cannot.' He agreed so eagerly, so pathetically, I could have wept in despair. I tried to cheer him with little silly ravings, saying, 'If soap could stick in the lav' like that, in what the plumber called a million to one chance, I *might* get such long odds again and win the Irish Sweep you know and I'd have off to Cook's and book a cruise and we would be off within a week.' His lips trembled as he suddenly thought of something and said, 'I'm sorry I was nasty about you "cooing" over the plumber', and I brought a watery smile to his poor face by saying severely, 'You're not, you know. It's just you think I should only "coo" over you, you big baby.' I felt so heart thankful Arthur is coming on the 31st. Dear God, what *would* I do if it wasn't for the thought of my two sons in the background. Cliff gets me cross and he loses patience so often with some of my ways – oddly enough those same ways are amongst the ones Arthur likes – but I always feel the strength of his affections cropping up. They are both 'always there'. 'What we have we lose, but what we keep in memory is ours for everlasting.'

Sunday, 5 March. I went down to see Billy and his wife. I've known and 'mothered' Billy for well over 20 years. He served his time as apprentice and always worked at the shop, except in the war years when he was afraid he would have to go into the Services and went on cement barge construction – *very* rough work, only knocking wooden shells and frames together – and though his wife and I haven't met often, I've always known her as a shop assistant in each of two shops I occasionally went, so I felt I *could* speak plainly. Billy has a queer dense spot. I've known all the time he was spinning out the work and either wouldn't or couldn't see the need we stressed for an early close down. Today I made everything clear – *no* strings to the business. Billy knows at £250 he is getting stock and machinery for many times that value and it's not that he quibbles, it's just that he will have to get the money from somewhere if he doesn't take that offer. I pointed out that the 'half of the profits' could mean a fraction of what the interest from borrowed money – from one of the firms that lend money on security – would be. We talked together. Ida has a more sensible head and could see my point when I suggested getting proper advice – a given period for this 'half profits', and the money to be returned at a given date. I can see Billy has no idea of book keeping, estimates, etc. or that people take their own time to pay bills, while monthly accounts are sent out by wood yards and travellers.

Slight contempt and dismay filled my mind when I looked round their decent but poorly furnished home, everything of the cheapest and poorest. Ida had no stockings on and her toes showed through holes in tawdry velvet slippers. Both had the cheapest and most worn indoor clothes, really ragged. The lovely little girl woke from her nap and cried to come downstairs. She certainly was no film star today. She had ragged woolly slippers on and a torn outgrown frock.* Only half rent for the little house. It's not as in the case of so much 'indoor' poverty. Nowadays, they are struggling to pay for a house. When they talked so pitifully

---

*Two days before Nella had written that Billy and Ida's 'lovely little girl of 2½ is dressed like a film star's child. White kid boots, white fur coat, etc., but I felt shocked at their lack of thrift.'

about never saving I said, 'You will have Savings Certificates, haven't you? You would be in a street saving group.' When Ida drew the corners of her mouth down and shook her head, saying, 'No. Billy and me said it was only a way to prolong the war and as long as mugs† scraped and saved "they" would keep on.' I thought of how they had both prospered all the war, and how the poorest had bought 6d savings stamps, thinking 'it will help the boys'. They hadn't *any* one fighting or suffering. I looked back on my own struggles, when the only money that could be saved was for years what dividend I got at the Co-op – and an old metal box I'd had from a child. The first ten years of our married life was bad going, for I'd never been used to thinking of money, or the shortage, but I and every friend and neighbour I ever had *could* have the feeling of security 'a bit behind us' can give. I wondered if this state of affairs was the new way of life for young people. Yet, on reflection, both Margaret and Norah Atkinson have that same attitude to 'independence' I had when young – 'If you have a pound you have a friend' feeling.

I rose to go. My husband was sitting in the car, round the corner. His poor head wouldn't have stood any more. I ran through all we had decided – the £250 had to be paid, no money lent, my husband had never on *any* occasions to be worried, he would never have to be regarded as the boss or adviser whatever happened, and I had to be approached always first in any little business matter that would arise before all was finally settled. I said, 'I hated to come and talk like this. Thank you both for being so nice to me. Things aren't any too easy just now.' Ida took my hand and said so kindly, 'Thank *you*. I'm glad we have got all settled on rock bottom level and we know exactly where we do stand. You know, Billy seems to have come back with *some* different yarn every time he has seen Mr Last.' I thought with a little sadness 'I'll bet!!'

I suggested we go over Walney and sit in the sun, but my husband rather surprised me by saying, 'No, Coniston Lake. I know now why you always want to go there and leave all your troubles. You know, I used to think you were fanciful when you said that.' We parked at our usual draw-in where the road widened a little and walked along the edge of the Lake in the sunshine, the beauty of hills and fells with the sunshine picking out greys, purples and tarnished gold of last year's bracken, the nut trees so laden with dancing goldy green catkins. The gentle lap, lap of the quiet water on the pebbly edge wove a magic of peace and serenity, making a quiet on my troubled mind. I'd have liked to sit quiet and still, letting it wash over me. It was one of those days when you felt if you did so sit, things would be made plainer, values get sorted out, dross washed out of mind and heart. We walked further than we thought and both were tired by the time we got back to the car. We walked with the westerning sun shining over the hill into our faces, and it picked out the branches of trees, etched against the blue skies. Suddenly I stopped and pointed to a lovely birch tree. Sure enough, tiny buds showed faintly on the slender spidery twigs and branches.

I was so 'away' with the beauty that was like a blessing, I had hardly noticed my husband's silence. He didn't seem any quieter than usual. When he spoke I gasped as he said, 'You know, I'm sure my head will go before long. You don't know how I feel sometimes. Look how foolishly I behaved over the business. Anyone "sharp" could have taken advantage and got me into a real muddle. When I go out tomorrow I'm going to put my Building Society Account with you. There will then be £1,800 in your name, and when all is settled, I'm putting all money in your name in the Bank. I'm not fit to be bothered and if I get worse in my head I might begin to give money away like Mother.' To say I could have sat down flat in the pebbly road was no exaggeration. For a few seconds I paused by a mossy wall and leaned on it for support. I said quietly, 'Well, just as you like, dear. You *must* avoid worry in every way.' But, I added, 'If you give me a whip I shall crack it, and I tell you plainly, if you don't get into this Convalescent Home I shall arrange a few weeks' holiday for both of us, and take you away somewhere, *and* spend as freely as I think best in other ways. I'll neither pinch or scrape or "draw in my horns", as you are so fond of telling me. Dear knows they aren't very long horns, and I don't see that being pinch-penny is going to help.'

It shook me so badly I was violently sick when I got in. I felt tired of my day, and longed for bed. Poor dear, he had made tea when I crawled down. Two cups of hot tea took a bit of the nervous chill away. Lately I have seemed to have such poor circulation – at times my hands and feet go wet-cold, and my finger nails dull blue grey, and my hands look soiled. Just nerves, no doubt. One thing, my wretched bones don't feel quite as disjointed now it's not so cold.

Monday, 6 March. It was like an April morning, sun shining, birds chirping. My husband went down to the Co-op offices by 9 o'clock, before he went to the doctor's, and got the recommendation for the Scarborough Convalescent Home. I *did* feel so thankful. I feel a complete change will do him good – both of us. Mrs Salisbury didn't come as I'd half expected. The house looks very upset, with stair carpets up, pictures down, etc., but I felt everything would get done sooner or later. I'll have a lot of spare time when my husband is away and it's possible he may go next week. Most people like and try for high summer in such places. He is beginning to feel himself that he doesn't improve much and is ready to take any chance.

Tuesday, 7 March. Times I crawl to bed thinking, 'Well, the day has been the most tiresome I've known', and day after day follows equally, if not more worrying and upsetting, and I get through more and more conscious of 'given' strength not my own but for which I so ceaselessly pray. Perhaps the upset, added to the turmoil of settling up the business finally, makes my husband increasingly difficult and I so often feel at a breaking point. Mrs Stable – Mrs Howson's mother – and Mrs Atkinson both asked me today if I'd 'be afraid to be alone in the house when Mr Last goes away'. They little know how the thought of blessed peace and quiet, able to 'stand and stare', and not have to watch and guard every word or action, is keeping me up lately! ...

Billy rang up and began a pointless 'He said, I said' talk, and asked if I'd like the safe bringing up – it was my father's and I let it go to the shop, but kept any securities etc. in it. I said it would have to come up to the house now and suggested to my husband it went under the stairs. I got out all nearby, not an easy task in a short time for I had to re-plan where they had to go back. Then he decided he would have it in a corner of the lounge where it's a real blot in the room. Billy has never realised how things upset my husband, but he and the other two saw plainly! To say anything only upsets my husband more and more – so there the big ugly thing sits. I said with what I thought heavy sarcasm, 'Now if I'd only a lace curtain or the like to drape over it, and put a geranium on top, it could be camouflaged'. My husband said, 'I bet you haven't such a thing and that when they went out of fashion you never even thought to keep one'. The look of utter amazement on young Gilbert's face would have made me laugh if anything would, but I felt so dead tired and edgy. I lost count of the phone calls – people who 'have just heard Mr Last is giving up business – you *will* see I get so-and-so done before he does, won't you?' One woman had apparently just discovered she needed new wooden sills on her upstairs windows. She used to come with a '*Must* be done straight away, I want the painters in' – but left bills unpaid for months in spite of being a well-to-do person! I felt it gave me pleasure to give her the shop phone number and say, 'In future that will be the number to ring'.

Wednesday, 8 March. My husband kept to his idea of putting his Building Society money in my name. Perhaps when he is away and I have the keys of the safe I can really find out our position, and know exactly where we stand. If and when I do I'll work out future plans. A parcel came from Cliff – it had lard and apricot jam and honey, casserole beef and a little box of such nice muscatel raisins and almonds. All went on the shelf except the last named – they will be welcome later. I've promised my husband to 'Take the first train if he feels he cannot possibly settle'. In return he has promised to try to settle for a month. I sighed as I realised how quickly things go out of his mind nowadays. As fast as I get one worry in the least solved, another crops up.

Mrs Atkinson called me. She said that 'Mrs Jones is back and I've seen her peering in your front window three times today'. I've known Mrs Jones from a spoilt pampered childhood, but only at all intimately in the war when she worked at Hospital Supply in the morning. She never had a friend amongst all the busy friendly women who served so busily. Her husband was twice Mayor and she 'mixed' surprisingly well, but for years her only 'pleasure' was going to different doctors, even specialists, with some vague nervous trouble no one seemed to solve – except one, a semi-quack who told her she had auto sclerosis and he gave her a course of expensive injections. I wonder lately if he could have been right. These last two years has seen a great decline in her mental health. She goes away to rest care places and seems incapable of settling in her own house. She met me several times and spoke of 'all the fun and laughter those days at Hospital Supply', and said she was going to begin calling. I wasn't enthusiastic. She was never likeable and I felt I'd enough with Mother at the time. Mrs Atkinson said, 'Keep your garage door locked. She is terribly queer since she came back this time.' I felt I would.

Thursday, 9 March. I heard a noise upstairs but took no notice, thinking I'd left one of the bedroom doors open and Shan We, who evidently thinks wind and storm ahead, and has been very flighty today, was jumping on and off the bed. Then I realised it was a step on the landing and feet began to come slowly downstairs. Odd how a feeling of danger spurs and stimulates. I glanced quickly round. My poker isn't very strong. I grasped the little brass tongs firmly and moved quietly into the passage, thinking I'd *have* to keep the garage door locked when I'm on my own. From where I stood I couldn't see who it was stood where I do when the cats need chasing into the garage for bed, not standing at the foot but behind the panelled stairs, so as not to frighten them back upstairs. Partly to my relief, partly horror, Mrs Jones walked down. She must have come in through the garage when I was in the garden (my husband said when he came in). She had been peering through the window when he went out and asked, 'Does Mrs Last live here?' Her mind seems to have quite gone. She said offhandedly, 'I'm looking for an old friend of mine, Mrs Last. We called her Lasty in the war at Hospital Supply, and she used to make us laugh. Do you know her?' I said, 'I think she has gone away. Won't Mr Jones wonder where you are? He will have lunch ready', and opened the front door and let her out. I felt my knees tremble and sat down on the stairs, feeling in one of those silly crying-laughing ways.

Friday, 10 March. My husband suddenly said, 'Don't look through the window now', and went on writing. I stole a glance from where I was sitting. Mrs Jones' distraught face was pressed to the glass, but she went as quietly as she had come. Poor woman. She had opened the garage door and gone right through. The kitchenette door had been closed and the key turned so the window cleaner could go through. Later I picked up a really valuable glove I recognised – real chamois – I remembered seeing her wear and which they had bought in Switzerland at a handicraft shop in a small mountain town. We were going to get the railway ticket, so I left it at the Joneses' house – it's only two streets and five minutes away. I'd not have known Mr Jones if I'd met him outdoors. He was a vivid type of man, with Welsh colouring and 'fire', a good speaker, and as Mayor twice, much in the public eye. Now he seems to have faded and shrunk with all the worry and care. He closed the vestibule door carefully behind him and said, 'Mrs Jones is sleeping and I don't want her to wake. She will only go trailing out again.' He laughed ruefully when I told him she had asked me if 'Mrs Last' lived at our house. He said, 'She doesn't recognise me always. She said the other day after repeatedly asking my name "The name seems familiar. I must know someone called that".'

My husband was in the car. Mr Jones spoke so sadly as he sent regards and the hopes of recovery with a holiday in Scarborough. He said, 'I've been *appalled* – that's the only word I *can* use – to have so many early breakdowns in mind and body brought to my notice lately'. I said, 'Well, you have been going to doctors and specialists quite a lot lately'. But he said, 'I wasn't referring to that. Go down into town on a sunny morning – you can see ten times more people looking as if they have crawled out to get the sun, and as if they are past work.' He always was an interesting man. He read everything but had his own theories too and he is convinced this world is 'aging' at a rapid rate and somewhere else a new one 'rising'. Hence wars to take 'young souls'. He said, 'Don't you think you can do any good by "friendliness" to Mrs Jones? Her mind has gone, I fear. Don't let her in if you are alone. She has some queer ways now.' Such a tragedy, for though she was always a spoiled woman who 'enjoyed bad health', they were reasonably happy.

Nella and Will were preparing for his journey to Scarborough, where Will was booked to stay for at least two weeks in a convalescent home. This would be a big departure from their norm of almost relentless togetherness. Both were worried, though no doubt for different reasons, and on Monday the 13th, when Nella 'left him as the train drew out and saw his pitiful lost look, I wondered how he would settle'.

Tuesday, 14 March. Mrs Salisbury came. Her first words were 'I can't stop all day. Little Billy isn't at school. He has styes on his eyes.' Knowing her slapdash meat and potatoes and onion, bread and jam, fried sausage or meat pies menu, I marvel they keep so well. They are all five robust children, tall and strong for their age, not liking milk, green vegetables or salads, and little fresh fruit unless when apples and tomatoes are in their garden and little greenhouse, and blackberries in the hedges. They have strong 'gypsy' flashing teeth, and never have many colds. Their hair is thick and shining, their cheeks rosy. 'It makes yer think' – wonder if vitamins and calories and 'mothercraft' *are* as we are told. Billy has shot up from a fat baby of four to a wiry stringy little boy of five, and just when free things would do him good, they cease. Mrs Salisbury never bothered to get orange juice or cod liver oil. Anyway, she has that 'If it costs nowt, it's worth nowt' way of thinking.

Wednesday, 15 March. Mrs Salisbury was talking about the couple in her rooms – only newly married. Each weekend she has put her joint in Mrs Salisbury's tin in the oven, and the potatoes have been boiled together, and tinned peas heated the first time. The second Sunday the young bride asked if Mrs Salisbury could lend her a tin – she had forgotten to get one. Mrs Salisbury couldn't, but she offered a little cabbage, but it was refused because 'Ah, I've never cooked a cabbage'. All week they eat eggs for the packed lunches, and again for tea when they come in – the young man's people keep a lot of hens. She cannot wash, bake, clean to any system. She works in a paper mill, where she does something in the wood pulp department. I wondered whatever she would do if she had a baby!

Saturday, 25 March. The sun pouring into my bedroom window this morning suddenly gave me the 'wanders' and though I did feel I was wearing someone else's feet and ankles, as I dressed I made up my mind to clear off for the day and go to Ambleside on the 9.30 bus. I took an orange and some chocolate, meaning to get lunch. It was a perfect spring day, one to make a poet sing. Woods and gardens golden with daffodils and forsythia, or purple with crocus and petunias, and the early almond and rhododendrons were a glory of pink. Little lambs skipped in the sunshine, old people and children sat on steps and low walls of cottage gardens. Windows were wide and doors propped open, as if everyone wanted to take full advantage of the lovely sunshine. The bus kept filling to bulging, then emptying a little as market people got off and fishermen, hikers and walkers, and people with children with baskets, eagerly talking of the daffodils they meant to pick.

The Ambleside bus from Barrow takes nearly two hours, and

there's a two-hour service. I decided to wait for the next one,
and sauntered through the town to the Lake. It was too early for
lunch, and I didn't feel like any of the proffered menus – made
up dishes mainly – so I bought a meat patty and a cake and ate
them, together with the orange and plain chocolate, down by the
Lake. I'd have sat longer in the sun, but when I'd no more bits
of pastry to throw to the swans, they began to come out of the
water to know the reason why, and looked a bit formidable, so
I walked slowly back to the bus terminus and got a cup of tea.
A pack of young huntsmen with about the most mixed pack of
dogs imaginable devoured big tea cake sandwiches of egg and
cress, cheese and lettuce or meat, and spoke of the rough going
over Coniston and Hawkshead fells. A girl walked slowly up to
the snack bar, leading a French poodle, and we talked of animals
as I lost my heart to the silly black-haired clown, who, evidently
realising how I admired him, did all his tricks. When he put one
paw on the side of his nose and peeped up sideways so roguishly,
I felt I could have taken him home – and chanced my spoilt cats'
reactions to him!

If my feet and ankles hadn't throbbed and burned, I'd have
waited for the next bus, but I knew it would go colder quickly
as the sun sank behind the hills. I was home at 3.30, and meant
to go downtown, but the settee in the sun tempted me and I
stretched out and read the paper.

Sunday, 26 March. It's been a marvellous day. I thought wistfully of Coniston Lake. I thought I'd better turn out the little
front room and air the mattress and pillows in the sunshine. If
as I suspect my husband will be coming home at the end of his
fortnight, I'll not want a lot to do. With working all morning I
could have a rest this afternoon whereas if he was home I'd have

had to go out, and even in the car, if I've had a busy morning, I'd rather relax.

Mrs Howson came to see if I'd go to church, and took my letters to the post. We had to be there by 6 o'clock. It's a small church, only holding about 300, and was packed before they rang the bell. It was a very good sermon by the Archdeacon of Westmorland, a simple sincere 'talk' rather than an actual sermon, on trying to see 'God's plan' behind everything. It could have been my old Gran speaking.

Will returned home on Monday, 27 March, as gloomy and 'nervy' as ever, and for several days thereafter Nella found little to be cheerful about. Her son Arthur arrived from Belfast on 1 April for a ten-day visit, so she could at least enjoy his company; but it was her husband's low moods and neediness that darkened much of her writing this month. 'As I sat I realised suddenly how all fight has left me nowadays,' she wrote on 15 April, 'to be replaced by a calm acceptance of the fact my husband dislikes most contact with the outside world, that his life-long shyness has somehow soured, and settled into a "keep out" fixation. Now I feel I don't want people to look at him in surprise when he says unthinking remarks, or behaves in a pettish way. I feel *I'm* growing reserved to a degree – a kind of pride no doubt. I hate people to pity me!'

Friday, 21 April. Mrs Higham had rung up while I was out, saying it *was* uniform for the WVS† dinner on Saturday. To hear my husband natter you would have thought I intended going as Lady Godiva. He thought I should have gone in my dinner dress and defied whoever had decreed uniform. I felt a bit peeved myself, but when they were all going to wear it I naturally fell in. After all, I feel happier in my old shabby frock and overcoat than in any Paris creation. It represents something in my life that is a mixture of effort, gaiety, comradeship and purpose that outweighed all the darkness and anxiety of war years …

My husband laid down for an hour and then decided to get out the car and go and sit over Walney. I'm sure he is suffering from a kind of poisoning from taking sleeping tablets constantly again. He was saying how ill all over he felt, and I said a bit crossly, 'You are the only one who can do yourself any good. You have drifted back to that state you were in before when you were over-drugged. You *must* stop taking them as a habit and concentrate on simple things like windows more open, drinks of water, reading when you cannot sleep, etc. You haven't any worries about the business wind-up – or your mother – to blame now, *and* you must take some liver pills or Fynnons.† They won't do harm if they don't do good in the way of making you sleep.' I tried not to be ungenerous but couldn't help wondering if he will be better after the St George's dinner is over. He does so hate me going anywhere he cannot go.

He wouldn't go for his usual walk in the sunshine. He said it was too windy, so we sat with the windows of the car open on the sheltered side. The sea was thundering in at high tide and smelled sweet and fresh. Several beachcombers staggered up the stones with good oddments of wood that had been washed up. Some of the squatters have been luckier than others, as if the RAF huts were in better repair than others. I noticed a group of huts were being repaired and the roofs tarred. That section had little gardens – even hen runs – cultivated, and rough fences from, apparently, driftwood. Other huts had been utterly demolished as soon as tenants could be put into Council houses. I suppose as this big new housing estate gets finished they will all have to go. They will find a change from the freedom of sea coast and wide spaces – *and* having to pay as high as 24–28 shillings a week compared to the 10 shillings they pay which now includes electricity for light.

Saturday, 22 April. Mrs Howson ran in to ask if I'd go down early to help receive guests [*at the WVS dinner*]. She had been helping Miss Willan and her sister set serviettes with wee red rose buds (cotton), fudge in little silver bonbon dishes, cigarettes, silver candlesticks with red and white candles, and had had a busy afternoon. It poured with rain, and kept several members away who had been last year. The organiser from Birkenhead was the speaker. I'd met her in the war, but wouldn't have known her. She had so gone to seed, not only put on weight but badly needed a decent corset and hairdo. She still wore her rather unruly hair in a long bob, most unbecoming when it is now grey – and she has grown fatter. She and Mrs Diss, who has put on at least three stones since wartime days, teased me with my 'girlish' figure, asking the secret. I said, 'Perhaps a nervy tummy that keeps me more or less on a diet – and I don't like chocolates', a little dig at Mrs Diss, who rarely has one out of her mouth, eating her husband's and son's share as well as her own! ... Perhaps I've so many real worries and problems nowadays, but the speeches about WVS seemed either a rehash of past efforts or a little 'make believe' effort to recapture the undoubted value of the move-ment. Perhaps in Barrow there isn't the need or call for 'meals on wheels', 'good mother' schemes – and the Hospital Outpatients Canteen and Trolley service seems like another leg on a cat.

Monday, 24 April. When Mrs Jones began knocking at the window and ringing the bell just after 8 o'clock, I felt my day had begun badly, but when she insisted on taking the two bottles of milk off the milkman and bringing them on to the window sill and dropped and broke one on the step, I felt really cross. It went off like a bomb and splinters of glass flew everywhere. The milkman gave me another in its place, but that didn't help clean up the

mess. To make matters worse a needle-like splinter got into Mrs
Jones' instep – she had court shoes on – and with it being so cold
the blood flowed quicker. I felt I couldn't be bothered with her. I
put on my coat and hat and took her home, telling Mr Jones what
had happened. He looked distraught. He has aged terribly these
few months and has the unkempt look elderly men get with no
woman to keep him up to scratch. Years ago, his perky, bustling
ways used to amuse us. His droll witticisms kept people laughing. Now his eyes look tired and have no humour, only weariness.
He said, 'I hope Mrs Jones doesn't worry you like she did?' I said,
'Oh no, don't worry. She loves our chiming bell you know.' And
when I saw a bit of worry lift off his face as he smiled goodbye,
I thought, 'Odd how a lie can make you happier than the truth!'

CHAPTER THREE

SNAPSHOTS OF SOCIETY

May–August 1950

Wednesday, 3 May. We decided to go tonight to the Coliseum, mainly to see Albert Modley's brother Allen, who was a comedian – very good too and a well balanced show [*billed as 'Strippingly Saucy'*]. I often think I must have a queer kink – the turn that interested me above all others was judged by most standards revolting! A supple limbed man with a toupee, but with the rest of his hair long, and with an unmistakable air of perversion, did little more than 'dress the stage' and join in generally. Then came his scene – two Chinese immobile opening curtains, a pallet bed piled with cushions on the floor, in a corner a table with a life-size silver idol with contorted limbs, silver mask with stiff upstanding spirals of hair. The curtains parted. A golden-haired girl came through and was helped off with a gorgeous fur coat, and led to the divan where she was given an opium pipe and settled herself to sleep and dream. The idol quivered into life and stepped down. His supple silver body only had a G-string with silver fringe. Few realised the utter perfection of his writhing as his arms wove bonelessly in what looked like a true altar dance. His body had lost the perfect sinuousness of adolescence needed for perfect interpretation. The music was marvellous and puzzled me at first as it whispered and throbbed with the true temple beat – a gramophone record of course. I heard a man behind say, 'You see a lot of this kind of thing in India, you know, but generally in back street shows'. The dreamer on the pallet bed tossed and moaned. The 'idol' with the perfectly masked face – like a real idol, so impassive, sexless, ageless – bent over her, and then sprang silently back onto the table as she stirred to consciousness. The attendants brought her coat and firmly led her to the curtains, which parted. She went through. They fell in silent folds. The 'Chinese' attendants tucked their hands in their sleeves and bowed their heads slightly. The spotlight flickered on the immobile silver idol, and the curtain fell quickly as the music died. A real gem of production, timing and performance. I suppose it *was* revolting. It was perhaps a 'wonder it had been let escape the censor's eye'. The half whispers round showed that people recognised what the man was by inclination if not an 'accident' of birth, but somehow the perfection lifted it above all else for me. Allen Modley is good. Pity he models his toothless grimaces on Norman Evans, and his witless type of humour – 'gormless'† is the Yorkshire word – on his brother Albert.*

Thursday, 4 May. The sun shone. I persuaded my husband to go to Ulverston market and felt glad we did for I got such nice fillets of sole and a halibut head for my cats – 1s 8d for the fish and only 3d for the good meaty head. Beside two country lorries drawn up in the square, a line of women queued. Feeling curious I went to the top of the queue to see – then hurried back to the end to wait my turn for cauliflowers when I heard the price – 1s for bigger and cleaner looking ones than for 2s 6d in Barrow. When it was my turn I said to the pleasant-faced girl, 'I wish you came to Barrow market'. She said, 'Nay. Dad and Mother say it's wasted

*Albert Modley (born in Liverpool in 1901) and Norman Evans (born in Rochdale, also in 1901) were variety entertainers and comedians.

time and petrol, and it means we can sell them cheaper here in Ulverston. We sell all we grow direct so our prices are generally about half.' She told me they had had plenty of young spring greens at 6d each but all had been sold. I saw onions on several stalls at 1s a pound, but they found few buyers. Women bought green scallions at 6d a pound. Though not so strongly flavoured, they were better value. Plenty of nice fowls, huge whole salmon, and every kind of 'good' fish in the fish shop where I got mine. I felt shopping was easy with a full purse! We had a cup of tea at a snack bar, and then were home by 11.30.*

Friday, 5 May. Mrs Howson came in after tea, in one of her very worst 'I've no time for *that*' humour, and sat waspish and bitter tongued about all and every subject that cropped up. I felt puzzled and wondered what had possibly upset her. I've not seen her quite so nowty since Canteen days. I think I found what was the root of her bad humour. I asked if she had filled in her Civil Defence form, and she snapped, '*Yes*, if there's any decent job going *we* might as well have them and not the folks who have only been in WVS five minutes'. She and I differ widely on WVS policy. She 'doesn't want strangers poking into meetings and dinners – folk that never helped when there was work to be done'. I feel we who have gone through the war have had enough and should encourage and help others to take over in the dreadful event of being needed again. Perhaps because I myself feel so depleted nowadays,

---

*'I love to wander round on market day in Ulverston', Nella wrote on Thursday 22 June 1950. 'Born and bred in a town, so much of my childhood's happiest memories are of Gran's farm on the hills, coming to market in the gig, meeting kindly country neighbours. The smell of freshly cut and dug vegetables or the sight of a patient shaggy horse is akin to the feeling I get by Coniston Lake – not exactly an escape as much as a reality, something firm and strong in my life.'

I think others will feel the same. She said suddenly, 'What do you think of that newcomer, Mrs Todkill?' I said, 'I don't know much about her at all. She was a stranger. Her husband is an Admiralty man, and she came to the WVS to try and make friends and when introduced to me I pounced on her and asked her if she would take over and help Mrs Higham in the trolley scheme, and be stand-in for me at the hospital outpatients' canteen.' I got *such* a look as Mrs Howson said, 'So *that's* how she got pushed into things – and now she is going to be organiser for the Civil Defence. *I* was asked but felt *I* wasn't smart enough, but *she* took it without demur.'

I laughed to myself at Mrs Howson's being asked. At the Canteen she gave frantic signals for help to the counter if a coloured man, a foreigner who couldn't speak English, or a lad who showed the least signs of having had drink came up. She got offended and was so touchy she had to be handled carefully, and disliked people at a glance. I wondered what job on her own she could have held. As for lecturing, she has no idea of speaking coherently, even about clothes and fashion. It's difficult sometimes to grasp the idea she wants to convey. I said without thinking, 'Mrs Todkill is a quiet little thing – but have you seen her firm decisive mouth? To me she looks as if she has been used to authority – perhaps been a teacher.' Then I got Mrs Howson's opinion of teaching, folk who were stuck up because they had been to college, etc. etc. I felt so out of patience. I felt she needed a sharp slap and a dose of syrup of figs like a disordered child, and I felt too I'd all the whims and moods to cope with that I was capable of doing. I often realise with a little sadness that I must have had a lot more patience in the war. Maybe, too, I felt more balanced. To make up for little annoyances and frets, there was the purpose, the laughter and the wide companionship, and the feeling you were helping – a pretty good feeling.

Saturday, 6 May. It poured as we went in the bus but lessened as we hurried down the road to the Odeon. People in every shop doorway showed by their lack of raincoats they had been caught unexpectedly. It was a really good mixed programme – a short comedy, cartoon, an interesting but very misleading propaganda short. A foreigner would have said, 'Ah, the *wonder* schools the English have. Now the Health Scheme is nationalised.' Twice the commentator spoke of 'free secondary schools for all', and by what I hear, parents have even more worry than I had! Arthur got in the Grammar School sixth in the town; Cliff just failed the written exam, but got in on the 'personality' test. I can hear of many anxious parents – generally it's mothers who worry most – who are waiting this week to hear how children came off last week when they had their interview. *The Big Steal* [*starring Robert Mitchum*] was the best picture we have seen for months – its action in Mexico alone would have been of interest – but the story, acting and production was all good. My husband has begun to take an interest in going to the cinema, and though I'm very glad I'd be more so if he could find something to do – to build. He used to care. He *could* make toys for Peter, he could paste snaps in the album, help a little in lots of little household tasks – even go shopping – lots of retired men do.

Monday, 8 May. A ring brought a dapper assured-looking man, with pencil and pad and the brisk manner of someone determined to have information. Yet he was only seeking customers for cleaning windows! I could only tell him two men did all the windows on the small estate and suggest he tried somewhere a little farther out of town. Such a nice friendly young man, really. He had just finished 21 years in the Navy, joining as a boy of 14. I can generally size up people. I said, 'Why window cleaning? I think you have been used to waiting at table.' When he said he had I recommended him to Thompsons, the brewers, who own a lot of the hotels in the district and where a cousin of my husband's is managing director, and I'd heard his wife say they were short of part-time waiters often. When he thanked me he said, 'A chap who knew Barrow said, "Glad you are going up there with the wife – there's a friendly crowd", but I didn't realise what he meant. I am grateful for the suggestion and will go right away.' He turned to wave at the gate – and for no reason at all I felt tears on my cheeks as I closed the door, and thoughts of Cliff, never far from my mind, rushed overwhelmingly over me.

Tuesday, 9 May. For curiosity I called in to see if my naval caller had been to see about a waiter's job. My husband's cousin said, 'He seems a very likely chap, and if he comes up to what he says of first-class waiting and understanding mixing and serving of drinks, he will have no need to think of a window cleaner's round'. I got half a bottle of whisky to have in the house – the first in a *long* time I've been able to get, in spite of my husband's connection with the managing director. Wines, rum and brandies as well as many brands of cocktails were plentiful, but sadly enough, no gin …

My husband, after wondering and wondering what to do, decided to go to see *Happiest Days of Your Life* [*starring Alastair Sim and Margaret Rutherford*], so after I'd washed up and he had relaxed a while, we went. It began so well, but as it went on seemed to lapse into the amateurish way of so many British pictures. We have such polished, experienced actors, marvellous photographic scenes – as good if not better 'types' for every imaginable crowd scene – yet so often, however good the story, I catch myself saying in my mind 'tich tich', let's do that again. The stars

I've blushed for from Gracie Fields, George Formby to Margaret Lockwood and poor Tommy Fields [*brother of Gracie*]. I'd have liked this picture run through again with frequent stops, to really find why, with everything to hand, it petered out. I wondered if it could be the attempt to blend rapier wit and flannel-footed slapstick. Then there was a travel picture of a London typist going on a Mediterranean trip on a cargo boat – boring and tedious and far too long. I love travel pictures of any kind, but when most of the film is taken on board and of people so commonplace in looks and actions as these, it seemed a waste of time. I felt that a lot had gone to destroy people's interest in pictures. When I see poor ones I long to remonstrate, if even by getting up and walking out!

Wednesday, 10 May. Such a lovely summery day, and the sun so warm. I got Mrs Salisbury to do all the windows and she seemed pleased to be outdoors in the fresh air. She had been to the Co-op dairies to find out why her eldest lad had been sacked, and was told it was because of his 'poor educational standard'. The manager *had* held forth about the lads he had sent from the Labour bureau. He told Mrs Salisbury the bulk hadn't the standards of a lad of 9–10 of the old days. He said, 'Twenty years ago boys took milk out, or papers, or took basket meals to the shipyard. There was no cheap meals or free milk yet youngsters were bright and intelligent *and* mannerly when spoken to and didn't pretend to know it all.' He told Mrs Salisbury she *must* send George to evening classes and see he sticks to it. He said, 'whatever he is, at least he wants to be able to count beyond 12, and write plainly, and at least spell simple words'. Mrs Salisbury said, 'I told you my lads were only workers and the extra year was no good to them at school' – and I could only agree. [*The school leaving age had recently been raised from 14 to 15.*]

Thursday, 11 May. After tea my husband ran Mrs Higham home
and then said he would like to go for the last time to the Coliseum, which goes back to pictures next week. I looked at the
orchestra – such good musicians but all grey headed. There isn't
any hope they will get another similar job. Two I know gave
lessons and I suppose still do. Life must be cruel to all musicians
– *and* stage people – unless they are on the top. A good comedian, several good turns and a 'Title' trained team of eight chorus
girls didn't compensate for the rest of the bill, which would have
been more suitable for the Windmill! I never saw quite so little
worn on the stage – and the really comic part was the pudgy
starch fed girls which instead of allure radiated bath night. Two
had definitely lost any virginal curves.* It was a shame to be in
on such a lovely night. We walked slowly home, the sun still
shining.

Saturday, 13 May. I had a chat with Mr Helm, my next-door
neighbour. I think Mr Helm is one of the most honest men I
know. One eye after an operation is sightless, the other is so dim
that he is blind in bright sunlight – and he has the awful uncertainty of success when he has the next cataract operation. Yet he
potters about his garden whenever the sun is not too high, always
working busily till dusk. He listens to talks and plays and news

---

*The Windmill Theatre in London was famous for its (more or less) nude
performers. Two years later Nella made her views on nudity clear. 'As for people
who have little or no clothes on, well, they haven't, and that's that. I never could
see anything shocking in nude or semi-nude figures, always provided they weren't
gross untidy ones' (12 June 1952). By the standards of her time, Nella did not
hold particularly rigid views concerning sexual propriety. On 1 February 1951 she
borrowed from the library a copy of D. H. Lawrence's *The White Peacock*, though
she did not report what she thought of it.

of every kind on the wireless, 'blessing it more every day', and is cheery and pleasant always. This morning he and his wife were full of concern about his brother, who has been in hospital with pneumonia. We talked about mutual acquaintances returning after being in India for over 12 years, and wondered how they would settle to life and conditions in England. The wife went to school with Arthur. Such a pleasant little gossip. I sighed as I saw my husband made no attempt to join in. He just sat back, aloof as always. I thought, 'What pleasant companionship there could have been between the two "crocks"'.

Tuesday, 16 May. My husband suggested going to Spark Bridge. I'd not sent Aunt Sarah her little parcel last week, for some dripping I had seemed [*too*] soft to send by post when it was so hot. I soon made tea so we could have an early start. There was enough cold meat I could have minced for sandwiches but my husband snapped, 'Oh give it to the cats' and we had cheese, lettuce, honey and bread and butter and fruit cake, and were off by 6 o'clock. It was a cloudy evening with a heaviness in the air that brought out the smell of hawthorn blossom, and as we neared Greenodd the wood smoke hung in the air and filled all around with that smell that always spells home to me, perhaps because my happiest childish memories are of my Gran and her quiet serenity, though the boys too always speak of wood smoke and the smell of baking bread as if it's part of them! Aunt Sarah and Joe both looked as cheerful as usual, though she had been baking and he had just put in a hard day's gardening. I thought at 85 and 82 they were as nature intended old people to be, full of memories, content to slowly go downhill, savouring every little pleasure or blessing coming their way. I had to hear all the local gossip. A confirmed old bachelor of over 60 had been to Manchester, his home town, and brought back a wife at Easter. As it's an isolated cottage, I can only hope the bride of 62 settles after a city.

Saturday, 27 May. I heard Mrs Howson come in and knew she had come to tell me all the news of the wedding. I made a plate of mixed sandwiches – tomato, cheese and lettuce, and cheese and grated onion, a favourite of hers – and there was sponge sandwich and bread and butter and strawberry jam. The bridegroom was a cousin of hers, a year widowed, and we knew the bride from childhood. She is older than Cliff but not quite as old as Arthur. There seemed to have been a little shadow cast by an unforeseen muddle at the church. The groom and best man and big taxi cab of guests had arrived at the church before a very sad little funeral was over – that of a three-year-old baby who had been drowned last week. The mother's wild cries of 'My baby, oh my baby' had echoed round the church as she was half carried out, to meet on the steps another lot of wedding guests. Mrs Howson said it was surprising what a gloom was cast, and the pouring wet and cold day didn't help, or the fact that ten more guests were squeezed in to the tables originally laid for 50 at a not too convenient café. I felt glad of her prattle about what everyone wore, how they looked, who had aged – or not – in the few years since they had been out of town. It helped hold my husband's interest without effort on my part.

Wednesday, 31 May. We relaxed and listened to *Twenty Questions*. I wondered as I sat if all the gossip in the papers about the effect television was having on the home life and make-up of American people could be exaggerated, and if we were in for a general change in amusement and entertainment, as in the rest of things today. We seem to have got into a whirling mad hurry that *could* carry us over the rapids to smooth strong waters, or draw us into a deep whirlpool. History seems to be 'made' in deeper and deeper swathes and spasms as each upheaval comes. I felt a sick shock to realise Australia is taking over in Malaysia, that there's a growing need for action if peace is to last our time, never mind the next generation. Such a dreadful thought. From where I sat, Cliff's tree showed at its best in the sunset. It's different from the laburnum trees in the surrounding gardens. They have tassels, it has a long golden-scented fringe that isn't at its best till the laburnums are finished, and has a long-lasting perfume. 'I'll see you again' – but I won't, not ever. Whoever I meet, if Cliff and my paths cross again, however dear, however he has fulfilled hopes and ambitions it's 'just the echo of a sigh' for so much, and the sick wonder if another generation of mothers and wives will anguish over loved ones – for nothing at all. Worriers are always losers.

Thursday, 1 June. Mrs Higham and I sat and talked. She spoke of all the undercurrents of unrest in the Yard,[†] as men wondered if their 'responsible' jobs would last. It's always been that the key men who attained a good position kept it till retirement, and didn't have to fear the axe from London. I laughed at little jokes the men in some offices had played on each other when petrol rationing was abolished [*this had just occurred*], like ringing up and saying, 'Interested in a few petrol coupons for Whit, Bob? I believe I could get you ten or a dozen for 3s 6d each.' They were largely accepted and 'Bob' went up to Mr Higham rubbing his hands saying, 'Thank goodness I've got fixed up for petrol for Whit. I've managed to get hold of a dozen coupons.' He joined in the laughter at the leg pull, but Mrs Higham said there had been a strong rumour rationing *was* being abolished the day before, and real offers of 'bargains' in coupons were being made.

I thought of petrol at 3s plus 3s 6d for a coupon and gasped, but Mrs Higham said, 'My doctor was in debt to the garage for nearly 200 coupons, and it's been a general thing at some garages to pay your money and then hand over coupons and say casually as you fingered a 10 shilling note, "This any more use to you than the coupons?" – and it more often than not worked'. I began to feel a very simple kind of bumpkin!

Saturday, 3 June. Bowness was a throng of milling people being decanted from coaches and seeking hotels and cafés where tea had been ordered. I don't think there would have been much chance of a meal without ordering. We went along to Ambleside Road. There was no chance of parking the car in Bowness, except in the big park, and we sat a while, and then strolled along the tree shaded road by the Lake. Our 10 horse Morris was the poorest car in a group of bigger and newer cars when we returned. We had parked in a little clearing where several big trees had been recently felled, and it looked as if it was a well known spot for car picnics. We felt very surprised at the type of people who like ourselves had brought tea, and the good stoves and little collections of picnic oddments showed it was not just a sudden idea but they were used to taking meals. One big car that held three abreast was full of luggage and wraps in the back seat. I felt amused at the couple who began to light the stove while the third (looked like the son) got out folding chairs and cloth and laid out the meal. They looked more the type to roll up to a super hotel and demand a good meal. It made me look round and notice similar well-to-do types contentedly picnicking and contrast it with the definitely working-class types getting out of the coaches or eating in the top class hotels where beautifully laid tables and men waiters could be seen through the windows

from the road. It was 9 o'clock when we got home. I quietly
made excuses for leaving till all the heavy traffic had gone. That
sweet quiet peace was over all – residents out, yachts stealing out
like moths, or bright red butterflies, replacing motor and steam
boats, white clad chefs outside back doors of hotels, tired walkers
returning to hotels and boarding houses for a bath and meal. We
came down the quiet still Lake as in a dream, hardly a soul on
the road. It compensated for all the rush and noise and I could
relax and not wonder what would rush round a hidden bend and
upset my husband.

Wednesday, 7 June. We found Aunt Sarah relaxed on the couch.
She admitted she was 'a wee bit tired' – she had washed two
blankets and a heavy hand-knitted counterpane† and laid them
on the grass to dry because 'they felt too heavy to lift on the
line'. I went out and hung them where the air would dry them
better today. Joe was busy working in the garden – so awkward
as he used his left hand and arm, and cheerfully said, 'This pesky
rheumatism takes all the use out of my right arm sometimes'. I
felt at 80 and 84 they were indeed a marvellous couple. I don't
want to live to be old but if it's my fate, I pray I can grow old like
my serene busy little auntie, so content with all small blessings
she thinks it is a sin to complain of things that would get a lot
of people down altogether. I had to listen to all the bits of village
news and gossip and *yell* my news – it was one of her very deaf
days, poor old pet.

We were home before 5 o'clock. I poached eggs and made
toast, and there was bread and butter, apricot jam, shortbread biscuits and cherry cake. I'm having my yearly perm in the morning
and had to wash my hair. Anyway, it wasn't fit to go out far –
rain threatened but there was no heavy fall. We listened to the

wireless … It's a lot colder tonight and we felt glad of the fire I
made to dry my hair. I always pay for things like a perm out of my
own money, and draw it out of the bank, but tonight my husband
said when I mentioned it, 'I've some money in the safe. I'll give
you the two guineas.' I felt I gasped. He is changing so rapidly I
feel at times I'm living with a stranger.

Monday, 12 June. There's a lovely sailing ship in for repairs. It
was made nearly 30 years ago in the Yard for Brazil, to be used
as a training ship, and has come back for some refit or repairs.
The youths on it fascinate me. They look cultured and assured,
as if from good families, and have the manners and deportment
of well educated and poised people. Their clothes are cut so perfectly – ordinary sailor rig, slightly musical comedy in detail.
The mariners have scarlet tunics. The officers I'm sure had their
uniforms made by a tailor-artist. They have this and that all
over – cords and medal ribbons, chevrons and rings – and are
in grey-blues as well as navy, and all of superlative material and
cut. But it's their faces and colour that so fascinate me – deepest
chocolate, though every tone of café-au-lait to pale ivory, and all
are young enough to have a haunting adolescent beauty, or the
smiling candour of a happy child. It's plain to be seen that where
they come from there's no 'colour bar' as we understand the word.
I look at each couple or group and wonder what mixture of race
and colour, tribe, 'aristocracy', way of life and thought, and religion have intermingled to form their perfectly cut features, the
different noses, mouths and brows. It makes my theory that some
day there will be one race with no warring element of barriers
that fear and greed make, and understanding of each other's ways
and thought.

Saturday, 17 June. Margaret Atkinson came in.* She seems to be looking forward to beginning housekeeping in a house of her own, but said a bit thoughtfully, 'It's going to be a bit strange having to ask Arthur for money. With working a year after marriage, it will seem worse than if I'd begun being "dependent".' We talked of the queer unrest in the Yard [*managers were being laid off*]. She said, 'No boss feels safe. I can tell the way they talk they wonder round our office who will be next.' Margaret is near enough the Cost Office to know the real undercurrent of worry for the future for work. There's no more lines in view, and we don't build the cruisers and submarines now that made up the orders before 'private' ships were built. Within two years, unless other big orders are obtained, or fresh subsidiary lines are developed, it looks as if Barrow will have had it. We will be worse than Jarrow in the big slump, for beyond the steel works – working at a loss and on the borderline of being closed within a short time – there's practically nothing. What few small industries there are rely on the Yard's prosperity.

Nella sometimes remarked on the state of the wider world, and usually with alarm. There was a lot to be distressed about, not least the threat of atomic weapons. On 17 May – her wedding anniversary – she was thinking about 'the account of 70 foot atom proof shelters being built at Stockholm, recalling a forecast by Naylor the astrologist, quite 15 years ago, that humanity was approaching an age when they tended to go underground, and build deep in the earth to work, live and "play"'. These were, once

---

*Margaret, the younger daughter of the Atkinsons, a great favourite of Nella's in the 1940s, had married Arthur Procter, a schoolteacher, in August 1949. They were soon to move to a new home near Bacup, Lancashire, in the South Pennines, near the border with Yorkshire.

again, and so soon after a world war, troubling political times. On 29 June
she and Mrs Higham 'talked so sadly of the news, both with a sick feeling
that *anything* will happen, wondering if Korea will start the war in the East
that is to destroy civilisation as we know it, talking and conjecturing about
Russia and what she may have behind the Iron Curtain, recalling half forgotten memories of our war work together, or air raids, blackout, shortages.'
Civil Defence became, once again, a major concern, as it had been just a
few years earlier.

Talk of war was much in the air, particularly because of the crisis in Korea
(a country that many people had barely heard of and probably could not
locate on a map): on 25 June the North invaded the South, and the United
States responded through the United Nations by organising resistance to
this aggression, as the North Korean action was widely perceived to be. At
the end of this first week of crisis, on Sunday, 2 July, Nella and Will drove
to the Coast Road. 'A group of elder people sat near where we parked,
not near enough for me to hear clearly their conversation, but sentences
with "Korea" and scraps of conversation about the Navy and RAF and "our
Robert", and their expressions of concern, showed their thoughts were on
the future, and what it would bring. I wonder if this "firm gesture" *will* put
a stop to Communist drive and urge.' (Perhaps she had in mind the words
of John Gordon, 'Why America Must Not Fail', in that day's *Sunday Express*,
p. 4: 'Britain responded with inspiring swiftness to the call of America and
the United Nations. It was a tremendous gesture we made. But, in fact,
no other course was open to us. And in the crisis every man in Britain
stands behind the Government.' Britain had, among other things, promised
immediate naval support to the Americans in the Far East. In response to
the Korean crisis, the period of National Service was soon to be increased
from eighteen to twenty-four months.)

Monday, 3 July. It was a glorious day for the seaside – the tide
at full and a land breeze. The cadet training camp is full of boys

14 to 18, some from Bolton and some from an approved school.
It seems the policy to mix the latter with ordinary youths. In
healthy windswept Barrow-in-Furness we are too young to have
history of any kind, especially industrial. I looked at some of the
young badly built youngsters with real horror. They looked as if
they had been badly bred for generations of tired warped parents,
few really nice-looking, some who shambled along with dull eyes
and aimless limbs looked subnormal. I like boys. One group were
throwing stones for an eager little dog, and I suggested a stick so
as not to chip the dog's teeth as I'd often seen. I said, 'No national
aid for dogs' teeth and when they cannot chew their food they die
young'. I expressed surprise they went swimming or bathing and
was told, 'Want us in jankers,[†] I can see. But I wish you would
talk to our sergeant. He doesn't like water himself and hates to
see anyone else have fun there.' The crowd who were unable to
bathe seemed to just lie round and I was horrified to see how some
of them chain smoked, with the ease of long practice. Others
bought mineral water of the colours of red ink or a hideous greeny
lime, ice cream and sickly cakes from a trailer 'café' that was sta-
tioned. A penny was charged on each bottle, but many who sat
fifty yards or even less from the 'café' set the bottle on a heap of
stones and aimed till broken, and left the glass scattered.

I fell into a train of thought as I wondered where the curious
lack of responsibility to others began. Our generation taught
children 'Don't leave gates open or the poor little moo cows will
get lost and not find their mammies and be cold and lonely at
bedtime', 'Let's bury this nasty sharp glass so no one will cut their
feet', '*Such* lovely flowers, but we will only pick some for the glass
jug and leave the others to grow – they like growing as much
as little boys and girls', 'It's ugly to be dirty – look how pussy
washes herself and then begins to purr and sing because she feels

so nice when she has washed herself'. Now they talk of 'repressions' and 'fixations' and hidden things in children's minds. I'm old-fashioned enough to think a child is less complicated than the clever ones think. The security of comforting arms, a sharp slap when needed, busy hands and minds and the example of elders would be better for growing children than all the new and clever ways.

Tuesday, 4 July. Mrs Howson and I both had shopping before going to the WVS Post-War Club meeting. I got potatoes, pears, tomatoes, apples, apricots and a quarter pound of mushrooms – only 9d today – and so my shopping bag was full and rather heavy. We had *such* a good speaker, a local farmer's sister who joined the YMCA at the outbreak of war and went overseas. She told of her experiences in North Africa, the desert towns and northern Italy. She had had a wonderful experience. She is a most attractive woman, now about 35 but looking less, for she is so gay and vital and must have met thousands of eligible men from all over the Empire as well as the British Isles, but in spite of all hasn't even an engagement ring. I wonder why. I'm sure she must have had *some* offers of, if not marriage, that 'understanding' that leads that way. I wondered if 'Clogs weren't good enough and shoes never came her way', as they say in Lancashire.

Before the war she kept house for a farmer brother, who got married and left her rather at a loose end, and she had never been far from the district so it was a wonderful experience. She gossiped about people and places and her work, and made us rock with laughter at her 'most embarrassing moment'. In a very full YMCA in Italy, a slightly tipsy soldier lurched up to the counter, stared hard and shouted, 'Hallo, aren't you going to speak to me?' His friend asked if he 'knew the lady' and he bellowed, '*Know* her

– she was my last mistress in England'. She said, 'The silence that fell on the group round the counter could be felt. I leaned forward and said – making matters sound worse – "I'm afraid I've forgotten exactly who you are, or where we met". He said, "I was your brother's cow man and was there the year so many heifer calves were born. You *must* remember me, Miss Coward. You used to laugh at my checked shirt."' Miss Coward said it sounded as if a sigh of relief went up!

It's the first Civil Defence meeting to arrange training classes on Thursday evening. As we moved into groups for a cup of tea, we began to talk of the beginning of the last war. With a half humorous, half dread of tomorrow, Mrs Higham and one of her neighbours made us all laugh as they related their experiences with a very 'superior' lecturer. He had everyone so in line, doing every precise action with the stirrup pump, moving limbs to allow 'full action of muscle' etc., while others trotted up with full buckets of water for 'chain' service. He said, 'Now I want you to watch this carefully so as not to leave a gap in operations while the empty bucket is changed for the full one', which entailed a finger put in one place and the stirrup pump clasped a certain way. The homely little woman who had hurried up with the full bucket of water looked at him and said quietly, 'Wouldn't it be better if I just poured this water out of my bucket instead of fiddling with the stirrup pump being lifted out of one bucket into another?' Mrs Higham said the look on that man's face as he agreed was 'something to see'.

Thursday, 6 July. I got ready to go to Civil Defence meeting, and was down for 7 o'clock. With the exception of about half a dozen women, all the rest were WVS and we feel a bit put out and bewildered to find we will have to go through the whole Civil

Defence training – gas, bomb training and disposal, rescue, fire fighting, etc. etc., and do a *three years* course! There's no WVS member in our lot who can either stand up to such a course or feel it necessary before they can do all the homely jobs they did all the last war. In fact many very valuable members blinked at the notion of jumping out of windows, going through gas chambers, working in 'teams' at rescue work, etc., and everyone, including myself, said we would never have joined if we hadn't been misled! Mrs Diss looked dismayed. WVS Regional had told her we could take our training in the afternoon. There was an air of complete dissatisfaction on every hand. As a whole, none of us were capable of such rough, tough training. The two youngest women were Mrs Howson and Mrs Fletcher. The latter has asthma bad if there is any untoward smell and said she 'would leave it to chance' whether she got gassed, but wear a gas mask and 'play around' she wouldn't and couldn't. Mrs Howson even surprised me by her outburst in the porch as she talked of 'Did you ever hear such darn rot? Anyone would think war was coming *any time.*'

Friday, 7 July. I got such a shock of surprise in the grocer's. It will be some time before I forget it! A customer and I spoke of having had one or two bad eggs recently in our dozen or half dozen. The proprietor's wife said, 'You should have mentioned it to the girl who served you'. I said, 'I *did*. I told her my eggs were costing dear when out of six I'd one really bad and one so doubtful I didn't use it for cooking'. When she came through she put a bag on the counter with half a dozen eggs in and said, '*That* will make up for them'. I said, 'I shall begin to believe in Santa Claus after this' ...

My husband was busy clipping off dead roses. When I see him occupied in any way I feel so happy for him, and he had cleaned

1. Nella and Will Last, and their dog Garry. Nella once wrote of Will's attachment to his car: 'after me, it's his chief anchor to life and living'

2. The Lasts' elder son, Arthur, with his wife Edith and their sons, Peter and Christopher, around late 1952

3. The Lasts' younger son, Cliff, a sculptor in Australia

4. End of a shift at 'the Yard', Barrow's dominant industry

5. The daily exodus from the shipyard

6. The WVS collect clothes for flood victims in Eastern England, 6 February 1953

7. Flooding on the Coast Road, where the Lasts often drove
to Ulverston and the Lake District

8. Nella Last on a pier on Morecambe Bay, Christmas 1958

two pairs of my shoes I'd put out to clean when I came back – so beautifully too. I wonder why men often get such a much better shine on shoes – more weight behind their rubbing, perhaps. I had vegetable soup to heat, and potatoes and peas to cook, to eat to corned beef. I made custard and stewed some prunes I had, and when I packed tea of cheese, lettuce, tomatoes, a loaf and butter, I put in a jar of fruit salad by adding a few prunes to the stewed apricots and segments of apple. I wanted to change our library books. I got a 'Crime Club', and one of Muriel Hines' novels for my husband, feeling another little thrill of thankfulness when he has settled to reading more, and got used to his glasses better. We went to the Coast Road and sat on a rug on the shingly shore. The tide crept slowly in, no wind at all, and the air heavy with the scent of hay going past on carts and lorries, so lovely and 'green dried'. We had tea and walked on the sands – it was only low tide – and I settled to read a while.

My husband seemed so much less despondent. He said suddenly, 'Do you remember anyone called Clamp? The wife came several times about air raid damage and I once heard her tell you her daughter was getting married. Mr Clamp worked in the gas showrooms.' I knew then who he was referring to and nodded. He went on in such a queer thoughtful manner. 'He went past when I was in the front garden when you were out. He too has had to retire through nervous trouble and he is younger than me.' There was a pause and then he went on, still in a wondering tone. 'He spends most of his time in the park. He says if he stays in, he and his wife quarrel fiercely and she isn't a bit sympathetic. She dislikes sickness of any kind and loses patience when he has no memory for anything.' I said, 'Well, it takes two to make a quarrel. Perhaps he is bad to do with. You cannot judge till you hear both sides.' I thought a bit grimly of the many quarrels

we two could have if I didn't keep self-control, didn't pray so
earnestly for patience and kindness, but felt tears rise in my eyes
as the poor dear went on. 'You've always been so understanding,
such a *pal*. It's good when sex dies to feel there's something even
better.'* I nodded, and realised as often, it's always been a mother
he has needed as much as a wife.

Saturday, 8 July. Two cars only were parked in the 'draw in' space
where we like [*to stop at Coniston Water*], and I could tell they were
a party of friends. One was an old lady with such a lovely smiling
friendly face that seemed vaguely familiar. As she hobbled slowly
along looking for flowers for a little nosegay she was making, she
kept looking at me as if she expected me to speak, and then suddenly someone called, 'Nellie, I think your mother wants helping
down to us', and a plump elderly woman I *did* recognise came
up and took the old lady's arm – only as a guide though; she
planted her feet firmly and chattered happily as she went to join
the group on the shore. I made rapid calculations, and with a
slight gasp jumped out of the car and joined them and said, 'Why
Mrs Thompson, you haven't altered a bit – in how many years?'
The sweet old face crinkled in delight as she said, 'A good many
years – and I knew you at once, Dearie. I knew it was Lord before
you were married.' I looked in real awe as she went on to speak
of my father's people, of mother when she knew her first, before
even her first marriage, of little events when I was a lame child
who didn't get about and used to sit and talk to her in the little
sweet shop she had on the corner. I turned to her daughter and
whispered, 'How old is your mother now, Nellie?' I thought my

---

*On his initiative, Will and Nella had ceased to sleep together, and probably
ceased to have sexual relations, by 1942 at the latest.

whisper was very quiet, but Mrs Thompson heard and said gaily, 'I'm 96. It was my birthday this week, and that is Annie's boy and *his* daughter.' She would have been a pretty active 76, and her mind was clear and nimble as ever. She was a delight to be with. I remember her always as 'old' to my childish imagination and somehow she had not aged much. I had some Callard and Bowser butterscotch and gave her some, and when I said, 'Good isn't it? But not as good as the butter toffee you made', we began to talk of treacle toffee and peppermint sticks, stick jaw with nuts in and toffee apples we loved and which she made so well.

Much as I enjoyed our meeting, I think the old pet enjoyed it even more, and there was no hint of 'not exciting mother' as all laughed and egged her on to tell of bygone days. My husband was amongst us, enjoying it as much as anyone. He said, 'I thought your Aunt Sarah was wonderful for 84 – but 96. It would be grand to be old and enjoy life still.' I recalled the bitter struggle Mrs Thompson had had till she raised her family of four to help. I could feel the warmth and laughter and the friendliness packed into that tatty little sweet shop on the corner flow even across the years. Little scraps of memory thronged my mind – bits I'd heard Mother say. How her family loved and clung to her, her in-laws as well. Both daughters are widows. One son 'went' in the First War. The youngest, a technician of some kind who volunteered his services on some kind of radar, was torpedoed in this last war. She has not escaped troubles, she has 'rode' them.

Thursday, 13 July. To say my feelings are mixed is to put it very mildly. My husband has found an interest!!! Wood beetles. Nasty little brown 'woody' bugs that bore round worm holes. We had a basket chair in a bedroom, and last year when Arthur and Edith were here, they carried it on the lawn and broke a leg as Edith

sat down heavily when it was wobbly against the rockery. Such
a train of minor destruction seems to follow Edith and she is so
'unlucky' with electric irons, cups and saucers, etc. I didn't think
much when Arthur said, 'The leg is worm eaten. No wonder
it snapped.' Later I noticed little clusters of round holes at the
top of my good oak panelled doors, and used Flit, and nagged
gently on and on, finally saying I'd get someone in to see to them
if my husband wouldn't tackle them. Still he didn't bother. He
had that 'couldn't care less' attitude, till there was something on
the wireless last night. He had done the tops of the doors with
Cupressol, a mild form of creosote, but after hearing the serious-
ness of neglect, I got really on the war path today, and the house
looks as if stirred with a stick. He found signs in a wardrobe
and a dressing table back, and both have been ripped off and are
waiting hardboard. He says three-ply is the wood that encourages
them. Clothes from two wardrobes strew the bedrooms, mats and
carpets are rolled up or askew, there's litter as if for removal. BUT,
I heard my husband whistle for a while!! ...

I packed tea, raspberries and a little evaporated milk, a loaf and
butter, cakes and two flasks of tea, and we went off to Walney,
though black clouds were rolling up from all directions. Few had
gone to the beach for the half holiday. We walked on the sands a
while, before it rained, and then had tea. On the way home, I got
off at the schools where Civil Defence classes are held and found
the rain had held up a lot from coming where a bus wasn't handy,
and it made a late start. It was more of a 'settling in' than learn-
ing anything, and *seven* gas masks were fitted. The sergeant said,
'More will be available lately, but I don't know when.' I felt faintly
sick as he talked of 'zone' and the possibility of Barrow being considered as such, and I watched the gas masks being fitted with a
sick pity as I thought of all that had happened since I last was at

a school where we got ours, that fateful Munich year, wondering 'Is this another Munich warning?' It's the dreadful acceptance of many people that chills me most. When the sergeant spoke of the effect of an atom bomb on a place like Barrow – destruction with a 5½ mile radius, and the evacuations to a 'cushion' belt – and the remarks of the morbid, pessimistic London man who sat beside me, a queer 'sooner it's over, sooner to sleep' feeling stole over me. Ordinary people can do so little – only pray.

Saturday, 22 July. When I was coming up in the bus I noticed some nurses from the Hospital sitting opposite me, in the long seats by the exit. As the bus stopped at my bus stop a smartly dressed, coal black African girl rose from the front of the bus and prepared to alight and I idly wondered if she was visiting the African oculist on Abbey Road. As she reached the three nurses sitting opposite one said, 'Hallo – thought you were going shopping. We would have waited if we had known you were coming this way.' The black girl murmured something and the nurse said, 'Always changing your mind, daft cat' and gave her a friendly slap – a *chummy* slap – on the rump of the girl, who laughed so jolly and happy in return, as if colour and race were one.

We walked side by side. There's three or more African nurses and I don't know one from the other, so speak to all. I was really surprised when the beautiful honey voice said, 'Beginning to think about your rag bag babies yet?' Granted I'd met them twice on Xmas Days I'd gone to the 'visit of Santa Claus', but was surprised when she had remembered I made them. She said, 'Matron often speaks of you when she gets a hoarded dollie out of the cupboard. She likes to keep a few back. Last week she found a cowboy for a badly burned little boy and gave it to him. If you could see how your dollies are loved you would think your work worth doing.' I felt tears start to my eyes – dear knows why. I said, 'How nice of you to tell me, my dear. Are you still happy in Barrow?' She paused at the gate where she was going to call at the African doctor's and her wide mouth split into a huge happy grin as she said, 'I've never known such happiness I've found here. The memory will linger all my life.' I said, 'Matron is the most wonderful person I know – and I've known her for over 30 years.' She nodded as she said, 'Yes – but we have found happiness and kindness everywhere. The children love us, and we had been warned small white children might fear us because of our colour'. I said, 'Children are the best judges of people. They would soon realise your kindness and love. Matron told me she wished she could have a full African staff of nurses, if only for the warmth and love of nursing you all had, as well as your sunny dispositions.' She said, 'Now it's *you* who are nice to me'.

The house door opened and my little happy feeling seemed to sour. A lily pale woman [*the wife of the black doctor*] stood in the doorway, with a tiny coffee-coloured baby in her arms, a darker-skinned little kinky-haired girl, and a really dark, goggle-eyed 'nigger' little boy rushed excitedly down the steps in welcome. Whatever the views I hold of '*some* day, one colour, one creed', the sight of half caste children seems to strike at something way deep down in me. I *say* I've no 'colour bar', but wonder if really I've a very deep-rooted one. I could work with coloured people, enjoy their society, attend their wants in Canteen, fully admit them to positions of trust and service, but know, *finally*, I'd have *died* before I could have married one, or borne coloured children. So perhaps I *have* a 'colour bar'.

Nella had earlier disclosed some of her racial prejudices and mixed feelings, when she made her usual Christmas visit in 1948 to the hospital and encountered two African nurses, one of them the nurse she spoke with on this July day. They were, she wrote, 'the Basuto type – their uniforms intensify their really frightening ugliness. One was helping the one-time little patients into coats and scarves, her huge capable hands seeming to attend several children at once. They looked up so "inaffectedly"† as if a hideous black face was the one they would have chosen to hand over them. She passed where I was standing and impulsively I put out my hand and said, "A very happy Xmas, nurse. I hope our cold grey skies don't make you home-sick for your lovely sunny land." A soft, rather guttural but very pleasant voice said, "Oh no, madam. We *love* it here. England is a wonderful place and we have met nothing but kindness. No one in Barrow seems to have noticed we are coloured."' Nella and this nurse agreed on Matron's virtues, which led Nella to write that 'the enveloping clasp of that huge black hand, its firmness and warmth that was not only physical, made me say, "Why my dear, you have something Matron has always had – perhaps it's what is called being a born nurse". It was such a feeling of strength. I'd have felt every confidence in the little black thing.' Later Nella spoke with Matron, who said. 'It was kind of you to talk to nurse. She is a really splendid person – they both are. I'm amazed to find such understanding and quick intel-ligence in people who have so recently been "civilised". They put a lot of the rest to shame' (25 December 1948).

Three and a half years later Nella again pondered her confused feel-ings about race after visiting this black ophthalmologist at his office in his home, whom she portrayed as 'clever, patient and well liked', and who was married to a French woman. 'I felt what wonderful people the Africans – and coloured people – were. In one or two – three at the most – genera-tions, they have bridged such a gap between primitive and civilised ways. I'm not consistent. I've *no* colour feeling, no shrinking from black hands touching me as head was turned and lenses fitted, no feeling of revulsion at all; yet when those really charming half caste children leaned against me – the little girl of three climbed on my knee – I felt something in me shrank away' (1 August 1952). It was the 'mixing of blood and race' that unsettled her, and which she found hard to digest (5 January 1950). In the same passage she had written of 'the shock I got the other day to read how many half caste children were the result of the American negro soldiers' short stay in England'.

Saturday, 29 July. We set off [*for Coniston Water*] at 1.30 to avoid the congested roads of 2 o'clock onward, for it was the Agricultural Show at Ulverston, and the rush times from the surrounding countryside are early morning and early afternoon. I'd have liked to go, but it's a strenuous affair with so much walking and standing. I felt I couldn't have stood much, and for my husband it was unthinkable. It was one of those crystal days of loveliness that [*Hugh*] Walpole loved, and only he could find words to describe. A sweet peace on every shadowed fell and hillside, muted slap, slap of water on the edge of the Lake, the gentle breeze hardly stirring the leaves, woody smell of earth and trees perfumed with meadowsweet, soft carillon of wood pigeons, which must be a pest to the farmers this year, their numbers are so increased. We parked at our usual spot on the East side of the Lake. Few cars and no bathers about today – perhaps the regulars have gone on holiday ...

I never saw nuts so plentiful. If they only ripen there will be a bumper crop, and blackberries promise to be more plentiful than last year even. I picked handfuls of sweet wild raspberries and ate them as we walked. I looked at the green tender shoots and leaves and thought of the bags full we picked as children for Granny to dry. Those days every expectant mother drank raspberry leaf tea. Mother and Aunt Eliza, both London-trained nurses for midwifery, scoffed at such absurd ideas. Now it's one of the clinic's instructions. I often wish I'd collected Granny's simple recipes. Not even Aunt Sarah thought the faded crabbed written 'cures' and recipes worth keeping. I let my mind wander to 'turnip syrup', thin slices of freshly dug swede turnip, sprinkled with demerara sugar and stood in a warm place and the syrup given to 'chesty' children. I chuckled as I remembered the gasp of astonishment I gave when once as I was hurrying to get ready to go to Hospital Supply I heard it given out in Housewife 'hints' after the 8 o'clock news! I recalled the flavouring that gave to Granny's cakes at Xmas, something rare – hawthorn blossom gathered when the sun was bringing out its heady sweetness, and after the green stalks had been slipped off, it was packed in a glass jar with a tight-fitting lid and covered with brandy. As the flowers wilted more flowers were packed in, more brandy added, and long as the 'May blossom' lasted. Kept in a dark place, well sealed, the flower went to the bottom and the syrupy brandy decanted into small bottles about November. The residue was pressed through muslin and went into a different bottle for 'heavy' cakes – Xmas and Simnel[†]. I thought of all the sachets – elderflower, sage, marshmallow[†] – small 'eye bright' ones for styes on the eye. I rambled on and on, till I said, 'Sorry dear, this won't interest *you*', but my husband had been both interested and entertained. He is like the two boys in his interest in Gran and her way of life and living and tales of a day that seems as far away as the 'golden age' of Elizabethan days, yet measured in years, isn't so *very* far away.

I spread a rug, and we had tea, watched eagerly by several impatient sparrows, who hopped about waiting for crumbs. Wild birds do seem to like 'artificial' food, as if they too come under the restless urge of change of today. I sewed lazily at my wool work – this cushion is getting finished quicker than Cliff's other two – and we came back slowly, and were home before 9 o'clock. We felt we wanted to linger in the perfect evening, knowing well the rain storms that would follow.

Friday, 4 August. We went down the Coast Road again. It was a lot cooler, and looks set for a change. The fields were being prepared for the reaper and binder to begin harvest. Down the edges, two sides, men cut and tied a swathe – it does look a poor thin crop, and I can hear it's much worse over the Duddon estuary in Cumberland. The incoming tide was dotted with bathers. Happy family groups round little tents everywhere on the grass verge looked as if they had been down all morning. Cars with numbers from every part of Scotland and England passed or paused a while. The number of Scottish cars increases each summer. The other day when my husband was getting petrol at the garage where he generally deals I said, 'The news and situation in Korea makes us wonder how much longer petrol will be off ration'. The proprietor said, 'I think it's found its level. The trade say only 10% more was sold, and that includes part of the holiday traffic, you know. My son says our sales haven't gone up a lot, but people will be buying petrol further afield, as they take longer journeys.' We walked along the sands before the tide was full. The air was sweet and fresh. We met several people we knew and had a chat, and had tea in the car ...

The news of retreat and yet still further retreat in Korea is bad. It seems to play right into Stalin's hands and give him such cause to crow 'America – pooh – why *Koreans* can send them packing. They would never have a chance if they struck at ME', and it's not good Westerners should lose face. I had a fearsome little remembrance of 'The last war of all will start in the East' and vague oddments of revelations that were 'being proved every day for those with eyes to see' and such like – hangovers from a nosy childhood when there was nothing for curious children to interest their minds as now, and a street orator *was* a treat. I can see plainly as I write a figure I'd forgotten long ago, only coming back now as his wild prophecies of the 'end of all things' was shouted at indifferent adults and enthralled children. Not one corner of this lovely world is safe or secure. I wonder what this dreadful H-bomb *is* like in its effects. It will be a fearful 'adventure' to set off a trial one. I wonder if America *will* set off the atom bomb in Korea. To do so could set the whole Eastern world against us. As Stalin *would* be able to say, 'This is what the West means to you, death and mutilation on a wholesale massacre'.

The war in Korea had attracted Nella's attention on several occasions recently. On 26 July, 'When I heard the 6 o'clock news I felt faint shock – that we were sending troops to Korea'. Hundreds of thousands of British families were bound to be alarmed, as their boys of military age faced the prospect of being sent, once again, into battle. 'Fear and concern is coming to mothers of boys who will be due for National Service', Nella wrote on 28 July, 'for now it sounds as if they will be soldiers from the start, liable for overseas, and all it can mean, by the time they are 19.' Moreover, the current crisis raised for the first time since 1945 the potential use of atomic weapons, and Nella was gloomy about Britain's post-war weakness in a world dominated by the two superpowers. 'America has the A-bomb – and is young', she remarked on July 27. 'We would have little or no say whether one had to be dropped in Korea, and if such a dreadful thing *did* happen – and Russia *has* them – all hell could be easily let loose. A terrifying outlook.'

Wednesday, 16 August. I called in the library to get my husband a book and then took the bus up to Croslands Park. Miss Butler [*recently returned to Barrow*] still must have a lot of money. She is not the type to live on capital, but to buy and keep up a house rated at nearly £40 a year, have a car and telephone, a day girl – she would like a resident help – travel, dress and spend as she does, her income must be good. She still has the lovely furniture

– or scraps of it – her parents collected. Some a collector would like. Her father was a local solicitor, her mother a wealthy Bradford merchant's daughter, her two darling brothers of 19 and 20 killed in the First World War. Now beyond cousins scattered, she has no one but a little Corgi dog. She is rather a 'difficult' person, to have begun life for herself at over 50 when her mother died, and the mother belonged to that real Victorian-early Edwardian type who demanded a 'prop for my declining years', 'someone to close my eyes', etc. Miss Butler was so joyously happy to help in Canteen. I thought at the time it was pressure from her mother that made her leave. She was unwilling HER daughter should mix and work in such company, although she was goodness itself in giving to charity.

We sat and talked of loneliness, and what a searing thing it could be. She said, 'People like you cannot know what it means'. I said, 'Well, I've had two sons, but see little of them, and my husband has always been so quiet and reserved. I've felt lonely in spirit often.' She said, 'Yes dear, but never in an empty house, looking out at passers-by, go to bed lonely, rise the same – you could never plumb such depths. You look too serene to have known what I mean. You speak to people – the way Foxy took to you shows you are friendly – I'm not you know.' I said, 'You might be a lot friendlier than I am really. I know I've always been "individual" more than "communal".' She knew what I meant, and said, 'Do you know that I think I *would* have been "communal", as you call it. Being alone has no appeal to me. I've never known what it was like till these last few years.' I recalled she was right. They had four or five indoor servants. She was driven into town with someone to carry her parcels, etc. She isn't the 'malleable' type that you could pop in to see, take a book, ring up for a chat, suggest coming down to Civil Defence or any WVS

activities. She kept showing me little 'treasures', opening boxes
and drawers. I saw nothing of handiwork or sewing, knitting or
embroidery about, no books or papers, and she complained of the
poor wireless programmes in summer.

Saturday, 19 August. I tidied round quickly after breakfast and
we sat waiting about 15 minutes for the taxi. Being such a big
wedding [*of her cousin's son*] and so many to bring from a wide
district, even with a fleet of taxis it was a rush to get everyone to
church in time. The bride lived at Rampside, a small village on
Morecambe Bay, five miles from town. The church was beautifully decorated with pink roses and tall pink spikes gladioli, and I
don't remember seeing a lovelier bride and attendants. Nancy had
a medieval plain cut dress with long tight sleeves, flowing train
in stiff corded silk, and wore a family veil. The bridesmaids had
stiff striped brocade of blending pastel shades with a silver thread
between each delicate hue. They were simply made but cunningly
cut and so different from the usual bridesmaids' dresses. We knew
nearly everyone. Miss Ledgerwood, who worked with us at Hospital Supply, is an aunt of the bride, and there was the usual big
turn up of relations rarely seen between weddings and funerals.
Mary Rawlinson was there, beautifully dressed, serene and aloof,
parrying enquiries about the break between her and Cliff Crump,
after a long drawn out courtship of nearly ten years, when she had
kept putting off her marriage, saying 'There's plenty of time', and
now he has tired of waiting. Perhaps because I asked no questions, she told me, 'We grew to have less and less in common,
and anyway Nell, I think I'm like your Cliff – too content on my
own'. I said, 'Well Mary, you are so like my own mother in looks
and ways. I think it's as well for either a husband or any children
you might have had that you don't marry. I know Mother would

have been happier if she hadn't married my father, but put it
down to the fact that the "real" life of her died when her first
husband did. Now I wonder if she was like you – a kind of Rhine
maiden.' She wasn't at all pleased, but she knows well I've known
several of her half finished romances in all their details. It's as if
she seeks a perfection in human relationship almost impossible
to find, and the comic part is that she is more full of whims and
whamseys[†] and more difficult to understand than most.

We didn't go to the station to see the bridal couple off, first to
London to spend the night, and then to Newquay on the Cornish
express. It was too late to make the journey in one day from
Barrow.[*] Instead we went to Spark Bridge to tell Aunt Sarah all
about the wedding. Other days, others ways – she was so disappointed her share of the 'wedding feast' and a glass of wine hadn't
been sent. Useless to try and explain the difference of hotel catering and that of the old-time personal attention to everything. I
recall country weddings when I was small when any old or sick
who couldn't go had their share of goodies put aside – someone
took it and told of every detail. Ruth is staying in the cottage

---

*On Monday the 21st Nella was back in Rampside to view the wedding presents.
There was no sign of austerity, and she was much impressed. 'I never saw such
a collection of "covetable" things. It looked as if the cream had been skimmed
from every good shop in town – latest model wireless set, Hoover vac, a full set
of Community tableware. Cheques had been pooled and dozens of everything
bought. There were fish eaters and carvers, Prestige kitchen gadgets, antiques,
electric toasters (2), coffee percolator, kettles (2), trays, cut glass, blankets and
linen and towels and table linen to last them for years, an electric clock for the
bedroom and two for downstairs rooms, luncheon sets, two tea sets and a small
dinner set to match one of them, every type of useful oddment like heavy pans in
aluminium for a gas or electric stove, bread and cake tins and set for the pantry
shelf, all in cream and green, eiderdowns – it seemed nothing they could need or
desire had been left out. We had a cup of tea before we came away.'

next door. She came in to hear all about all that occurred. I felt shocked to see how suddenly she had begun to look her age. Her lecture tour in America was so strenuous and she did so hate New York, saying 'Never go there if you can help it. It has the least soul of any place I've known.' I can tell she feels gloomy about the way things are going in Korea. She seems to have got atom bomb and total destruction of civilisation pretty bad. I said, 'I've got past it, Ruth. I've a growing Sayonara – "if it must be so" – a feeling we are all in some great and intricate "Place", that "it's not life that matters, but the courage we bring to it"'.

CHAPTER FOUR

FRAGILITIES AND FAMILIARITIES

September–December 1950

Saturday, 2 September. I got ready hurriedly to go and see a wedding – my grocer's only child, whom I've known all her life. Mrs Howson and I had planned to go, but when it was a fine morning she and Steve had taken the chance to go off by an early train for a day out. I looked round the church wondering how much money was represented, even amongst those I knew. The bridegroom, an accountant, comes from Glasgow and only a small group of his relatives and friends were there. The church was beautifully decorated with tall white lilies and white gladioli, but it looked colder than the soft pink roses and gladioli of a fortnight ago when my cousin's son was married, and I much preferred Nancy's plain well-cut gown in thick heavy silk, although her slim slight figure could have worn anything. The bride today is plump and rather thick set, and her billowing and flowing gown made her look a bit pudgy, and the diamanté[†] trimming twitching in the sunshine looked too Hollywood for my taste. Her mother looked sad. Newcastle, where the married couple will live, 'seems a long way off', though the other day I pointed out it was much nearer than Northern Ireland or Australia! …

As we ate lunch I asked my husband, 'What would you like to do, short of putting your head in the gas oven?' He looked aggrieved at my flippancy, but wouldn't give any kind of answer.

But when we got out, he perked up and said suddenly, 'Let's go to Kendal'. I felt surprised. He has never suggested going since Robert was here just after Xmas. I said, 'I'll be delighted if you feel up to it'. We went slowly. It's not much more than an hour's run from Barrow. Everywhere in the high wind and fitful sunshine farmers were busy. I saw many ricks being covered with tarpaulin as if some grain on higher ground had dried sufficiently. Hay too was being cut, and quite a good crop if it only dries. Two hikers hailed us for a lift. They had huge packs on their backs but my husband wouldn't stop. He had read an article or letter by a motorist in the *Express* the other week saying, 'Why should motorists, who are taxed and have to pay so dear for petrol, pander to some people's desire and determination to get a cheap holiday by hitch-hiking?' My husband pointed out that there was a very good bus service, and just before we came along a service bus half empty had paused to pick up passengers, and the two hikers had not bothered though it would only have been a few coppers to go as far as Kendal.

There was the usual life and bustle of a county town. Kendal has been as unfortunate for weather as the rest of Lakeland. In two shops where I went – one for a lettuce and celery, one for elastic – they spoke of the 'terrible weather for August'. We came round by Bowness and parked by the Lake to eat tea, from where I could see into cars round about. Most of them were having a picnic meal – and some really large expensive cars. Perhaps the price of petrol hits more people than one realised! Fewer cars and only a very short line of motor coaches in the big car park. Perhaps Morecambe illuminations will take most coach trips now. We were home by 7.30, already foam over the Irish Sea. Banks of rain were rolling in. It's only been a 'borrowed' day.

Thursday, 7 September. There was wild confusion of piled furniture and carpets in some side streets of Ulverston, brought hurriedly from houses never been flooded in living memory, and a great deal of damage to two bridges and roads had been caused. A 'river' surged through Ulverston station, washing all before it. Passengers from Whitehaven to Euston were taken off the trains at Dalton and travelled by road round the Bay to Carnforth, and we didn't get papers till noon as all had to be brought by lorry or bus. Low-lying fields were lakes. Others I never remember seeing flooded were under water, any stooks of corn that didn't float submerged altogether – a pitiful sight. I'd not dared to look at the poor garden before I left, and hardly knew where to start when I got home. I had a promising crop of pears and James Grieve apples – half were on the ground – herbaceous plants flat, rose branches torn off completely, the lawn was covered with branches and pieces of Michaelmas daisy, chrysanth plants, etc. With the dry spring and too wet autumn, stems and stalks were too spindly and thin to stand up to much. I looked at apple blossom, spring rock plants, aubretia and polyanthus in bloom, and could not remember so freakish a year. I felt spent and exhausted long before I'd made much tidy, so left it to heat cream of chicken soup and fry fillets of hake to make a handy meal.

My husband I could see didn't want me to go down to the Civil Defence meeting. I felt if I didn't get out for a while, I'd be really ill. I felt like an old glove – nothing but the outward shape. I couldn't eat much but had a rest. He nattered about 'being glad when this silly fad is over and your Civil Defence lectures finished', and wondered 'what can I do all afternoon'. I lost patience as I pointed out the lecture was an hour, and another 30 or 40 minutes to go there and back, and suggested he went to the cinema or go over Walney. I can never understand his attitude to

the car. Most folk use a car as a help to get about. He won't take
it out if he thinks it will get wet, or leave it in a car park, however
public, in case someone scratches or damages it. He wouldn't hear
of going down to the pictures and leaving it unattended, but with
one of his most hurt expressions decided to go over Walney and
sit and watch the sea. I said, 'Well, that *will* be cosy and uplift-
ing – enough to give anybody the miseries on a day like this', but
I went off thankfully on my own.

Odd how differently people look on home. To me it's my real
'core' of life and living. I can always relax and read or sew happily
if I'm on my own, and would like to have people in rather than go
out looking for change. My husband has his mother's deep horror
of being in the house by himself, and only wanders around unhap-
pily, looking out of windows, watching the clock and timing my
return. I often feel I took a wrong course of action somewhere or
he wouldn't have got quite so bad ... Mrs Higham 'wonders how
on earth you keep so serene and calm. I'd go mad if I was you,
cooped up as you are' – and says, 'You will pay for all this, you
know', as if life was all ruled in little routines with rules made
for every condition. I said, 'Well, things *do* get me down at times,
but I firmly count my blessings, and I've a lot you know, including my queer intelligent cat friends, who are unbelievably good
company'. She said, 'Cats! – fah!' I said, 'Well, add books, my
letters and the regular arrival of the boys' letters. Many women
don't have even that link with families, you know.' She said, 'I
repeat, you lead a most unnatural life, and will pay dearly for it
some day'. I began to argue. As I pointed out, nothing or no one
could hurt you if you didn't allow things to eat into you, and she
got out of patience with me and said, 'Only visionaries and cranks
talk like that. I repeat, you will pay for repressing yourself. Much
better to begin to face it.' I felt sardonic amusement as she talked

and reminded her that we 'all march to our own drummer', and thought secretly that, when done, I'd not change places with her. It must be very bleak not to have a family when you grow old.

Tuesday, 12 September. Anybody I met downtown seemed agog with the gramophone broadcast at 4.30 yesterday by William Chislett, our magistrates' clerk – a well known solicitor – who went off with a young married woman, and now keeps a bookshop in Oxford. It was a nine days' sensation, and sides were taken. As I disliked his whining 'child wife' who at quite 50 talked baby talk and whose mother and aunt had shared their house and interfered for years, I took his side. I felt so impatient today and would have liked to be rude to several people who got so sanctimonious. After all, it was no business of anybody's but those concerned, and if reports speak truly there's a queer enough lot of people work for the BBC another wouldn't be noticed.

Barrow had been abuzz with amazement in the early spring of 1948, when this extraordinary elopement became public knowledge – 'It's been years since such a thing – or anything – has stirred everyone', Nella had written on 31 March 1948. (The episode is mentioned in *Nella Last's Peace*, 11 April 1948, where the surname is given as 'Chislet'.) A few weeks after the elopement, on 6 May 1948, Nella wrote of the aggrieved wife. 'I was going through Croslands Park, and ran slap into Mrs Chislett, who is taking a house not far from Mrs Higham's. I didn't know whether to speak. Last time I saw her to speak to, in the air raids, she was very rude to me, really passing on her spite to me because Mrs Diss wouldn't let her have a permit for a WVS uniform, saying she had better apply to the Ulverston branch when she had gone to live there – they were sleeping on the floor of Mr Chislett's office, though he was Head of the Home Guard! She planted herself in front of me and said mournfully, "Ah, Mrs Last, how nice to see you. I suppose you have heard how dreadfully I've been treated." I felt any faint liking or sympathy fading, as she talked. I felt her lack of all dignity and reticence distasteful in the extreme.' During the war, according to Nella, the Chisletts had left their home in Barrow for the relative safety of Ulverston because 'both were so terrified. We used to wonder what would have happened if invasion had come!' (31 March 1948). The scandal got a second wind in late August 1948. 'I heard Chislett's name mentioned for the first time in weeks. He has a baby daughter now, and has a bookshop in Oxford, and is "very happy". There was the same heated arguments as to whether his wife should divorce him with a slight bias to "I'd *never* let a man free to marry another woman" etc.' (31 August 1948).*

Wednesday, 13 September. I noticed my husband get up from reading the paper and begin to chop some wood we didn't really need. I baked bread and turned out the pantry and kitchenette cupboards. I keep wanting to get curtains and two blankets washed but couldn't dry them indoors with my husband always about. I'd made vegetable soup with a little scraggy end of the weekend mutton, so it only needed heating, and I cooked potatoes and turnip to the cold mutton and made a baked custard. I felt tired yet longed to go out. It was no use suggesting the cinema. Every picture this week seemed too 'thrilling' to suit my husband. Luckily I'd got him a novel by Berta Ruck which I'd skimmed through in the library to make sure it had a happy ending and no deaths or partings, and he settled with it. I got

---

*All this gossip may have been prompted by false information, for there is no evidence from the BBC Written Archives that William Chislett was in any way connected with this broadcast on 11 September. The writer of 'The World of Movement' on the Home Service was a Martin Chisholm, and this could be the source of the error.

out my dollies but felt too tired to sew for long and relaxed on the settee. I wish the appointment for the interview with the psychiatrist would come soon. Times I feel desperate as I look at my husband and see him ageing and letting go of so much, shuddering to myself as I wonder what he *would* be like if I didn't sternly remind him to use his handkerchief, etc. I insist on him changing his clothes or I'll not go out with him, and keep an anxious eye on him altogether, and try and push all memory of his mother out of my mind, though she poor old thing is 83 and not 62. Shut in day after day, when he thinks and thinks about every symptom, every ache and pain, he hasn't the chance of fresh ideas and interests, and he does get despondent. By tea time today I felt I could have climbed the wall. My hands shook – I sliced tomatoes for a salad to eat with cheese, and I cut my finger. Mrs Howson came in with her knitting. I breathed a heartfelt sigh of relief as she settled to talk about clothes and shopping. I'd have welcomed anyone who read the railway timetable out, and she is the only person whom my husband doesn't resent ever. I think he sees always the little girl she was when we first knew her.

Mrs Howson was 20 years younger than Will. Four days earlier Nella had remarked on his unsociability and how 'people don't like it. Mrs Atkinson has stopped coming in. If she wants me, she calls me to the back garden fence, and if he is in the garden never pauses for those little "aimless" chats that can help brighten women's daily round' (9 September). 'He has an unfortunate way of making people feel unwelcome,' she later lamented, 'though I know well he doesn't mean to be as rude as he seems and would often now like people calling' (7 October). While Nella was sometimes critical of Mrs Atkinson, perhaps unfairly, and had complained of her borrowing ways (see *Nella Last's Peace*, especially pp. 143–4), friendly chats over the fence were common, and on one occasion Nella rose to defend her against

Mrs Howson. 'Yes, she isn't backward in asking for what she wants, *but* she tries to pay back in other little ways – it's not altogether one-sided – and I know well if I ever need help in any way, I could rely on her' (25 October). Nella also lauded Mrs Atkinson's 'glowing vitality' (27 October).

Wednesday, 27 September. Power was off two hours. I'd not anything in the oven as it happened, and my bread was slow rising, but it meant Mrs Salisbury couldn't vac, and I had to bake small coconut cakes to put jam and 'Serocream'[†] in, and a tin of crispies, and I had to work longer than usual. Before getting washed and changed, I made a little fruit cake too. I'll have to place oddments that won't go stale in airtight tins, and bake bread after tea. To read about the wasteful lights at Morecambe and Blackpool doesn't help! Mrs Salisbury was full of 'blue sun and moon'. Her old stepfather quotes Revelations, and quite expects the end of the world comparatively soon, speaks of Russia as the 'eagle', and the Chinese war when it first started as the 'war in the East' that would creep over all the West, and says the last world war was only part of the conflagration soon to overwhelm the world. She said in awe, 'I'm keeping away from our old fella for all week. I know he would get excited about the "strange sign in the sky" as soon as I saw it.' I soon finished baking for I'd all ready, and fixed bacon and egg for my husband, and heated tinned soup. Meals *will* have been a problem where electricity was the only means of cooking.

I got washed and changed and felt I would have time to relax before Miss Butler came, but she was here soon after 2 o'clock. For short periods she is a good companion, and as we all have a small town background and know people and incidents in general, we can gossip aimlessly and pleasantly, though I utterly lack the intense interest in the royal family and the 'social register' that is an inheritance for her from her mother. I see the same knowledge and interest in Aunt Sarah, and Aunt Eliza had it too. 'Poor relic of something sweet and serene that has passed forever', I thought. She *is* sweet, and at 60 has the loneliness and helplessness of a child. She never went to school, but had clever governesses, and was reared to be 'mother's companion' and when her two young brothers were killed in 1915 and one of their friends she showed interest in was killed later, the gates clanged behind her for life. She is not by any means the first to be reared with three maids – a cook, governess, gardener and coachman, later chauffeur – and who stepped into today's bustling stream. She dallies on the bank, utterly helpless, lets her house go lost and dirty when she hasn't a daily help, and confessed swiftly she 'lived in the back kitchen with its combustion stove always making it so nice and warm' rather than make a fire and enjoy the comforts of her two other beautiful living rooms. She enjoyed her tea, with a healthy schoolboy appetite for sweet things, complaining plaintively about 'never being able to learn to manage the stove'. Perhaps if she had married things would have been better for her. She would have grown and developed, in spite of her height and increasing weight.

I felt motherly towards her as she spoke half fearfully of growing old. She asked me if I didn't fear old age, 'when no one wants you'. I said, 'Well, candidly, I've often more worry to *push out* of my days to add any more. It's so much better to fill each day, "do the best you can", as my Gran taught, and "pass on".' Unless anyone was fond of running a home entirely and didn't mind Miss Butler's utter 'sloth' of mind, she would find difficulty in sharing a home. Miss Butler speaks so longingly of a 'clever bright companion' – someone to go about with, laugh and talk with. The wind howled and sent leaves flying. The paths were covered when she went out.

We talked of crisp bright autumn days, and wondered where all this rain is coming from. Mrs Howson came in with her knitting. I felt I'd rather have spread out my visitors – Mrs Higham coming tomorrow. Mrs Howson was in one of her sharp-tongued humours, wanting to know 'What does Miss Butler want? I hope you aren't going to try and sort things out for her. She is such a negative lump.' I said, 'Well, we enjoyed her company. She is kind and pleasant, and we found lots of "Do you remember so and so? Wonder what became of them?" and though everything seems against her making friends, she is *not* snobbish and stand-offish as you say. I think her aloofness exists more in people's minds as they remember her snooty "exclusive" mother, who, dear knows how, was "presented at Court" and never forgot it.'

Miss Butler was a new personality in Nella's diary. Her first appearance had been on 16 August 1950 (see above), her second on 28 August and her third on 8 September, when items were being collected in aid of charitable causes, including Barrow's famine relief shop. 'It's only the Edwardian "sheltering" ways that has made her so utterly useless', Nella wrote on 28 August. 'I gave her a label they had sent me, and told her of my "sacks" and suggested she gave me any warm or useful cast-offs for displaced persons, or better still get one of her own and worry folks to give her things. I said "People *would*, you know. Look how marvellous everyone was in giving to the Red Cross shop, your mother amongst them." She looked at the picture of hungry children and said, "I often think of your belief in reincarnation and 'things coming right somewhere'. I loved working in Canteen amongst you all. You all seemed to argue and think. Perhaps next time I'll have babies and a family of my own." I thought of how in the First World War she and a friend of her brother had been so "friendly" and how he hadn't been thought good enough, and how it had been considered her duty to stay at home with her parents when her two brothers were killed, and now she is lonely and a bit eccentric at 59.' Miss Butler was, thought Nella, struggling to fit in. 'Her people were so wealthy – *and* snooty – that lots of people who would be friendly fear a snub. She will have to pick up threads herself. It was a mistake to stay away so long if she intended making her home in Barrow. One thing – I've got her interested in Oxford Relief, and she has got some friends and relatives interested too' (25 September).

The next several weeks in the Last household were fairly routine and unremarkable, punctuated by outings in the car and such small rituals as Nella's weekly filling out of the football pools – though she considered herself 'a complete dumb wit at football' (25 November). Consequently, only a few selections are presented for this period, before resuming a fuller recording of her writing from 30 November.

Thursday, 12 October. In Ulverston I met an old friend from Greenodd and we had a chat about old times. She has one of the loveliest – and dumbest – girls I ever met. Her gorgeous corn-coloured hair, perfect complexion and limpid blue eyes never seemed to make up for her rather raucous voice and real twaddle of small talk. Yet she is a good hairdresser with a little business of her own in Grange. Mrs Barrow was always rather a silly person herself, and put the idea in Maisie's head that her really exceptional beauty would ensure a very good marriage. I've heard her say proudly to the exquisite little girl, 'Our Maisie won't have to work like I've done – not with that lovely face'. Today she complained that 'Our Maisie never seems to get an offer and she is now over 30. She will have to meet your Cliff when he comes home.' I smiled to myself, feeling a bit wistfully, 'Well, after all, Maisie would be better than him not marrying anyone' but realising too there didn't seem any likelihood of Cliff marrying. He likes his own way too much and, like several of my father's brothers, at the heart of him he is a rover, both bodily and mentally.

Thursday, 19 October. When rain began to fall in a soft curtain of drizzle, I didn't expect my husband to go to Ulverston as usual. He felt restless, though, and when Mrs Higham rang up to ask if we *were* going to Ulverston could I see if a stallholder there had any checked 'suiting' weight material, he said he would go as usual. I got a nice bit of English lamb – 3s 8d – and a good sheep's head and some lights for my cats. As I picked up my parcels of meat I felt something different in one, and Bob whispered, 'There's a little present from Alice in that – she thought you looked real poorly when she saw you the other day', and he winked and nodded his head as if it was a good joke. When I got into the car and opened it I couldn't believe my eyes – half a pound of fresh country butter! His wife was my hairdresser before the war and till the call-up took her into the Yard, and we always liked each other, but her kindness amazed me, and I felt glad I'd got a dollie made for the baby for Xmas. I couldn't see anything to suit Mrs Higham, but did wish I could have bought a Harris tweed coat length for Edith and a sports jacket length for Cliff and Arthur for their Xmas present – only 15s and 18s a yard. It amazed me to see such good woollen material and no 'rush' buyers who saw the value. There were really amazing bargains in oddments on every stall, especially for anyone who could make things up themselves.

Sunday, 29 October. I grieved to hear the fire last night was a disastrous one on the *Oronsay*, the new Australian liner, due for her trial trip next March, so she will be partly furnished, and the cork insulating slabs would burn like wood. We went to church, and when we came out the smell of burning wafted on the chilly wind, which was south-west and blew straight over the town. I heated cream of chicken soup and had a little with toast, and then had celery and bread and butter. My husband had soup and bacon and egg, ate bread to the latter, and finished with a cup of tea. I put tea up in the flask and when he went to lie down picked up my book – a Crime Club, *Murder among Friends*, by Elizabeth Ferrars – quite good, but I wish the whim for 'crimes' would pass. Oddly enough, when I'm really well I dislike them. My husband wasn't well. I notice he never is if he motors above 20–30 miles. Yet I don't feel it would be wise to find fault with anything he takes a fancy to do. It's when he just sits that makes me worry so much. I feel a curious feeling at times that all vitality of the room dies, not only in myself, when those deep depressions sweep down over him. I'm sure too he is growing a little deaf. So often he takes no notice at all when spoken to, and I noticed at Mrs Higham's he let her remarks pass.

The sun shone and he insisted on going out, but wasn't pleased when I said I wanted to go and look at the *Oronsay*. When I said, 'Well, don't come – I'll go and return on the bus', he seemed to think I'd only meet people to talk to and 'stay out all afternoon', so he got out the car. All roads seemed to lead to the dockside – cars in a stream, walkers, and every bus going that way was full. It looked as if the fire ship had drawn half the water in the dock to pump into her, but the fire still smouldered below. Outside, except for a strong list, there was little to be seen, except a squad of men busy propping stays to prevent her keeling over on her side. The side of the High Level bridge was lined about six feet deep – lots of youth and young children you would have expected to create some kind of noise, but a hush was on everyone and voices were low. Barrow people love their ships, not only those people who create and build, but all of us who see a shell launched and brought round to the dockside, where day by day it is built and people can see it in passing. Two men quietly discussed the possibility of an electric fault causing the fire – the refrigeration plant had recently been installed. The thought of any kind of sabotage didn't occur to them. We came away feeling a sadness at the waste and destruction, hoping it wasn't as bad as at first thought. I don't like any kind of mishap in building.*

We went round by the Coast Road home. Sea birds flocked as if feeling a storm out at sea, and settled in the fields. The sky had a coppery glow that showed our little sunny spell might be ending. I made tea. My husband had cheese on toast. I wasn't hungry, and had toast and a cup of tea. I settled down to stitch my felt oddments, and made two pair of large dollies' shoes, finished the bonnets and partly made up the rabbit. The wind rose and howled mournfully over the chimneys. I didn't feel well, and after the 9 o'clock news came to bed.

Monday, 6 November. The Town Clerk was late for the WVS Club meeting. He had been on the selection committee for staff for the new old folks home, and he gave a most interesting talk on 'The Ups and Downs of a Town Clerk's Life', suggested by Mrs Diss instead of the talk on Civil Defence originally planned for two months ago when we should have had a meeting and there was a 'drive' for it. Few people fascinate me as he does. I could watch him talk for hours. Everyone has two different sides to his face. I've seen faces 'rearranged' by taking two left or right sides on the print and they all looked amazingly different people, but

---

*Two days later Nella's tone was more buoyant. 'We were so glad to see the *Oronsay* riding proudly and straight in the water. I hear they are going to endeavour to get it finished on the arranged date, so there will be a lot of overtime for many men' (31 October). The *Oronsay*, at 28,200 tons, was reputed to be the largest passenger liner then being built in Britain.

never did I see such a perfect Jekyll and Hyde face as his. He has
been in the town since long before the war, and of course is a very
prominent man in the affairs of the town, but never once have
I heard anyone say they liked or trusted him, and as for things
said against him, 'hypocrite' is the mildest. He brought an idea
of morals and lady friends which might have passed unnoticed in
a city, but which shocked a provincial town and started off badly
when public opinion practically forced him to marry a hairdresser
who was expecting his baby. Rightly or wrongly, his treatment
of her – cold, callous, sneering, etc. etc. – was blamed for the
coming baby being an idiot. Many men could have lived it down,
and not gained the contempt he did, if he hadn't such a face. One
side of it is that of an amiable actor, wide eye, mobile pleasant
mouth, and cheek that curves into a likeable smile; the other is
evil, much smaller eye, mean twist to mouth, and a startlingly
sinister look. If you saw him on the screen it would be in a vil-
lain's role. Yet he took his sea-going motor boat, with one man
to help, and helped in the evacuation of Dunkirk. I felt a strange
pity for him today. I felt I could almost *see* his two warring personalities as he spoke really brilliantly.

I helped wash up and pack dishes away. We felt so awkward
in a new kitchen, and as Mrs Howson, Mrs Host and Marjory
Fletcher were on my Canteen squad, they seemed to think if I
helped all would be done quickly!

Saturday, 11 November. Billy Newington called in – the man who
bought the business. He wanted some advice on War Damage
claims my husband had dealt with nearly two years ago. I
reminded him he hadn't finished Mrs Howson's mother's gate,
and he said he had been 'rushed to death – could do with another
man, and had heard of one'. I couldn't but wonder why my

husband said, 'there isn't a man to be had anywhere' yet Billy has had no difficulty. He went on, 'We have the Laundry work now and have worked Saturday afternoons and Sundays on some jobs, which had to be done when machinery was stopped.* By heck, I've struck a gold mine. I've averaged £30 a week clear every week since I got settled, including of course all my overtime'. I wished he hadn't come. My husband began to brood on 'all he had lost'. I knew sympathy would have only made him worse. I said sharply, 'It's no use looking back. Do you think it's any easier for me than you? You have no one really to blame but yourself and no one but yourself can begin a cure. If you tried to think of bright things, you would feel better. Morbid grizzles breed fast as flies, and anyway, if *you* had £50–£500 a week what pleasure would it bring you? You are growing more and more of a hermit. Soon you could live in a cell without missing anything. All you want to do is eat and sleep and drift. Good luck to Billy in all his "wasting time" playing cricket, watching football, filling up coupons and twice a week at the pictures. At least he has other interests to take his mind off work.'

I think the knowledge we were due out at 2 o'clock helped him throw off his mood, and after a short rest for him we set off. I insisted firmly on going by bus. Knowing how upset he can get, I wouldn't risk him driving after hypnotic treatment, not being very sure of the results. When I saw the annexe door locked and no nurse in attendance, I began to think there was a hitch. After a reasonable wait I began to make enquiries – not easy, for there's no connection between Moor Hospital at Lancaster and the North Lonsdale; the former only come and go for appointments. The

---

*Power cuts were frequent this autumn in Barrow. Nella's neighbourhood experienced at least one or two cuts almost every week from mid-September.

only thing a Sister and I could think of was that Dr Wadsworth had not made a note of the interview and it had quite slipped his mind. We could do nothing but come home. It was after 3 o'clock, and any programmes at cinemas half over or I'd have dragged him in, but we just came home, and the look on his face appalled me. He might as well have had his death sentence instead of only a broken appointment. Nothing lifted his gloom.

Thursday, 16 November. I got a small half shoulder of Canterbury lamb, and some good steak bones for my stock pot, and we went to the Martinmas fair at Ulverston. The town was thronged with smart but serviceably clad and shod young fellows, keen and intelligent as well as healthy looking, and so widely different from the brutish country bumpkins of a few years ago. I felt that there was a few things in this swiftly changing world that were brave and splendid. I never saw such a number of really marvellously furnished and equipped trailer caravans – coal stoves, expensive carpets and furnishings with beautifully polished silver on the tiny sideboards. Nor did I ever see so many fortune tellers and palmists. Six of the best equipped and largest of the caravans had placards with 'testimonials'. Lea's, Boscombe's and Smith's, and a tawny eyed beauty of little more than twenty eagerly offered from her caravan step to 'tell your fortune, lady'. The age-old surrounding houses of the Gill [*the site of hiring fairs*], the dark-eyed unchanged gypsies – except for better clothes – the merry-eyed happy children tumbling round, the tawdry splendour of old-fashioned shooting galleries, roundabouts and sideshows, swung me back more years than I could count. If Mrs Higham hadn't been coming, I'd have loved to linger in the crowded little town, where, it seemed, everyone from the surrounding countryside had flocked today. I felt I'd have liked to be able to 'dream back' to when the fair first started – a church near by goes back over 1,000 years. I wondered if the fair did. I get fish from a very nice fishmonger at Ulverston – a Tynesider who went all through the war in the Navy but has a hint of small town ways, likes to chat about Ulverston, cats, the weather, etc. He surprised me today by asking, 'Isn't there any old history books of this place?' I couldn't tell him. Any I know are contemporary, except those Norman Birkett wrote, and they tend to leave out so much you feel you would like to know. I told him of Collingwood's *Thorstein of the Lake* – from Greenodd up the Crake River to Coniston, in the time of the Norsemen.*

Saturday, 18 November. We had to be at the Hospital for 10.30. I hurriedly dusted and shook the rug, washed up and made beds, and we set out by 10 o'clock. I felt far from happy. My husband rose looking ill and was in one of his silent brooding moods, and I knew he dreaded going. After he went into the smaller room of the annexe with the doctor, the nurse-receptionist and I settled silently, she with her knitting, I with a rather tatty magazine off the table. Our silence contrasted with the noise of all kinds of traffic noises, cars being reversed or started in the Hospital quadrangle, shouts of children. After what seemed a long wait, Dr Wadsworth came out and spoke to the nurse, who hurried off and returned with a pillow. She mouthed at me 'Can't get him off'. Then followed another long wait till the door opened again, and looking across at me the doctor said quietly, 'Will you come in please, Mrs Last'. I had that awful feeling when the blood all

---

Thorstein of the Mere: A Saga of the Northmen in Lakeland (1895), by W. G. Collingwood (1854–1932). Norman Birkett, an eminent barrister and judge, was born in Ulverston and educated at Barrow-in-Furness Grammar School.

seems to drain into the feet and makes them heavy as lead, and
the rest of the body feather light and giddy, and for a split second
I felt incapable of moving. It was only a few steps to the door of
the inner room, and I saw my husband in one of the worst nervous
shaking attacks he has had. I crossed over and took his very cold
hands and rubbed them. The doctor got some kind of tablet and
dissolved it in a glass of water, and I soothed and 'petted' my
husband until the dreadful tremors passed, knowing so surely
there was wild terror and some kind of memory behind them. I'd
seen my poor old Cliff like that often, when he was first home,
and the horrors of war hadn't faded out of his mind.

Dr Wadsworth said, 'We will leave Mr Last to rest quietly till
his tablet takes effect', and he took my arm and gently propelled
me from the room to a chair by the radiator in the anteroom and
began to talk. He said, 'Does your husband get so easily upset at
home? He was only being asked a few routine questions, and he
reacted so badly it was impossible to hypnotise him.' He seemed
to be able to put leading questions so simply. I recalled afterwards
he must have been able to build up a very clear cut picture of
my husband's habits, moods, and approach to life in general, not
only now but for years. He said, 'Would you agree to bring your
husband to the Moor Hospital at Lancaster some evening?' I said,
'Doctor, I'm beginning to feel so desperate I'd take him to China
if I thought it would help him'. He said, 'Something *will* have
to be done. I can see he is worse than when I saw him first. His
life cannot be worth living – yours either if I may say so.' I said,
'Tell me please, doctor, am I right to give way to his moods to
avoid such attacks of nerves, or should I, as his doctor suggests,
"rouse and stimulate him, and quarrel with him if it's the only
way to jerk him out of himself"'? Dr Wadsworth pursed his lips
and slowly shook his head as he said, 'Any course at present that

helps to avoid such distressing attacks is your best policy, but rest assured, everything in my powers will be done to help him'. Once an attack is over, my husband seems himself, often better, seemingly, than I feel after one!

Thursday, 30 November. Mrs Higham spoke of vague unrest in the WVS office. As I get little chance of going in the office I hear little – and feel I care less. When a prim old maid school teacher, fast getting a little 'woolly', grabs the news, I feel *anything* could happen. I feel sorry and understanding for Mrs Diss and her somewhat weary attitude. She wanted to give up long ago, and it's a mistake to persuade people beyond their feelings or wishes. People got so tired after the war years. New ones were needed and should have been sought. I'd expected a power cut for tea, and prepared candles in my brass as well as glass candlesticks, but the cut must have missed our part of town. Mrs Higham went early, and we settled to listen to the good Thursday evening programmes, but Mrs Howson came in and stayed till 9 o'clock. I felt I'd rather it had been Mrs Higham, for you can discuss any subject with her. Mrs Howson utterly refuses to talk of any war worries, the effects of rearmaments, anything she considers deep or worrying.

Sunday, 3 December. Everything was thick with snow this morning, and soon after breakfast it began again. I never remember such an odd effect. Big feathery flakes the size of pigeons' eggs stuck to the windows till the heat from inside melted them off. Poor Shan We sat on the window sill chattering like a monkey, and looking so distressed. I'm always puzzled with the gulls and rooks on really bad mornings, and cannot but think they have a 'memory' and also a way of telling other birds they know a place where some kind of a bite will be given them. Always they sit round on the trellis and fence waiting, while none can be seen in the surrounding garden ... I felt so bewildered and depressed by the news from Korea. What *can* we do against such hordes – and such cruel ruthless 'savages'. I shuddered to think of poor wives' and mothers' feelings in America who read of GIs wounded being burnt. My deep fear that another atom bomb will be dropped grows daily as I can see no other weapon against such odds.

Nella had read John Hershey's *Hiroshima* (1946), a gripping account of the ruinous impact of one atomic bomb. On 4 December she heard another opinion about the crisis in Korea. 'My hairdresser is a young married woman whose husband works in the Yard. She was full of the conviction of the men in the Yard that the atom bomb – or bombs – would be certain to be dropped, that unless they were used American and British troops would be pushed back into the sea, and there would be no Dunkirk rescue.' The following day, with her sister-in-law, Flo, 'We talked of the black shadow of war looming'. 'It's a queer and mad world when prices rise and rise,' she wrote on 22 December, 'and the only things we *do* seem to be able to afford as nations are armaments and atom bombs to further destroy and kill, not only peoples, but the gracious lovely things of life.' As a result of the war in Korea, there was to be a major increase in military expenditures, to the detriment of the domestic economy; Britain was under heavy pressure from Washington to rearm.

Wednesday, 6 December. It's been an evil day of sleet and rain and North wind and all turning to slush. Mrs Salisbury came round by the bus, which cost me 6d extra, but I felt so glad she came I didn't grudge it. She has never complained of being so hard up – says, too, that she years ago, when she had two small children and her husband only had the dole, had more in her purse that wasn't 'condemned' and could be 'spent' instead of just for weekly bills. A lot of her troubles even now are of her own making. As I often tell her, if she made soup and porridge and baked more instead of tinned soups – for six of them – and didn't rely on cornflakes always and silly little bought cakes that were stale the next day, she could economise on her Co-op bill. Where she lives there's only one other shop on the estate and it's easiest to get all 'on the bill' and pay each Friday.* I washed a few oddments so as not to have a real wash day with a lot of wet woollens etc. drying in the house, for my cough still keeps bad…

I'd remembered in the evening that Mr Attlee would speak and Mrs Howson asked if I 'would bother to listen'. When I said, 'certainly', she went with something about 'No time for that'. I listened with real respect for the dignity and restraint of Attlee's speech. He couldn't have said less – or more. I felt that never before in the world's history was so difficult a situation facing men, or countries. Whether to leave all our gallant soldiers with no hope either of more troops to help, or a Dunkirk, or withdraw and lose face but 'live to fight another day', always with the sick fear that whatever we did would be wrong, but with the certainty of Stalin's deep laid plans to engulf Europe, and, if Europe, the whole of the world. Beside Stalin, Hitler seems a boy scout. *He* is the Anti Christ and not Hitler.**

---

*'Mrs Salisbury has *no* idea of diet and is an atrocious cook', according to Nella on 18 October, though she did not fault her for lack of effort, which included taking in boarders. 'In August when the couple she had living with her left, she couldn't get another – it's rather far out for Shipyard men. She was talking of Xmas, rising prices and her increasing efforts to make ends meet. She *does* try in every way for her family, and she is such a friendly faithful little creature.'
**The Prime Minister was in the American capital for talks with President Truman and senior American officials. Britain was striving to contain the

Thursday, 7 December. It's been such a nice sunny day. I rose feeling out of joint generally, but the sun was like a tonic. I got what bit of tidying round needed doing and was ready when my husband came back from the hospital. I'd sent Matron the Xmas dollies – only 1½ dozen this year, and not up to the usual standard. Bits and pieces get more scarce every year, and scraps for stuffing too, for each dollie takes quite a lot of scraps cut finely. Gone are the days when Matron used to say, 'Ask for whatever you want. As long as it is coming back to the hospital, it is quite alright.' …

Mrs Howson had said, 'Come early – don't forget it's a little party' – she had had her 25th wedding anniversary at the weekend. She had invited two other friends. Before they came, we sorted out some oddments of fur cloth and felt. She is making a monkey at evening class with a bought 'mark', and I've always wanted to make a monkey, so I'm copying it, hoping Edith won't get vexed with the clutter of soft toys I seem to make for little Peter.

I knew the couple invited very well. We spent a pleasant if a bit grim afternoon discussing Korea and our fears. Jack Hammond is certain the atom bomb will have to be dropped – 'the only way to stem the onrush of Chinese, drunk with power, who otherwise will wipe out our troops mercilessly; and remember, those self same troops may soon be needed in Europe'. I see every argument for dropping the bomb, or bombs, yet I grow sick and cold with horror when I think of the results on the innocent as well as guilty – and 'guilty' in that soldiers are pawns in a game, hardly considered as human by the ones who wage wars. We took the

---

increasingly dangerous conflict in Korea (China had actively intervened in November) and discourage the use of atomic weapons. The speech Nella refers to was probably the one Attlee gave at the National Press Club in Washington that day (*The Times*, 7 December 1950, p. 4b).

Hammonds to the Ribble bus stop – they live near Ulverston – and we came home. I felt somehow lonelier than usual, not bodily as much as mentally lonely. Talking doesn't solve world problems, but to talk out things always eases worry. My husband never liked to talk or argue. In fact, most things have always passed over his head and his argument has always been 'Don't worry so much. It does no good and you cannot help things.'

Mrs Howson came in and I felt so impatient at her concerns and worry because she cannot get grey shoes anywhere. She has 19 pairs of shoes already, all colours, mostly Joyce or sling backs, or 'peep toe' sandals. A more expensive doll-eyed collection I couldn't imagine, and not a good pair of walking shoes or bootees, not even Wellingtons for snow and wet. I didn't like the idea of grey accessories to the deep ruby red coat she has anyway, and the expensive grey hat looks definitely wrong. She got up hurriedly when I turned on the 9 o'clock news and grabbed her coat, saying, 'I'm not going to listen to any old war news. They make too much of it anyway. There's never anything else nowadays.'

Friday, 8 December. Every day this week there's been a power cut. It didn't come this morning at breakfast time but at 10.30. We got out the picnic Primus stove and I can boil a kettle and heat my husband's porridge – I prefer cornflakes with cold milk. I'd got the rabbit stew cooking, with carrots and onions, so lifted it on the side of the dining room fire and later added potatoes and sprouts to steam on top. Celery soup too finished cooking by the fire, and later I made custard and stewed dates. Mrs Higham said when her sister was here at the weekend for her wedding anniversary she told her she had been lucky enough to get a gas stove in place of her electric one, and hundreds of people thronged the gas showrooms in Liverpool making enquiries about a changeover.

The man emptied our meter this morning. I had £3 0s 1d in the meter and was handed back 15s 5d and the 1s of course left in. We spoke of the 'good old days' when I'd have had quite half that £3 back! He knows I've only one fire, the rest electric, and said, 'Considering your stove in which you bake all your bread and cakes, and the fact you have an immersion heater, I think you haven't used much electricity'. I pointed out I never used the latter when I had a good fire, for with the boiler being behind the dining room fire I had all the hot water I needed. He glanced at my gleaming pans as he said, 'But you do all your cooking on the stove?' I said, 'Yes, but again, one ring keeps three pans simmering once they have come to the cooking point. Electricity is too dear to waste.' I was amused to find him so interested till he mentioned they were on the lookout for any tips to save electricity, which were passed on to the girl in the showroom, who answers all little baking and cooking problems and has little 'demonstrations' from time to time.

Saturday, 9 December. A parcel came from Edith and Arthur with my husband's birthday present, and our Xmas gifts to be put aside. When I handled my husband's soft parcel I decided to unseal one end and see if my fears were justified. They were – and I felt really cross to find a woollen scarf. Arthur had written asking what to buy, and a scarf was *not* included. It was the same last year. Edith ignored my suggestions and bought a very unsuitable light fawn scarf, far too thick to sit under an overcoat collar. I've asked Arthur if it's possible to change it for something he needs – socks or a tie would be better. Before he got last year's, he had two they bought at different times, both hardly worn!

Monday, 11 December [*Will's 63rd birthday*]. We stuck to our plan of last night, that I'd do any shopping I need while he had the car out. I got some chocolate biscuits – on points – and a shaving brush for one of his little Xmas presents, and we went for his watch, but was again disappointed. He dropped it and it was to cost 10s 6d, so he asked for it for his birthday gift. When I was in Boots I noticed few expensive cosmetics were on Xmas shopping lists. It was 'Something about 5 shillings, please' or 'Have you that in a smaller size?' Last week they had such a good choice of children's hot water bottles made like bears, cats, etc. Today all had gone, and 'they hoped' to have more in before Xmas. Mrs Diss was in the greengrocer's when I was in. She was in one of her least attractive moods, when in a loudish voice she gave her order, as if to impress listeners with the fact 'Money is no object, as you know!' It isn't, either. But to see pots of cyclamens, orange-berried plants, lovely azaleas – at 28s! – ordered in several of each, four very small fir trees – '*We* like a decked tree in each room' – to see the long list of frozen foods, from dressed crab to fruit salads, cauliflower at 2s – 'About four, I think; no, better make it half a dozen' – was to feel you saw in your mind's eye every coin in your purse and knew how far it should go! She spoke of having 'No patience with people who gave up making a fuss of Xmas'. I looked at her critically as I thought, 'Not one worry or trouble in your life. More money than you know what to do with. Two maids and extra help – hmm!' I felt slight annoyance when she never even asked how my husband was, and when I said, 'If I don't see you again before Xmas, all good wishes for both Xmas and the New Year', and she said offhandedly, 'Thanks', silly and childish of me to feel hurt when she didn't return my good wishes. I often feel I've lost or am losing my sense of humour entirely!

Tuesday, 12 December. At Spark Bridge I went up the road to see how much I owed a farmer's wife. I met her some weeks ago in Ulverston and asked her if she would take any eggs' points when she killed a pig and an extra pint of milk, for I thought it the best when I couldn't get up each week. Although I knew Aunt Sarah had had a lot of odds and ends, she would only take 10s, and I had difficulty in making her take that. She recalled I'd shopped with her points when she had difficulty in feeding extra hands. The wind blew off the snow-covered hills like a knife, and I felt sorry as she spoke of Greenodd people not having a resident doctor. The one who had come had only been able to get accommodation quite three miles away, on a very bleak moorland road. The original doctor, who was well liked and who has been there for a number of years, had no private means and found under the National Health new scheme he couldn't possibly rear a family and is down at the hospital in Barrow. I felt it wouldn't do to look for a cottage at Greenodd if my husband always needed medical attention. Anyway, while he is going to the hospital twice a week we couldn't very well go far out of town. Sometimes I feel I don't want to make a change at all. I wonder if any change we could make would help him, and I know I'd miss what few contacts I have.

Friday, 15 December. We hadn't the snow of many parts, but the roads were like glass. We have a stupid Council. They never seem to take precautions of sand or gravel except in the main bus roads, and at that not in the night, to help traffic for the Yard. I made a pan of vegetable soup which will do three days, washed some towels and woollens, dusted round, and sat down to finish my monkey. He is quite the cutest thing I've made, in his little green felt jacket embroidered round the edges with red and yellow, and his red fez with black tassel. I'm sure Peter will love it. Posts *are* good. I sent the scarf back Tuesday. Arthur must have got it the next day, changed it for two pair of socks and posted them back and I got them today. No parcel yet from Australia. I hope they arrive next week, especially the one for Belfast. I got the monkey finished by the time I had to prepare lunch. The soup was ready, and I fried bacon, boiled sprouts and potatoes and heated rice pudding I had in the fridge.

When my husband went to lie down I wrapped up warmly and went to the General Post Office. It was so crowded, and I saw one parcel that had been so badly tied it had been pointed out to the woman posting it that it wouldn't stand the journey to Glasgow so she went off to buy string, after holding all up while she argued it was 'quite alright' – and something like a tie could be seen at the end of the parcel already. The ambulance was starting up where there wasn't houses where anyone would have been likely to be carried out. I asked a passer-by if there had been an accident and was told an elderly man had collapsed with the cold. I didn't wonder. I felt chilled to the bone when I got in, and glad to make a cup of hot tea. I'd left the kettle by the fire. My husband rose cranky and irritable. He seems depressed because he has had no word to go again to see Dr Wadsworth. He pinned such faith in the 'wonders' of hypnotism.

Saturday, 16 December. So bitterly cold again, but bright sunshine helped me tidy round so we could go shopping to the market. I wanted to get kapok[†] in, given its rapid upward rise in price, before it rose higher. It was 5s 6d a lb at Woolworths and two finishing shops but when I went to the Co-op to enquire I got it for 4s 9d. And last supply three weeks ago was only 3s 9d. The man who served me said in a puzzled tone, 'I don't know what it's being used for. We are nearly sold out there has been such a

rush.' My sudden brainwave wasn't as original as I thought! I got
5 lbs. My two really good eiderdowns had 3½ lbs of 'eider' at 10s
6d a lb and are 'plump' and well filled, but I got the 5 lbs for I
plan a quilt to tuck in sides and bottom of the small single bed,
and I'll see how it is going in the making for I plan, too, to make
a fairly thick pad to go over the mattress. There's only a pad type
over a well sprung wire one – it's the type that the legs unscrew
and go away in a corner if not in use … So even with the two or
three reels of Sylko[†] (4½d each) I'll have a super cover that will
be as warm as two ordinary blankets, with perhaps some kapok
towards the mattress pad – for about £2 15s 0d.

My husband had one of his near fits, grumbling about spending money. These moods of his make me desperately sorry for
women with no resources at all of their own. My tiny income
makes me airily independent if I think that way. When he had
looked at horrible flock filled eiderdowns of the usual size priced
at over £5, he slightly altered his views! We couldn't decide what
to buy Mother for a little present. She has plenty of everything,
and too many sweets and chocolates are not good for her. She
never had an affection for any kind of 'pet' or interest in books,
and never used perfume. I saw some bowls of bulbs at 10s 6d and
12s 6d, just about an inch through the fibre, and we bought a 12s
6d one, although she always said she was 'not lucky' with plants
– she forgot to water them often. I thought bulbs needed no
attention. Eggs are scarce. I'd not had any for two weeks although
a few had been in, but today was lucky and I got four, and an
unexpected quarter pound of tongue as well. There were plenty
of tomatoes, but I don't like them 'box' ripened – they have little
flavour whether for table or soup. We got a nice bough of holly
and only paid 1s. Next Saturday the price will be at least 2s for
smaller, and a big rush for it.

In the 'pets' corner, poor shivering frightened puppies yapped, or sat in dumb-eyed misery, most far too young to be taken from the care and warmth of their mothers to be handed over to unthinking children as pets, none with pedigrees, most being chosen for their 'cuteness', none house trained. I thought, as I looked pityingly at the helpless things, how much unnecessary and unthinking cruelty there was in the world – most would have been better drowned at birth. Sorry as I was for the kittens, I always think cats have more sense looking after themselves, can keep themselves clean, etc. Chickens, rabbits and hares were in abundance, notices that 'Geese can still be ordered for Xmas', but no signs of turkeys. There's never been any big demand in Barrow, perhaps because, being a working town – except when big bonuses or a lot of overtime at the Yard – women have considered a goose or a couple of ducks better value.

I'd left my piece of frozen mutton simmering in a bed of celery, leeks and carrots. I added potatoes to steam while soup heated and was eaten. Tinned peas were well rinsed and drained, and a shake of pepper and dab of butter added and tossed till hot over the fire. We have always said, 'Thank goodness, no power cuts today' on Saturdays and Sundays, but there had been one of nearly two hours when we were out. I was glad I'd not relied on the stove – it was thrift that made me leave it by the little fire. I very reluctantly bought a new pan this morning. One of my two 7 inch pans – the most useful size now there are only two of us – has been giving out round the base of the handle for some time now, and I've kept dabbing 'stick solder' on. In view of the fact aluminium pans will soon be scarce, I made up my mind not to wait any longer – and began to think I'd left it too long to get what I wanted. I could have got a real bargain – one of the very thick pans that last a lifetime – but it was too large. At 24s the

price was little higher – they were always very much more – than
the ordinary ones. Shop after shop had the same remarks, 'Only
those few oddments, or sets, mostly steamers', and even pressure
cookers were sold out. Then I got just what I wanted – real old
stock when the proprietor was turning out the shelves in the
warehouse and putting *all* out for sale, including lamps and one-
burner oil stoves he had written off, and even the old-fashioned-
looking lamps, some slightly shabby with dust and rust, were
best sellers. I only paid 6s 6d. I'd been asked 7s 6d for the same
quality in too small a size for my need in a shop up the street. We
laughed as we recalled the turn out of shops and warehouses in
the war as supplies got worse. Mr Diss and his father before him
never seemed very good buyers, and in the big warehouse behind
the Disses' high-class jeweller's shop were shelves and cupboards
stacked with real junk, doll-eyed jam dishes and jars and bric-
à-brac more suited to present shops in seaside resorts. Brought
out gradually, together with good but unsaleable clocks, watches,
ugly presentation plate, etc., *and* at increasing prices, he made a
small fortune – out of stuff that had been a debit for at least 20
years!

I had got all Mrs Salisbury's plum pudding oddments ready,
and added my own, and planned to make them this afternoon
when my husband went to lie down, but he said, 'Let's go out a
while and I'll rest when we come in'. I jumped at the chance to
take two little presents and pay visits I only seem to do about
Xmas. My butcher's wife, an old pre-war hairdresser friend, lives
on the Coast Road and I'd made her baby a dollie. An old friend
of Hospital Supply days who lives in an outlying village got a
dozen chocolate cornflake dainties in a box, and a bottle of pears
in syrup. With making a snap decision, my husband hadn't time
to think up objections and I felt really happy to be able to make

the two little visits. We were home by 4 o'clock too, so he had his rest before tea. With everything to hand I soon made the two puddings, and the two pans with the basins in simmered on one hot plate of the stove, and I just managed to get the almond paste on my little cake by the time he came down. I made such a nice Xmasy tea – tongue and celery, bread and butter and raspberry jam and crisps, shortbread biscuits and chocolate dainties, some made with puffed wheat, others with cornflakes. We were both hungry, and my husband seemed in a bit less despondent mood.

CHAPTER FIVE

GETTING BY, GETTING ON

December 1950–May 1951

Tuesday, 26 December, Boxing Day. My husband's cold was still bad, and he said at breakfast, 'I don't know what was the matter with me last night. I couldn't get to sleep for thinking.' I said, 'What were you thinking about?' and he said, 'Ah, when the boys were small in the war and even when we were courting. You know it doesn't seem over forty years ago since you used to wear that white fur cap and stole.' I felt surprised. He doesn't often reminisce. I only dusted round and washed up. Margaret came in, then Steve Howson, whose cold is really alarming. I'd be making him stay in bed, fearing bronchitis, if I'd anything to do with him. He *did* look ill. I didn't bother with much lunch. We had the last of the boiled fowl I had in the fridge, bread and butter, celery, tea and a piece of Xmas cake each. It had not much fruit in, and is a much lighter cake than I've made other years. It was very cold. I'd nothing to take me out, and had a really good thriller by Christianna Brand called *Death of Jezebel*, and when my husband went to lie down I pulled the settee near the fire and curled up till 4 o'clock, when he came downstairs. His cold is still bad, but today he looked better of himself. There was ice cream to the rest of the sliced peaches, bread and butter, mince pies and almond cheese cakes.

Wednesday, 27 December. Mrs Atkinson and I filled a bucket of coal between us, and she carried it while I took three fire bricks each and some sticks I could spare to an old neighbour across the road who has just come out of hospital. We agreed we didn't give it with any generous spirit, but we couldn't see her without coal. She has money enough to live in great comfort, but she has a real miser's spirit – burns a candle to save electricity, rations every slice of bread, every potato. She cried today when we went in and moaned about 'being all alone, no one to care whether she lived or died', etc. I said, 'You should have let your sister end her days with you when she was over from New Zealand. You knew how unhappy her married life has always been, and how her husband would rather live with the two children of his first marriage and how he longed [for her] to end her days in England. It would have been an ideal arrangement for you both.' The thin lips pressed waspishly together as she said, 'But I would have had to keep her – and food costs money'. I said, 'And you have it, Mrs Townsend. I know all your circumstances, know you got £7,000 for the farm and land and cottages as well as all you had before, and you haven't anyone to leave it to, you know.' As Mrs Atkinson and I said, 'It's a religion to a certain type of person to so revere capital' – and don't I know it. I see storms ahead when *we* draw money from the Building Society, or sell War Savings Certificates.

Friday, 29 December. I saw Gilbert, the apprentice at the workshop, who had come to mend Mrs Howson's mother's gate. Only 19, he was hurriedly married to a girl of 20 recently, and they have a baby 5 weeks old. My heart ached for his queerly set face – he was so boyish for his age. I felt all youth had been wiped from his face. He looked so cold. I said, 'Hallo, Gilbert. Aren't you going for lunch?' And he said, 'I brought a meat pie and a cake.

It's a good way from home and I've a lot of little jobs up here.' I thought Mrs Howson should have offered him a hot drink, but I said, 'Pop across, love, when I wave and have some hot soup'. He seemed the happy lad who cut the lawn for me and frolicked with Shan We. I'd a teddy bear dollie still in my box, kept for some new baby. I wrapped it up and put 4s 6d in an envelope with 'Loving wishes for Baby Michael, some socks', and when he came across Shan We made more fuss than ever of him, though he hadn't seen Gilbert since early summer. My heart ached so for the lad, living with his wife's parents, who was a spoilt fanciful child and girl always. I felt I did so hope they could 'grow up together' after their bad start …

The hurt and anger is passing from the latest trashy sensational bit of journalese Cliff sent. The most annoying aspect of these interviews, with their different and wholly inaccurate blurb of Cliff's background – but accompanied by such good photos of surprisingly good work – is that I wouldn't dream of letting people read them, people who know we haven't exactly sprung from the dregs of a Lancashire mill town, or that Cliff fought single-handed against odds, and people who apparently threw every obstacle in his way, or at least never took notice of him. I make every possible allowance for the silly inaccuracies, but cannot but see that there's *some* fault in what Cliff told them. Another thing that wryly amuses me – I've laughed so often at odd little ways of mother's people who for some reason were always termed 'the proud Rawlinsons', laughed because so few had much to be proud about. I realise that proud streak runs deep and wide in my make-up, difficult to explain in myself as in some of the others. It's the kind of way that doesn't like silly lies, that 'holds their heads up' not for achievement or possessions as much as conduct. To read articles supposed to be dictated by Cliff making my quiet dignified father – or *his* genial well-spoken Londoner father – sound as if they were something akin to tramps makes me wild for their memory. For Cliff to make out he had a home where presumably he was ignored and thwarted makes me bewildered – or else long to smack his head! I had to cut off the pictures and burn the silly articles that would have only hurt and upset my husband.

Tuesday, 2 January 1951. An unexpected ring on the phone sent us both hurrying into the hall, both with the same thought – that Arthur was ringing to tell us about Edith.* I didn't feel too pleased when it was Mrs Howson's sister from Windermere. She went to a funeral and couldn't get back, and calmly asked me to 'go and tell Evelyn'. Mrs Howson *was* cross. Steve has had two days in bed, and now her mother has flu, and she has an appointment at the hairdresser's in the morning, and Mary promised to catch as early a bus after the funeral that she could. I had to climb over frozen snow that lay in banks, one side off the pavements, the other thrown up by the snow plough. The road was like black ice. Any sand and grit has been kept for main roads and streets. No one was walking. It would have been impossible to go far, and when a taxi came slowly down, fearing a skid I climbed back over the frozen snow. The roads out of town must be dreadful. I settled again to my merry job [*of sewing*] – and there was another ring. Sure it must be Arthur *this* time, I hurried to the phone, but an unfamiliar voice spoke, wishing me a Happy New Year and hoping I'd not been disturbed. One of my pet hates is not to know to whom I'm speaking on the phone. I asked, 'Who is

---

*Edith Last was about to give birth to her second child. Christopher was born the next day.

speaking, please?' The voice said, 'Well, that's the trouble. If I say I'm Margie Robinson and live in Furness Park Road you may not be any wiser, but I'm hoping you'll do me a little favour. I'm speaking from Kendal, have rung several people I know and they are out or something, and I'd like my mother to know I've decided to stay till morning. There's a dance here.' She giggled, 'My auntie says I've an awful nerve, but I said "Oh, WVS and all that, you know"'. I said curtly, 'I'm inclined to agree with your aunt, Miss Robinson. I've already been out to take a message for a friend, and that was only across the road, and I found walking dangerous. I couldn't possibly go to the top of Furness Park Road. It's a ten minutes walk at the best of times. I don't know how long it would take tonight.' She said, 'Well, do you know anyone else on the phone who would be likely to go for me?' I could only suggest she contacted the police station, and the policeman on the beat would probably call. I'd heard cases where they had done in case of need. I wondered how many she had rung up! I felt it was asking too much of even a WVS – equivalent to MUG so often – to ask them to risk a broken limb because she had decided to go to a dance!

Wednesday, 3 January. Mrs Salisbury came. She looked washed out and said she had been ill at the weekend. Poor thing. She is so worried about her husband – he is only a labourer at the Yard – and says he hasn't done a decent full day's work in the last six weeks, and every week fears he will be paid off. There's a big pay-off due, and finishers like carpenters, joiners, painters, etc. won't be needed now there's no more liners to build. I baked bread and some queen cakes, made leek soup, heated tinned peas, and cooked potatoes, and we had the rest of the cold meat. My husband was in one of his worst moods – *nothing* was right. I felt thankful when he said he would go out a while, though it was only to draw his sick pay at the post office.

Friday, 5 January. Mrs Atkinson came in to tell me something that shocked and saddened me. A brilliant boy of 18 at the Grammar School, intended for a university soon, has, with a boy of 16, been committing weekly burglaries. It was in the *Mail* tonight. Margaret's husband coached him for an exam – he had been off with a football accident – and he described young [Dennis] Veal as 'impossible – a rank exhibitionist who has been thoroughly spoiled and pampered all his life'. He verged often on the eccentric. Once he rose from his bed in the depth of winter, climbed down a spout, walked 1½ miles in pouring rain, climbed a spout and shed to enter his friend's house – to leave a note pinned to the sleeping boy's pyjamas, and carry off his hair brush as proof of his visit. Sixteen or not, if Cliff had done such a thing – Arthur would have been too mature minded at *eight* for such an escapade! – I'd have taken a stick to him! What puzzles me is where, in a small detached modern house, he could have hidden jewellery, bottles of wine and spirits, and hundreds of pounds. His mother cannot have any discernment. And how *could* a boy of 18 be out all hours of the night with no reasonable excuse?

There were, the Chief Constable said, 'a number of other cases against them in which several hundred pounds worth of property was involved. He objected to bail, saying that the house-breaking offences would probably be continued if the youths were not remanded in custody' (*North-Western Evening Mail*, 5 January 1951, p. 7).

Monday, 8 January. I didn't feel keen on the WVS Club meeting, knowing it would be a somewhat noisy 'romp', as it was styled

'Song and Dance' and a dancing teacher was coming to 'get eve-rybody dancing'. I never could find attraction in 'hen parties', dancing and making merry. In the war when I had to arrange social afternoons for Hospital Supply, I steered clear of dancing and found cabaret shows better. Quite a number of the younger members had a good time, though, and we who preferred to watch and talk enjoyed ourselves quietly, and it's always a pleasure to meet old friends and talk. Mrs Diss is still in bed. She had a New Year party to see the New Year in and celebrate her daughter Julia's engage-ment – and shared the flu she already had with a number of others. Four of them are in bed who were staying in the house, and another five are ill who were at the party. Mrs Howson and I did a bit of shopping, and walked slowly home. The worst of me once getting out is the 'What the heck' feeling I get. My husband was getting fidgety and worried but I didn't feel as repentant as he thought I should be. He had tea ready. I'd said we would just have cheese and celery, honey and bread and butter and cake and biscuits.

Mrs Howson came across to talk over the afternoon. Her mother is downstairs again, but far from well, and at 75 flu can be a real shake up. We talked of young Veal, an 18-year-old burglar. It's amazing how that young fool has broken into so many houses, and sad he has led off a 16-year-old boy. Veal's parents intended him to be a doctor. He was a brilliant scholar till lately, when wild unhealthy excitement seemed to have seized him, to set him off on his mad escapades. There was an upset at school 18 months or so ago when he stole a lot of expensive chemicals and pleaded he 'wanted to experiment', and the Head didn't let him cut short his school career. It made him into a kind of Robin Hood hero in the eyes of a lot of boys. I wonder if that unwholesome hero worship egged him on to later escapades. Mrs Howson says even Leo [*her well-behaved teenage nephew*] regards him as his hero!

Thursday, 11 January. I got an SOS from the WVS office to go and help at the clinic with the blood donors. I'd not bothered this year when I could see the list made up, but flu has laid so many people up. Mrs Newall asked if I'd go this afternoon ... I went off feeling glad of my unexpected afternoon out, even if it did mean work. I like meeting people, and today the doctor in charge, together with, I think, six nurses altogether, and two such amusing drivers, *were* so interesting. The doctor came from Belfast and seemed eager to talk about home. The drivers could have joined Frisby Dyke in *ITMA*.* They were so 'Liverpool' as they talked through their nose, and to add interest there was a lovely Australian sailor whom they had met in a pub last night and who 'came along' and was delighted to tell of Sydney and the sunshine. Mrs Newall said, 'My God, it's like a "To start you talking" with you around, Lasty', but we enjoyed our afternoon in spite of the little 'rushes' and two men fainting and one being so bad to bring round. They seem a lot more careful about taking a pint of blood nowadays. Three who had had flu recently, two 'high blood pressures', and one man who had just recovered from jaundice were told 'not this time'.

Nella's response to Mass-Observation's Directive† for early 1951 revealed something of her feelings about world affairs at that time. She was especially concerned about 'the supreme power the Americans grant to [Douglas] MacArthur. He seems to do exactly what he likes, and should never have

---

*Frisby Dyke was a slow-witted Northern character, played by Deryck Guyler, in the famous radio comedy programme *It's That Man Again*, starring Tommy Handley (it was cancelled after his death in 1949). See also below, 11 March 1952.

gone over the 38th Parallel and brought the Chinese into the war.'* There was talk in some circles of resolving the Korean crisis – even the danger of Communist attack elsewhere – by means of atomic weapons, and this possibility horrified Nella. 'I firmly believe that any atomic or H-bomb knowledge should be kept very much to some kind of [international] "control". It's a dreadful knowledge and should never be in any way regarded as part of warfare, or come to be considered lightly in any way.' Occasionally she reported other people's fears of this extraordinary new technology. 'I met two couples who had read, as I had, about the "atomic" snow that has fallen in America, and which "might" reach England this weekend. I felt a bit overwhelmed by the way each couple greeted me – a kind of "Here's Mrs Last; *she* has been to Civil Defence lectures; *she* will know whether it will be dangerous".' Nella's reply was that nobody could know (3 February 1951).

For the next two and a half months Nella's diary discloses less variety and incident than previously. Consequently, the following selections for early 1951 are less abundant than those for the early months of 1950.

Tuesday, 23 January. There was nothing on the wireless very entertaining till 8 o'clock, when there was an interesting discussion on the cost of living, though it was very inclusive and mainly reviewing. I fell into a train of thought, realising our own position was worsening. My husband still gives me £4 10s 0d a week, but everything with the exception of petrol and car insurance and licence has to come out of it, and more and more things from the chemist. I pay my rates weekly – 10s – and water and electric stove rent runs 17s 6d a quarter. It's impossible to clean

---

*The military situation in Korea was to stabilise in early 1951, partly through the sound direction of General Matthew Ridgway. Nella's disapproval of General MacArthur was shared by most Britons. President Truman was to fire him, although he was a darling of the American political right, in April 1951.

the upstairs windows from inside. I pay 1s 6d a fortnight. I've had Mrs Salisbury for half a day a week, up to now 5s, but realise I cannot have her much longer. I'll have to face up to leaving what polishing I cannot do, and do with a mop what I cannot do on my knees scrubbing. Four or five cwt of coal a month vary slightly in price from slightly under £1 to about 24s, and I put 5s every week in the meter and get a rebate of 8s or 9s. A three or four weekly trip to the hairdresser's costs 5s for shampoo and set, or 3s 6d if I wash it myself. I bake bread and any cakes or biscuits I can but any saving is offset by two pints of milk a day. Sanatogen, Phyllosan tablets,† rubbing cream or embrocation†, Allenburys Diet often work out over 5s a week over the weeks.* I try to buy a pound of soap, a tin of jam, syrup, meat or evaporated milk each week to prepare for Cliff being here soon, but even more for rising prices or in the dreadful event of war. All clothes, renewals, cleaning, shoe repairs, church or charity collections come out of my money, and oddments for the garden. I send only sheets, tablecloths and pillowslips to the laundry. I buy few sweets. We don't smoke. My one 'extravagance' beyond my dear cats' fish bits – with more potatoes boiled than ever before when they are boiled – is 1s a week for a football coupon. Started thinking it would interest my husband, and he would 'study' teams and do the pool form. I kept on when he lost interest.** I've tried not to

---

*As Nella noted some weeks later, 'rising chemist's bills' for all these medications and supplements were 'never budgeted for before' and were now very much straining her household economy (8 May).

**'I don't know why I *do* spend 1s on a postal order every week "in hopes"', she had written earlier this month regarding football pools. 'I think I'm the type who always has to work for what they get!' (10 January). A few days later she was thinking of booking tickets for 'the *Show Boat* by Barrow amateurs. I would so have liked to go, but it would have been 11s for us to go, and bus fares and

cut actual food bills, though we often get less meat, and fish is more expensive. I feel my next 'economy' will be Mrs Salisbury.

When my husband gets his very gloomy fits, he talks as if we are going to live to be 100, and our capital be exhausted. He even talks of selling the car and I *don't* want him to do that. I know that if he didn't have that he would speedily crack up. It means something more than 'just a car'. We don't need it, but it takes him out of himself however little we use it except in summer, and I know well he would never go out as much then and take walks on the sands or relax sitting by the sea. I would be very much against him parting with it.

Thursday, 1 February. I'd taken a beaker of hot milk to bed and settled to write up my M-O diary when I heard frantic banging on the bedroom wall from next door and jumped out of bed to rap back to let my adjacent neighbour know I heard, and would be in. Her husband has been in bed a month, first with a very severe cold, and then he seemed to go to pieces. He is nearly blind and worrying whether a cataract operation on his second eye will be a success. He had haemorrhage of the eye when he had the operation on the first eye and lost the sight altogether. I was speaking to Mrs Helm the other day and told her to knock if he was worse, whatever the hour. I was hurriedly dressing and there was a ring. My husband was still up and he answered the door and I heard Mrs Helm say, '*Do* come. Mr Helm has fallen out of bed and won't speak and I cannot lift him.' My husband said, 'I cannot come – it would upset me too much – but Mrs Last will be there as soon as she is dressed'.

---

programme another 1s 6d, and I just haven't got it to spare. I hoped he would be sufficiently interested to say he would pay' (2 February).

I followed her almost immediately and was struck by a pungent smell of burning – like feathers. Mrs Helm always has catarrh but either she did not smell it, or the opening of the bedroom door made a pillow which Mr Helm had clutched as he fell and which had rested against a portable radiator burst into flame. I snatched up a rug, put the burning pillow flat, placed the rug over and stamped on it, and then dragged the smelly charred mess on the landing. We couldn't lift Mr Helm – he's a big heavy man – so tucked blankets over him as he lay, and I ran downstairs to phone the doctor and Mrs Helm's daughter and her husband, and all three quickly came. Knowing Mrs Helm and how very upset she gets, I'd slipped a bottle of sal volatile in my pocket, and after she had some she felt better. I made up the fire in the dining room, and had the kettle boiling on the stove, and everyone, including Mr Helm, had a cup. After a discussion with Dr Miller, Mrs Helm at last consented to shut up the house for a while and go to her daughter. Elsie said she would stay the night, and I tucked her up on the settee and made up the fire to do till morning and came home. My husband always says, 'The slightest upset wakes or keeps me awake', but when I peeped in his room he was sleeping peacefully ...

I thought how lucky Mrs Helm was when they *could* go and stay with their daughter, and she could help look after her father. I began to wonder if they would come back to their house, if we would have new neighbours. They have always been such quiet reserved people. Beyond seeing them in the garden and exchanging a few words, the dog occasionally barking, or being asked to take in parcels or messages, we hardly heard them.

Monday, 19 February. I sighed to hear a ring and to see Mrs Howson come in with her knitting. She is very difficult to converse with.

She shies away from 'topics of the day' or conjectures about the future. She never reads a book, and buys two 3s monthly woman's magazines and 'never bothers to read anything but the fashion articles'. I *did* feel out of patience tonight. Most times I can feel secret amusement as she talks of 'wishing I could clear off and live in a town where no one knows me. I'd have my eyebrows plucked and wear scarlet nail polish without sending Mother and Mary into a pig's fit, and I'd *love* to get a pair of those new corsets that make you have a small waist, and I'd pad my coat basques† like in *Vogue*'. As her figure is round-shouldered with tummy thrust forward to counterbalance her shoulders, I felt the result would not be as Vogueish as she imagined ...

I was feeling a bit nowty as I thought of one of our favourite programmes, *Twenty Questions*, and even more were we looking forward to *David Copperfield*, when at 8.10 Leo rang the bell and told his aunt that some visitors had arrived and 'Gran would like you to make supper for them', so after all we listened as we planned. Of *all* authors, Dickens has something magic for me. I can remember my father bringing me the first few I had of his books – *David Copperfield*, *Martin Chuzzlewit*, *Nicholas Nickleby* and *Old Curiosity Shop*. Badly printed and on very poor paper, they were a special offer at a Boots shop. I would only be about nine, at most, but had been a good reader for a long time. Being lame, I'd not a lot of 'amusement'. The thrill and magic of other ways of life and living was as fresh as ever tonight, every artist so perfectly cast. We sat entranced as children. My husband had complained of 'not feeling well at all', but he seemed to forget everything as he listened.

Wednesday, 21 February. It's been wilder and colder than ever, and hail has rattled and beaten against the windows and the gale wind

howled over from the Irish Sea. There hasn't seemed to be any
warmth in the house, in spite of a fire. Mrs Salisbury said a lot of
people round where she lives have neither coal or coke. She has
got two men boarders – she really has to let rooms for a while. I
had difficulty in concealing my amazement when she said they
were paying her £2 5s 0d each. They are brothers and share the
same bed. One is a labourer, the other an engineer at the Yard,
and they have lately come from Scotland to work. They live in
with Mrs Salisbury's family. How they get into her tiny living
room I don't know. One is a vegetarian and doesn't even eat eggs.
A big bowl of porridge and bread and jam does him for breakfast.
He takes bread and jam and cake for his midday meal. The other
has brawn etc. in sandwiches and cake. Neither eat fruit. The vegetarian takes no nuts, bean dishes etc. Their weekend meals uses
up the 8s of meat. The rest of the week sausage, black pudding,
kippers or haddocks seem to be the evening meal. I've heard of
poor food in lodgings. I realised these two lads of 21 and 23 must
have had some poor places when they were so delighted at the
'good home' they had now. Both are very religious and joined a
Methodist church and attend several times a week.

Tuesday, 27 February. I felt I could have 'sat the fire out' as I pondered all the little issues that flooded my mind. Such undercurrents
there seem in life today, such upheavals. I reflected on the changed
path in life of many country people I'd known from childhood,
where it was an accepted fact that the girls went into one of the
several big houses near Greenodd, and the boys were gardeners,
coachmen etc. One old gardener, long since retired from 'gentle-
men's service', has a son, a veterinary surgeon, and two daughters
went in for domestic science, and one has a 'super' post in South
Africa and helped put her brother through his schooling.

I thought nearer home of Mrs Salisbury, my faithful kind little help who comes half a day a week. She belongs to that desperately poor type of family. The mother was left a widow with a delicate lot of children, and they were reared by grudging charity of relatives, themselves grudgingly poor. I doubt if I'd have had the courage to have Mrs Salisbury for domestic help if I'd not been so in need in the war when a very good girl I had had to go into the Yard. It's about 8 years ago. A friend passed on some answers to an advert, and Mrs Salisbury came. Small and ragged in appearance, quite frank in her admission she was 'only used to farm service' but with a family and no farms very near she couldn't get day work, or offices to scrub. Something about her bodily cleanliness and her anxious strained expression made me say, 'Well, if you will try to do my ways, you can come, and see if you can get used to domestic work'. She nodded vigorously and said, 'Ah, I *will*. I'd like to work for you.' Herself a half gypsy creature, her husband a big uncouth illiterate countryman, they had few standards of living, but a fierce honesty and pride. She has been a jewel, only leaving me to bear and part rear a baby, before [being] glad to come back. One boy is a bit unteachable, but she was determined he should have a trade and he is now serving his time as a joiner in the Yard. Her plans are now for the next boy of 14, and she hopes the only girl will fancy a 'nice trade like confectionery or hairdressing', while little Billy is only 7 as yet. Everything she can do to 'give them a good start off – not just be farm servants with nothing, like me and their father'. No thought of herself as she goes out working and has two men boarders. She too belongs to that 'uplift in aim and thought' that is the ferment in life today.

Saturday, 3 March. My husband announced he would like to go to

Bowness, 30 miles or so. I could only stare, but I never cross him in any effort he proposes. It was a heavenly late winter day, no buds of course on the trees, but every living branch was vibrant with life. I saw my first little clump of coltsfoot flowers. We had halted to admire the long vista into Windermere – like looking into a dream today, as a faint haze half obscured hills and fells, but left all in misty perspective. I bent to pick the vivid yellow daisy like flowers, and then changed my mind. They were growing on a little heap of gravel-soil by the roadside, where passers-by couldn't fail to see them. It seemed greedy to take them for my own tea table in my little crystal vase when they could flaunt and shout their yellow joy to motorists passing. Bowness shops were gems of 'luxury' goods – grocers' windows with every size of tins of ham, chicken, hors d'oeuvres of every kind, liqueur and wines, marrons glacé[†], etc., little gift shops stocking already for Xmas. I couldn't walk round as I'd have liked. My feet weren't so good. We went into a little café and had tea and biscuits. I generally take a thermos flask of tea but we left in a hurry and I forgot my little habit of last year.

We were home soon after 4.30, sunshine all the way on our faces from the westerning sun. My husband looked tired but not nagging tired. I made up the fire and made tea. Thousands of people had flocked into Barrow from all Cumberland to see Workington play Barrow [*at rugby football*]. I never remember seeing such a number of cars and coaches, and they thundered up the main road at the end of the street for some time after we came in – and there were five special trains as well. I said to my husband, 'There's something lacking in me – *and* Arthur and Cliff. I don't think we would get a scrap of pleasure standing or sitting all afternoon on a cold day to watch anything. We would have to be "in" a thing for that.' And I began to reflect just how true my passing remark was. Even to walk or read a book was preferable to just watching. I think just that lack in us would account for us never being wild about television. Me, I like to sew happily, with a discussion, play or music as a background, seeing something grow or take form under my fingers.

Tuesday, 6 March. I started the day badly. It was bitterly cold with sleet falling. I'd had my windows open and the room was like a vault, and I couldn't dress by the electric fire for there was a power cut. I heard the announcer's voice say Ivor Novello had died suddenly, I'd a sadness as I thought of so many men who could have been better spared. We need gaiety, and *some* world of make believe and 'happy ever after' today. Yet as when Tommy Handley died, I thought how good God was to them, and to let them go on the crest of the wave, never to let them feel their power to entertain fail them ... We listened later to Ivor Novello's *In Appreciation* programme. A queer thought that this time last night he was so well and gay crept into my mind.

Ivor Novello (b. 1893), composer, actor and playwright, had been an entertainment star for three decades. He died overnight. 'I never thought Ivor Novello's plays and music came up to Noel Coward's,' Nella wrote two days later, 'but he had one thing the latter always lacked – the ability to get on with others and make friends of all with whom he worked.'

Saturday, 10 March. We were at the Hospital before our appointment so my husband didn't get that lost and bothered feeling he so soon gets, and Dr Wadsworth was there in the consulting room, and I waited for what seemed such a long time, and other patients began to arrive. When he came out I saw he was very upset, and we had to sit in the car for 15 minutes while he stopped shaking and trembling. He said, 'Dr Wadsworth is very concerned with the way I've worsened in health, and still have those dreadful dreams'. I said, 'Could you remember one to tell him?' And he nodded and said, 'Yes. I told him of that very bad one I had last Saturday night, that I was walking in an ordinary street when there was a loud explosion and people were all flung about like sawdust stuffed dolls. I was thrown onto a narrow ledge and was clinging tightly to the edge when a woman was flung up and dropped on top of me, and her dreadfully mangled face was near mine and I couldn't move to get away from it.' I wondered if he *did* worry about atom bombs and another war, in spite of his lack of interest in the paper or news, and his refusal to discuss or listen to any.

Dr Wadsworth had apparently looked distressed and said 'That's *bad*', and when my husband spoke of his heart either racing or hardly beating at all after similar nightmares, Dr Wadsworth had said, 'It's such a pity, Mr Last, that you cannot mix with others and get into cheerful company, go to the cinema, a football match – or a pub'! My husband had answered, 'I never could. I never liked or wanted to go.' Dr Wadsworth had said, 'And your wife? I think she has a friendly way, and would like the company of others.' My husband said, 'I told him we had always been such good pals and you didn't have people in when you knew I didn't like it, and didn't want to go *anywhere* I didn't, except WVS meetings.' (!) I said, 'And what did Dr Wadsworth say to *that*?' And he answered, 'I don't think he said anything. He just screwed up his mouth as he does, and looked at me, and then wrote something on those pages of foolscap he seems to keep for each patient.'

There will be another appointment next weekend, to try to hypnotise him, and endeavour to find the real root of his terror dreams. He always amazes me by being able to drive – cautiously and well.

That afternoon, Nella reported, 'I drifted off to sleep, and was roused by the sound of whistling, and feet coming downstairs. I was astounded to see how he had thrown off his mood and by the suggestion we went to Ulverston and "took advantage of the sunshine"', which they did, and he returned home in brighter spirits.

Wednesday, 14 March. I felt really worried as I hobbled downstairs. I'd bandaged my foot before dressing or I couldn't have borne the weight on it. I felt a bit better when I'd got my low shoes on, the right one tightly laced, and I managed to bake, kneeling on a stool most of the time. I got brown and white bread made, some oat crispy, shortbread biscuits and a little cake for Easter, with some candied pineapple, cherries and sultanas in. Mrs Salisbury was very excited. Recently a bachelor brother of her husband's died and at the funeral it was said he had left his money to be divided between his sisters and only brother, and it's £117. Mrs Salisbury's great hope is that they could go in for a smallholding. She was always used to pigs and hens, ducks and geese, and Mr Salisbury misses an allotment he gave up when they moved to the house they are in. She said, 'Edward is set on being a farmer too. He is only 14 but knows a surprising lot about poultry, animal feeding and gardens. He reads a lot and will always give a hand to the farmer up the road.' I intended managing my spring cleaning, or rather each half day a week letting Mrs Salisbury do the cleaning – I'd manage with what bit of help my husband felt like doing. Now when my foot and ankle make my knee bad as I walk awkwardly, I felt I'd have her an odd half day. Suits her – she said she would stay on [*till 3 p.m.*] each Wednesday beginning Easter week ...

I've no sewing cut out, and I decided to begin embroidering dollies' faces. They only want doing once anyway, and if I have them done when I want to start making dollies, it will be a help. We listened to part of *Henry Hall's Guest Night* and then to the *Charlie Chester Show*, and then to the debate between [Tom] Driberg and Randolph Churchill, the least interesting pair so far, and I feel no pride in the latter. He 'blathers', as an old Scots neighbour used to say. Poor dear – it must be a great handicap to have so forceful and brilliant a father.

Saturday, 17 March. Yesterday when Mrs Atkinson was in, we discussed the case of the Southport man who had been stopped an hour's pay when he left his job painting the pier and went to the assistance of a man trapped in a sand bank. We only discussed it shortly – didn't give a lot of time to it – and I'd not realised my husband was listening or else, perhaps, I'd not have said even as much as I did. I have to guard *every* remark. I often feel like a child chewing gum, who pulls it out in a string, looks at it carefully, and then takes it back into its mouth. I have to count ten before I give an opinion, and be careful never to disagree with anything he says, but I wasn't prepared for the terrifying nightmare of drowning and sinking deep into quicksands, and the pitiful cries 'Oh save me – I cannot swim' that were so difficult to soothe. He rose this morning looking like death itself. I felt sick with despair, though glad we had to go and meet Dr Wadsworth this afternoon. He felt better after a shave, and decided he wanted a very light lunch and offered to go for fish. He could only get a tart piece of Aberdeen cod and a very small handful of scraps to boil for the cats. Fish is *very* scarce this weekend. I packed the parcel to send to Ireland and tidied round. My foot was painful. I rewound the crepe bandage after massaging it again, feeling

I walked on the bare bones of my right foot, and walking a bit awkwardly made my knee ache. I heated cream of chicken soup, poached the fish in milk, made custard and stewed apples, and we ate bread and butter to the fish. My husband wouldn't hear of any vegetables being cooked today.

I felt glad to see my husband wasn't in one of his worked up moods when we set off. I've insisted he took his mild sedative these last few days and it has helped his nerves a little. I was glad too that Dr Wadsworth was there when we got to the Hospital so there was no time to get edgy. After a while I heard a monotonous murmur and tiptoed nearer to the consulting room door and could hear Dr Wadsworth's voice repeating 'Sleep without dreaming' again and again, and breathed a sigh of deep relief as I knew at last he had succeeded in getting my husband 'off'. When the door opened and he came out, he looked really happy, and when Dr Wadsworth came out and said, 'Well, Mrs Last, I've at last succeeded in getting to your husband's subconscious mind and now may be able to help him'. I felt a ray of hope, though sighed when I saw my husband's worsened appearance in the strong harsh light from the uncurtained windows, so much more noticeable than in our own house. We went on the Coast Road as a little run out.

Wednesday, 4 April. A tiring but worthwhile day, and Mrs Salisbury bustled in, in one of her working moods. She *is* a treasure. I always feel so grateful for her. We had a good laugh this morning. The Channel pilot on the other side of the road suddenly decided he would paint the woodwork on the front of the house. He borrowed ladders and bought black and white paint, and got two fellow pilots to come and give a hand. They came in cars and brought a dog each, and old Tippy, the pilot's chow, has been touchy, and dogs snapping and being scolded and loud happy laughter has filled the quiet road. I've known one of the pilots from a schoolboy, and this morning when I answered the bell he stood grinning, his cap on the back of his head. He said, 'Hallo Mrs Last – like to save the lives of two poor sailor boys?' I said without a smile, '*Nice* sailors?' He answered and said, 'Nicest lads you could wish to meet'. I said, 'Ah, *that's* alright. I thought at first you meant Andrew and yourself.' He roared at what he thought was a real joke and then said in a wheedling tone, 'Lend us some tea. Em hasn't time to go to the shop. She is busy painting. She said you can have it back by tomorrow at the latest.' I filled a little cup with tea from my caddy, and then was asked if I could spare matches, so I let him have a box. A ship must have come in on the tide. After lunch we saw one of the pilots go off, and before tea he was back, returned the tea, and brought a string of small codlings 'for the lend'.

We all seemed busy this morning, and I only fried bacon and eggs and heated soup, and there was creamed rice I'd kept from Monday's lunch. Mrs Salisbury worked till 3.30, and had a cup of tea and plate of sweet biscuits and cakes. She chased the last chocolate crumb round the plate and sighed, 'I wish you could win that bloody pool – I could come more mornings a week, couldn't I?' I said, 'You *could*' and she nodded. I gave her half the fish and a bit of dripping to fry them. I steamed two for our tea – lately my husband has shunned greasy food as much as I do for my often fickle digestion. The cats got one between them. I felt I wished those lads would be round oftener and want to borrow something. I thought over some of the day's conversation. Mrs Salisbury loves to talk over things that puzzle or worry her. Today we talked of rising and ever rising prices and costs. She said, 'Them there fellows are all liars. If they say "Only 8½ d each ration book" it very likely means two bob, and we can't live on just rations. Another thing – bread going up means at least 1s 6d, and I've had to stop the kids' school meals. I can feed them cheaper at home – it would have been another 1s 3d with the 1d rise, and I've no more money coming in. I've these two lodgers but am paying for a bed and mattress and a vac at the Co-op.' I felt glad it *was* at the Co-op, and not at one of the big Jewish syndicates. She had read, too, that the jump in the cost of wool had nothing to do with the jump in the cost of raw material, that when that was taken into account, knitting wool, and of course bought socks, would be twice the price. She said, 'How are folks like us going to live and clothe ourselves?' I felt it was indeed a problem – for all of us. I know we hadn't foreseen present circumstances when we spoke of living on capital ...

I got 100 fire bricks unexpectedly today. Although Mrs Atkinson and I got them for a number of years, lately none have been delivered. The coalman who has the agency has let all he has go to his reg' coal customers. At 13s 4½d they are not cheap, but they burn a long time, and one put at the back of the fire and covered with wetted 'stacks' means a fire for hours. Again, I feel I must try and get a stock of fuel, not only for ourselves, but to help Arthur and Edith. They have been desperately short this winter, and when they come over will start from scratch. Even if I had to send a box of fire bricks by rail, I'd gladly do it if it meant warmth for those two little boys. Arthur shares my dear love of a fire. This winter when his health hasn't been good he would miss a fire more than ever before.

Thursday, 5 April. Often I've noticed when I reached a certain stage of exhaustion I've 'stepped into a picture' rather than had a dream. I felt last night as I used to do sometimes in the war years – utterly at the end of myself, not ill as much as quite spent. Being sick was the last straw.

I dreamed I was in the dining room. [*This was unusual; Nella rarely wrote about her dreams.*] My husband seemed to be away. I'd just got washed and changed and was wondering whether to go down town. I seemed to remember there was something going on in town and thought, 'I'll go and see what's to be seen. I never have any interesting things to write in my M-O. It would be just the thing.' I made a cardboard folder to hold a small pad of typing paper. I write on one side, turn it over and write on the other, and place each leaf at the bottom, ready for tying together. Its light brown folder is not suitable for carrying out to make notes, but I put it under my arm and went down town. The town was thronged by Austrian-German type of youth, in leather breeches, embroidered braces and alpine hats. I've never seen any in real life – only pictures – but in my dream I knew every little variation in dress, the meaning of every scout like badge on shirt arms, and I began to feel very perturbed as I noticed the gay rollicking high spirits when groups walked in the centre of the road in full view, and the different attitude when small groups met on the sidewalks and dropped their gaiety. In the queer 'wisdom' I had about the different types, I drew into a doorway and made a few brief notes, then walked slowly down the street and called in my greengrocer's and got bananas for Jessie and ourselves. The proprietor said, 'How's that little Clifford of yours getting on?' I said, 'Little – he's 32'. He said, '*No*, I meant the new baby. Wasn't it called Clifford?' I said, 'No, Christopher'. He said, 'Perhaps this will do for his birthday cake. I turned it out of the showcase the other day.' It was a rather awkward little ornament with figures on top, and he put it in a box for me and I went out with it and my two bags of bananas.

I met two acquaintances and walked towards the market and we saw a big powerful working man standing by the half opened door. He was asking every woman something. I saw to my horror he had my brown folder under his arm and at the same time heard what he was asking – 'Are you Mrs Nella Last, please?' I would have hurried away. I realised I must have been followed to the greengrocer's, and when I put down the folder to pick up the bags of bananas and the little box forgotten it and it had been picked up. One of the women I was with said before I could stop her, 'Someone is asking for you, Mrs Last'. I turned in panic, trying to remember exactly what I had written, and realising my name and address were on the top of my diary, felt I daren't go back and spend the night alone. I decided to go back to the house where we lived before, and the vestibule door was open and I went in, but a woman pushed herself in after me and closed the door to. I said, 'What do you want?' And she said, 'Your shoes for a start, and then I'll know you won't get far away'. There was a clatter of horses' hooves and the creak of some kind of vehicle and the half drunken singing of men, and some kind of wind instrument badly played. I opened the door and looked out, various of the women urging me forward. I saw a high old-fashioned 'waggonette' fitted with gaily dressed youths who urged me to 'come for a ride'. A girl I know paused and looked longingly and said, 'I'd like to come, Mrs Last'. I snatched at the offer and said, 'Jump up, Edna' as a little rickety set of steps were lowered over the back and hooked on. She ran forward and began to climb the steps, but fell with the 'bang' that only a hard push could have caused and struck her head with a sickening thud. I heard a voice mutter 'Fool – that's not the one' and I turned and fled, round corners, up quiet back streets. My shoeless feet making no sound let me hear unmistakable sounds that someone was keeping up with me at a distance.

My mind worked ice cold and clear. As I ran I puzzled where I could find sanctuary, realising I was getting near and nearer the hospital. I saw a policeman in the distance calling from a police box. I put on a last spurt and reached him, falling against him, and heard my voice say, 'Call an ambulance quickly and get me to the hospital – I'm hurt' and before I lost consciousness felt his strong arm grip me and him saying, 'Hold on, a few minutes and the ambulance will be here', and everything faded. All the 'knowledge' of details, of suspicion and fear, were blurred when I woke, and I arose with the shattered feeling I often did in the war …

Mrs Howson and I both had been interested today when a man from quite a good bakery-confectionery in town rang and asked if he could call twice a week. Never since before the war have we been able to get much at the door, and in a residential area without shops very near, we would have often been glad of a van calling. Both Mrs Howson and I bake, so we did not want any delivery, and Mrs Atkinson and Jessie go to a favourite confectioner's and wouldn't change. We wondered if it meant trade was not *quite* so good in town. We had a visit from what surely must be the 'gentleman ragman' today – smart car, well dressed man, small balance scale in hand, asking for old woollen socks, jumpers, etc. I felt I'd seen everything now. Such funny times to be living in. So topsy turvy!

Sunday, 8 April. I've nothing in the sewing line except my moss green two piece and I'll wait till the cleaning is over, and I've got the buttons and belt made. I've a tablecloth started to embroider, but I felt tired tonight and relaxed on the settee, to listen to *Palm Court*. If anyone had said, 'Remember George Dunnan, the Fleet Air Arm pilot friend of Cliff's', I'd have had to consider before recalling his appearance. Tom Jenkins' orchestra played the *Warsaw Concerto*. My eyes were closed. I felt if I opened them I'd see that merry impudent lad – and the happy saucy face of Cliff, so young and gay. *How* they maddened me by playing it on Cliff's portable gramophone. George bought the Concerto record, one of Brahms' Cradle Song, and 'Whispering Grass' by the Ink Spots – they were a present for Cliff to take overseas. They must have been half worn out in the few days George was here, *so long* ago. I felt all the sadness of utter futility and waste sweep over me, just as in the war. Our little Peter and Christopher seemed part of the sad montage that swept over me, one of those desolate if fleeting moods when faith burns low, when I felt glad my life was ending rather than beginning, when human hearts feel less powerful than autumn leaves swept along in a gale, just playthings of Fate rather than captains of their souls.

For several weeks this spring Barrow was abuzz with talk of the fortunes – mostly successes – of its rugby football team, which had reached the Challenge Cup final. Rugby League football, which was widely played in the north of England, was at the peak of its popularity in the early post-war years. Holding the Cup final at Wembley was intended in part to give this regional sport greater national exposure.

Thursday, 12 April. Mrs Howson called in, really to tell me Barrow was all set for Wembley. She is so little interested in [*the*] wireless she didn't realise I'd had it on the Light Programme. Four thousand went from Barrow by train, and coaches and cars swept down the main road at the end of our road till well after 2 o'clock this morning ... I was talking to a shopkeeper today and he was a bit gloomy about all the money taken out of Barrow already by the rugby semi-final and replay. In the paper it said 40,000

went to Odsal [*rugby ground in Bradford*], and 4,000 to Hudders-
field for the replay. They couldn't do it at less than £1 a head on
the average, and tonight the fare to Wembley was announced –
54s 6d – and in another column it announced 10,000 tickets for
Wembley stadium would be allotted to Barrow. With little or no
overtime being worked in the Yard at present, if people *do* flock
to Wembley it stands to reason someone or something will suffer
… My husband sat in censure on 'rugby fans with no sense of proportion'. I said, 'Well, it *is* their own money. It *is* they who catch
chills etc., but don't forget they *live*, if only in wild enthusiasm,
which, after all, is no sin.'

The next day at the greengrocer's 'they were talking of some bridal bou-
quets being cancelled as the bride and groom had decided against a "posh"
church wedding and were getting married at a Registry office, and then
with the best man and the chief bridesmaid were going off to Wembley,
confident that they would see Barrow win the Cup!'

Friday, 20 April. I went to the hairdresser's for 9 o'clock – and
there was no power, and none came on for two hours. There was
hot water in the geyser from last night so I got the shampoo
and set, but sat with a towel round my head, glad of a rather
smelly oil stove. I said to the girl who does my hair, 'Going off to
Wembley?', really to make conversation and not expecting her to
say she was. She is working after her marriage to help get a nice
home and always has some little 'buy' to tell me she has bought
since I last saw her. She said, 'Yes, if the Tradesman's Holiday is
altered to Saturday. My husband says "What's the good of scrat-
tling[†] and saving, Edna, when in two–three years we might all
be blown up by an atom bomb? And anyway when this job's finished at Sellafield [*nuclear weapons facility*], in about 18 months,

if we are still living, let's think of going off to Australia or New Zealand".' He was one of many engineers who have left the Yard since there's the 'go slow' with no overtime, etc. She went into the next cubicle to begin 'winding' a permanent wave. I could hear all that was said with no buzz of dryers, and I'd caught a glimpse of the customer as she passed where I sat over the oil stove. She spoke of being glad she had decided to have her perm before Whit – 'It's going to just work out nice for Wembley'. I gathered she and her husband were going on a 'Cooks tour' when everything was included but the ticket for Wembley, and they had those. She said, 'I *was* surprised when my husband said after he had been to Bradford, "What do you say if *we* go to Wembley? Could you scrape up enough to pay for yourself if I pay for myself?"' And she had said, 'I'll get that money if we live on porridge and potatoes till the 5th of May. What with all this talk of rising prices, shortages, armaments for another war, I'm going to begin "living for today". No use saving for an old age few of us will reach if they start chucking atom bombs about.' Without altogether agreeing, I felt with a sadness how much in my life I'd been persuaded to let drift by.

My husband came down for me and brought the library books. He has decided he will read a novel if I 'get a good one'. As it's to be large print, no murders, thrills or excitement – *and* not too sexy – added to the fact I was never a sloppy love story reader, it's a bit difficult at times to please him!

Monday, 23 April. Mrs Higham rang up to say she was bringing the car and would pick up Mrs Howson and I.* We went

*They were attending the St George's WVS dinner. When Mrs Howson brought Nella her ticket for this event, 'I thought of the 8s 6d and would rather have

just before 7 o'clock to the same hotel as last year – but a different manager. He couldn't help having no coal, but I felt it was shocking management not to have electric radiators for the people staying in the hotel – it felt so cheerless and cold. It was a very successful affair, with good speakers, the chief one a Scotswoman called Mrs Darling from London Headquarters. I've heard a few queer little dodges to get to Wembley, but one tonight did make us laugh as a WVS member complacently told how she and her husband had managed. They belong to the thriftless type of shipyard workers. When money is good they spend it freely, never having much saved, and tell you openly it takes at least 15s for postal orders for the football pools each week, etc. Lately with the no overtime ban, they have only just managed, so had to think of a plan if she intended going to Wembley. She finally decided to sell her bedroom suite – it couldn't have been up to much, she only got £20. She took £10 to Cooks for two all-in tickets – railway journey, meals, etc. – and then went to Jay's, a showy deferred payment store, chose a bedroom suite and paid £10 deposit, and it was delivered the same day. She pointed out in high glee that they were having a day out, and she had got what she had been wanting for some time, and now overtime was coming back she would soon pay the rest of the money!

Wednesday, 25 April. Spring *is* coming, even if the wind feels iced as it blows over the snow-clad hills. I got shortbread biscuits, almond cheese cake and mince pies, and worked with Mrs Salisbury. I'd got the living room vac-ed and dusted, and Mrs

---

spent it on a bus trip to Ambleside. She said gloomily, "I'm not looking forward to it – are you?" I said, "not particularly. I dread taking off a woollen dress and putting on a thin silk one to sit in that big draughty room"' (13 April 1951).

Salisbury had polished the surrounding lino, and I'd closed the door, feeling one job was done, and my husband decided he would clean some smoky corners with a big soft rubber. Then it showed up the rest of the frieze and he began to tackle one side of the room. Bits of rubber and the 'dust' off the paper was everywhere. He said, 'Now don't worry. I'll vac and dust' – and had the vac when Mrs Salisbury wanted it, and she *wasn't* pleased. We work to a strict routine and through it get a really good morning's work. Mrs Salisbury was full of all the 'bargains' being offered in the Yard – 8 pairs of blankets, a washing machine, several rings, a gold wrist watch, and so many pieces of furniture she had lost count. Two Electrolux vax [*vacuum cleaners*] not yet paid for, a half finished caravan trailer and a small fishing boat on the Channel. It seems *nothing* is going to keep some people from Wembley! She said, 'One pawnshop has stopped taking jewellery except gold watches.'

The following week Mrs Salisbury told Nella that 'her sister, who is more often than not on Public Assistance when her husband is off work for long stretches with bad abscesses in his knee, is off to Wembley – "and her without a nightdress or change of underwear to her name"'! She has borrowed from a money lender, as have *many* more … Mrs Salisbury said shrewdly, "A lot don't really care about rugby. They don't want to see other people going – and them staying at home"' (2 May 1951). In the Challenge Cup final at Wembley on 5 May Barrow lost to Wigan in (it was generally agreed) a lacklustre match. The reported attendance was 94,262. Barrow did win the Cup in 1955.

Thursday, 26 April. Mrs Howson came to borrow a pinch of Sylko and stayed a while talking. She 'never reads the paper', 'doesn't like listening to the news – always something depressing to upset folks, much better not to listen'. Tonight she really surprised both of us by beginning to discuss two items in the papers, one of Russia having submarines equipped with atom bombs, the other a speech by the Head of Civil Defence in America to say Russia had planes and atom bombs ready and could bomb American cities, and the papers had better begin teaching people how to survive in an atomic raid – both secrets stolen from America. The poor dear was so morbid as she sat wondering if life was worth living – if we *could* go on! I pointed out there was just nowhere else to go, and after all it wasn't life itself that mattered but the courage we brought to the living of things, but she seemed really downcast. I couldn't but think of our two little boys when she had gone, wondering what lies round the corner for them, and what life will be like when they are grown up. I'd a sadness as I thought it seemed the way of it that I couldn't see them often, or my own two, and I was always so fond of a 'family'.

Tuesday, 1 May. I'd such a feeling of blissful content at Arthur's letter, in which he said someone was going over for three days for special Inspections, which will determine his promotion to Senior Inspector within two years. He is my own son, but even if he were not I'd say, 'Well done', knowing the honest work he has always done. He was not a natural 'swot'. Study didn't always come easy when he first started out. I used to grieve I couldn't help them more, send them to college etc. Things work out. They are both nice men, with an old-fashioned reaction to duty, their own ideals and rules of conduct. I felt a warm content to think that Arthur's steady 'keeping on' would be recognised, and soon he will get a transfer this side of the water, and soon I'll be able perhaps to see more of them.

Tuesday, 8 May. A money row is brewing. I only hope Arthur gets here to give a bit of moral support when the balloon goes up! Although it's nearly two years since he started to be ill and 18 months since he retired, we have never actually drawn on capital, that is to say, sold savings certificates or shares in the Building Society. I had money in the post office and there was money coming in from paid bills. Now we have a little block of savings certificates matured, and I've still the money in the post office. He hides my book 'for fear you draw money and give it away'. I was very curt, not to say rude, the other day as I begged him not to compare me with his mother who gave to anyone flattering her the right way. You never could reason or argue at all with him. Lately, if he has been crossed at all, he has bad nervy attacks, verging on hysterics. I feel *so tired*. My patience seems to have dwindled so much lately, as I often wonder how ill he really is, and how much is due to his determination to have his own futile way. The way he gasps pitifully that 'I won't be here much longer and then you *can* go flying off to wherever you want' nowadays often makes me feel physically sick instead of, as he confidently expects, 'brings you to your senses' …

After a nap I felt a lot better and would have gone shopping but it rained heavily. There's always such a fuss if the car gets wet I decided not to venture to ask for it to be taken out. I sewed on my woollen dress – it's about finished – and I'll have it cleaned and put it away. I made potted meat sandwiches, and there was bread and butter and honey, and shortbread biscuits. I felt happy about Arthur's letter. He seems to think this special viva lasting three days is a pointer he may get his Senior before he thinks. Whatever he gets or wherever he rises, he has earned it by conscientious steady work, even when ill, even if he is my own dear lad. I would say the same if he was a stranger. He has what is so lacking today – a strong sense of duty, and his own ideals and standards.

Thursday, 10 May. I felt so worried this morning. My husband says he has 'worse dreams than ever' and says he feels as if his heart will 'race itself out'. Sometimes he feels so dreadfully frightened. He looked ill, and I didn't know whether it was wise to coax him to go out, but he said suddenly he would like to go to Ulverston. I'd meant to bake bread, but with the announcement there might be cuts in electricity up to 1 o'clock, and going to Mrs Higham's meant I couldn't leave baking till afternoon, I said I'd buy a small brown loaf to do till tomorrow. The sun was bright and warm, but snow still caps the hills and puts an icy edge on the wind. It was so nice to wander round the market and the shops. I'd put a tight bandage on my foot and ankle, so got round better. Bedding plants of every description, plump fowls, noble salmon and oysters – in spite of no 'R' in the month! – as well as piles of 'best' fish like turbot and halibut, seemed to give a luxury air to the shops, and tinned ham in several size tins, from 10s 6d to £4 10s 0d, and tinned chicken made me realise what a lot more monied people there must be who shopped in Ulverston. On our way back I got my meat and beef and mutton for stewing and 2 oz of ham. I heated cream of tomato soup, made a salad to the two thin slices of ham and made cornflour sweet.

We went to vote [*in the local elections*] on our way to Mrs Higham's. It was so fine and sunny a day. They wondered in the polling booth if Mother had gone to Walney with the children on holiday. Things were so quiet. We saw Mother and Flo, who had been to vote, and my husband said he would take them with him to Walney to sit in the sun while I helped Mrs Higham cut out a dress and two sets of underwear for Gert [*Mrs Higham's sister-in-law*]. We had a really happy afternoon. Mrs Higham said she felt the strain of the last few weeks while looking after Gert, and when they go to Liverpool for Whit weekend she intends staying with her parents till the next weekend. She has been buying a winter coat piece, a length for a black suit, two woollen dress pieces, and enough material for a bedspread and to cover an eiderdown, and will be busy at night school and W.I. for some time.

We were home by 6 o'clock. My husband went into the garden and began to talk to the Helms over the fence. I saw his jacket had fallen off the hook – the one he had worn this morning – and as I picked it up heard the rattle of keys. I never know where he hides them. I gladly seized an opportunity I've sought for weeks, and like a flash had our Co-op and post office savings books out of the safe and hidden under the carpet and under the settee and the keys back. I'm sure being so worried and nattered over money lately has been the last push to make me so nervy, and it's no use trying to make him see reason just now. To attempt to argue would only mean a wild nervy outburst. He won't get hold of these books again. Every penny is my own savings, and we do have to live! My goodness, I never thought I'd have to turn sneak thief to get my own – *and* to keep the house going at that!* Lately I have felt things get beyond me. I am so glad that Arthur and Cliff will be soon here – they wouldn't actually 'interfere' – Arthur especially has that calm 'come *come* now' that often influences his father.

---

*'Thank goodness for a tiny income of my own', she had written the previous day.

CHAPTER SIX

SUMMER AND SONS RETURN

May–August 1951

Monday, 28 May. Just before 12 the post came – a postcard from Arthur in London saying he would be home on the 'whip', the last train into Barrow. He must be leaving London at 4 o'clock and have to change into the 'whip', which picks up coaches all the way from Liverpool and will be in about 12.30. He said to leave the key on the window sill … A parcel came from Edith and her mother, chocolates and two pound of sugar from the latter, and chocolates and sweets for Aunt Sarah. Edith sent five eggs in a tin and a *pound* of fresh Irish butter. I thought when I looked at the luxury – unless Edith keeps contact with her very good Belfast and district pals, she *is* going to feel the pinch over here! I'd a little rest, but had to rise when the coalman came – five weeks since I had any, and today only got four cwts at 5s, and poor looking stuff. Arthur loves new bread. I'd planned my baking so I could make a batch of white bread today, and kneaded it before going off to the hospital for my heat treatment.

Tuesday, 29 May. I decided as I'd left all ready for Arthur – a little fire with the kettle on the hob, and the table set – it would be best if I didn't go down. We would only have got talking and he would be tired and ready for his bed, so it was breakfast time before we met. He looked surprisingly well – 'happiness is a great beautifier' – and he *is* happy now he is on his way definitely from

Ireland, and knows it's only a matter of weeks. We sat talking.
My husband said he would slip out and get fish for lunch and
so he could get fish bits for the cats. I seemed to do little before
lunch – soup, small golden haddock poached in milk, bread and
butter, a cup of tea and queen cakes – as none of us felt we wanted
a heavy meal. We were delighted to hear Arthur was not going
back till Friday night, and my husband felt in a good way for
driving and said, 'We will go to Spark Bridge today and see them,
and take tea to Coniston Lake'.

We decided to go to the Lake first, and spent a happy peaceful
afternoon talking. Arthur and his father went for a little walk.
My foot was a bit bad, so I'd a read in the car and had tea ready
when they came back. We took the Primus and boiled water. I'd
packed the tea pot, milk etc., bread, butter, a salad, the rest of
the potted meat and some shortbread biscuits and crispies. We
chattered happily. I heard all about the little boys. Christopher
was much better when Arthur left – he seems a darling little boy
– and Peter is getting to such an interesting age now he is nearly
three. We called at Aunt Sarah's. Joe has rallied amazingly. He
got into the garden to supervise a neighbour who is planting his
potatoes. Dear old Joe. All my life, in his shy way, I recall how
he helped anyone laid aside – it's nice to think people are kind
to him in return. Aunt Sarah is 'surprised people have been so
helpful'. We didn't stay long. Heavy thunder clouds gathered and
it began to rain heavily and turned cold enough to have the little
electric bowl fire on.

Arthur wrote letters. I did some mending – the years rolled
back. It was like old times when Arthur's head used to be bent
over study. He wonders – and hopes – if he will get to Head Office.
He would love to be in London. Odd how both the boys should
so love London. My father's people were seafaring people from

Woolwich. My great grandfather was captain of a tea clipper. My own father, though born there, came north when he was a baby. Yet his love and knowledge of London was amazing. He used to go on business often, and it was his delight to wander round. It seems as if my two have that 'inheritance'.

Wednesday, 30 May. We went on to Walney and sat by the sea. It was wild and chilly, but the air was sweet and I was so glad to sit and hear Arthur talk – we always have so much to discuss. We both love talking about things that have interested us. My husband looks brighter for Arthur's visit, and though he felt a little tired after cutting the lawn this morning, looked better than he has done for some time … We lingered happily talking, mostly about the children. Peter *is* an odd scrap. It brought back memories of Arthur – he too was an 'interesting' if difficult child. We talked of Cliff. The laburnum tree, 'Cliff's tree', is going to flower earlier this year – generally it's about the middle of June before it's at its best. Now Arthur has children of his own he seems to understand so much. Tonight I said, 'Make the most of your little boys. Love them and give them happy memories, and always the feeling they can turn to you in whatever difficulty or problem arises. You know time flies so very quickly and they may go far away as you two have done. I only pray they may be the delight and joy and purpose that you two have always been to me.' Arthur has such kindly brown eyes. He said, 'Amen to that, and may I give them even half you have given to us – they would be blessed at that'. I felt tears rise to my eyes and fall on the pants I was stitching. 'God gave us our memories that we might have roses in December.' Few women have such 'roses' as I have.

Tuesday, 5 June. A glorious summer day. Mrs Atkinson laughed at me this morning. She said, 'This weather seems to agree with you and put you in a better working humour than you have been for months'. I got the washing off the line that had been out all night and soon had more out and put two blankets on Mrs Atkinson's line, and then got ready to go down town when my husband did. He made an appointment for the X-ray unit for next Tuesday morning. We were a bit surprised to get a note for him to go to hospital next Saturday morning to see Dr Wadsworth. It's only a month since the last appointment – not that he ever seems much better for going. I paid my groceries and got a dozen eggs, *and* another pound of sultanas at the greengrocer's. I got small filleted finnan haddocks and some fish bits, tomatoes, and a very poor lettuce for 9d, and the yellowed cabbage and leeks made me decide to get new carrots, though at 1s a pound – the fact they are going a bit woody made them a dear buy.

We had tomato soup (purée), haddocks poached in milk, new potatoes and carrots, jelly and cornflour shape,[†] and decided to pack tea and go on the Coast Road. We took two flasks of tea, milk, cakes and biscuits, cheese, and tomato sandwiches. We were surprised to see so many there – mothers with babies and small children in prams, and groups of young fellows who left early, as if on nights. The sea had begun to go back and left the sands golden in the lovely sunshine. Children frolicked in sun or bathing suits. Happiness was everywhere. No discord of sharp voices. It was as if the sun mellowed and blessed. We came home just before 8 o'clock. Mrs Howson came in with some papers and sat chatting while I got all my ironing done. Her holiday *has* done her good – she has lost her cranky fault-finding way. I often think there really are no bad-tempered people, only sick, tired or out of tune ones. My husband watered his seedlings. Growing seems at a standstill. All is so dry and the ground hard. I'd a letter from Cliff from Cape Town. It added to the happy feeling the bright day gave me to hear he felt well and was so far on his journey home.

Wednesday, 6 June. Another lovely day. Mrs Salisbury worked happily – but *sang*! Her singing has to be heard to be believed. I felt my head begin to throb at the harsh discords – and took two aspirins. Mrs Howson brought two pair of shoes to see if they would fit either Mrs Salisbury or her girl. I felt a gasp as I saw perfectly good shoes – the 'Joyce' pair cost 25s to go back to the makers to be soled, and the good brown walking shoes were little worn. They both fitted Mrs Salisbury who said, 'I *am* glad of them. I hadn't a pair of shoes that turned the wet.' I'm always surprised at Mrs Howson's lack of thrift and her attitude of 'grandeur', and it's a bit comic when she knows so well I know her and her family so well, and know there *was* no 'grandeur'.

This sunny glare makes my head and eyes ache when I'm out without a hat, and none of my hats have brims shady enough. Any wide brimmed ones I'd seen have been at least £1. This morning I'd a brain wave and got out a parcel of coloured crepe paper I had. I'd only orange and black in any quantity, but thought, 'Anyway, it's only for wear in the car or on the seashore', and as I worked I thought it out and cut 1½ inch strips of both colours and put them with scissors, cotton and a head band of petersham[†] in a paper bag, and tea and put it in the car – salad and cheese, cutlery and cups, saucers and plates, bread, butter, cakes and biscuits and two flasks of tea. I made vegetable soup for two days, fried bacon and eggs and boiled new potatoes, and we finished with a cup of tea and biscuits. We went on to the Coast Road and I plaited the crepe paper and got the crown stitched before tea. I worked busily. I had no 'guide', but knew what I wanted the hat to look like. My husband laughed at the gay carnival colours, but it will soon fade, and anyway vivid colours suit me with being dark-eyed.

We had tea, and it grew chilly, so we set off for home at 7 o'clock, and most of the people who had gone down by bus were off before. I got my hat finished and it's really quite nice. The edge of the brim has two strands of black, and one strand is inset. Round the crown is another strand of black with a small twisted bow to finish off. It will serve its purpose – and it cost nothing at all. I may decide to do an all white one if we have a really good summer. It would cost only 2s or so.

Thursday, 7 June. We were surprised to have our 'Savona' fire grate delivered yesterday and a phone call from the firm to say the builder would fix it this afternoon. We went down town shopping, and then to Dalton for the bit of meat – a rough looking bit of Canterbury lamb, best end of the neck – and 2 oz ham. No beef was in when we called. The butcher offered to leave it Friday night, but I felt I wanted to see what I was getting so said the mutton alone would do this week. I heated cream of chicken soup (tinned) and made a salad to the ham, and we had bread and butter, small almond cakes and a cup of tea to finish. The builder had said he would be here by 2.30. I'd a rest when I went to change. My husband said he would take me up to Abbey House, where a party arranged by Mrs Higham of helpers of the trolley service were to be shown round. Then he would come back while the grate was fixed. Abbey House is a huge mansion type of house, built by Vickers Armstrongs to accommodate foreign royalties and the like who were having ships launched that had been built in Barrow Yard. The King and Queen when Duke and Duchess of York once stayed overnight. Later Sir Charles

Craven lived in part of it and when he died it was left empty, and 'useless', for too much would have needed to be spent on it to split into flats, and they would have been a gamble in a place like Barrow where everyone works and there is no 'wealthy' people.*

Then the town bought it for an old folks home – and everyone gasped, wondering 'How the rates will stand it'. Today we were left wondering even more. It took a year of direct labour by the Corporation's staff to paint and renovate it – the solid woodware and parquet floors were perfect and look as if they will be for a hundred years. It has 19 bathrooms, all of which, except two, were in originally. Waring and Gillow supplied the super carpets, settees, easy chairs, linen and bedding and curtains – all of the downstairs curtains are heavy crushed velvet lined with thick silk (rayon). Centrally heated – even today. The kitchens are equipped with every latest gadget for preparing vegetables, chopping and mixing food, everything on the scale of a luxury hotel. We were proudly shown the best quality woollen pants and vests supplied to the men – and union suits† – and the vests and panties or combinations, nightdresses and good woollen dresses of the women. Only one measure had been applied to each and everything supplied – the BEST POSSIBLE. I looked at the poor derelicts sitting round and shuddered as I thought of the many busy happy old people I'd known – a bit of cooking, washing, dusting, knitting or sewing making their days pass. There were none looked happy. I asked the Matron what they did all day and

---

*Abbey House was designed by Sir Edwin Lutyens and mostly built just before the First World War. It was sold to the local Corporation after the Second World War and officially opened as a home for the elderly on 1 March 1951, after renovations that allowed it to accommodate 5 married couples and 45 single men and women (*North-Western Evening Mail*, 1 March 1951, p. 6, and 15 September 1978, p. 4).

she said in a brittle 'bright' tone, 'Just sit and enjoy themselves, poor old dears'.

With always living in Barrow, I recognised quite a number of the men, some of whom had been well known hawkers, one a cellar man at a hotel who was reputed always to be 'half canned'. Two women I recognised as always been regarded as 'mental' and when they worked it could only be scrubbing corridors or the like. I tried to imagine what type of person could possibly be happy in such gorgeous sterile surroundings. I felt a wish that was a prayer – that come what may, if I couldn't like my father get 'one clear call' and drop dead, I could be like Aunt Sarah and be able to potter round in my own place, even if it was one room. The Matron, a brittle artificial type who got the position – with her husband – of running the place and were disliked when they were Master and Matron of the one time workhouse, spoke of 'giving these poor souls a little sunshine in the evening of their lives'. I made a mental 'gertcha'† and thought of several I knew who would be like fish out of water – that was not allowing for any normal person being merely unhappy with nothing to do but sit round in such splendour. The Matron said, 'A doctor said it will put 20 years on the poor old dears' lives'. I couldn't believe it! I thought, 'This Welfare State is not only creating a new aristocracy, but making a class of idle poor to replace their old scorn of the idle rich'. I couldn't but think all proportion has been lost as I listened to the Master saying, 'This beautiful Home is typical of many others in different parts of the country', and I wondered deeply where all the money can possibly come from when it takes more and more to buy less and less. There were five bedrooms for married couples – not yet occupied. A few joking remarks were passed about 'booking one', and Mrs Higham and I exchanged glances. Later I said, 'You know my belief that we get out of life what we put into it? I cannot recall ever either doing or leaving undone anything which would merit such a punishment' – and she understood perfectly what I meant!

That evening Mrs Howson was 'shocked at my account of such wanton luxury to benefit only a few "chosen" ones'.

Friday, 8 June. I had to leave my sewing when, first, an old business acquaintance of my husband's called, and then one of the WVS members who was there yesterday. Like myself, she had thought the old folks home totally unreasonable. As we discussed it, we were agreed wholly on several points. If it had housed sick, blind or chronically ill people, it would have been a splendid idea. There's nowhere in Barrow for very sick old people, except the stark Roose Hospital, which was the workhouse up to recent years. She was bitter at such a big staff – eight residents, four domestic day cleaners and two gardeners, besides the two included in the 'residents' to look after thirty-one 'spiv' types, as she called the poor derelicts. There will be 60 or so later, and more staff taken on. They pay 21s and get 5s pocket money, and the women get their sweets free and the men 1 oz of tobacco or cigarettes. Mrs Smith spoke of the many who wanted to go in, but who had difficulty passing the Committee of four. I stressed the 'grandeur' and so sterile aspect, saying, 'I couldn't imagine anyone *daring* to sew or knit or appear to do mending!'

Thursday, 14 June. My husband wasn't well. He does and says the *darnedest* things. It's a daft way of all the members of the Last family – all the cousins I've met have it too. It's a kind of 'speak before thinking' and to one of my rather Quaker upbringing, when you were taught to 'go and sit down quietly and think it over', it's maddening sometimes, more especially when I've so often to straighten things out and explain.

When Arthur was here he spoke of allowing us a small income when he gets this next rise of £200. I felt flabbergasted when I found out he had only £40 saved, for he has been getting £1,000 a year of late years. He always had a thriftless happy-go-lucky outlook, while Cliff, that wild Arab, could enjoy life to the utmost, yet as he used to say, 'Thank goodness I've got your way of managing, and your fierce pride in always standing on your own, with something tucked away'. Arthur wouldn't listen to my refusal and said, 'Look at it this way. If I have it, I'll spend it. If you have it, you won't need to spend all your capital, and it will benefit both Cliff and I some day.' I left it open. My husband thought it a good idea. When I knew Arthur had *nothing* I said, 'You must be prepared to buy a house, I'm afraid', and he said he could borrow most of it from some civil service building fund or other. I had doubts. I said, 'You would need *some* proportion of it, but we could advance it', and my husband was all smiling eager agreement, sweeping aside any of *my* offers, doubling – no I don't think actually there was any limit!

Now when Arthur wrote to ask if an overdraft at his bank could be guaranteed, my husband had such a nervy fit I could have spanked him. He 'had no money in the bank except £40 or so', etc. etc. I reminded him he had wildly offered to lend Arthur £500 or 'as much as you need when you buy your house'. I said, 'You would have to get it out of the Building Society or somewhere', but after I'd lost all patience I said, 'Don't think any more about it. I'll get £200 out of the post office and get it paid to Arthur'. It's simmered for a day or two. Arthur wrote to say he only needed an overdraft in any sudden emergency, and he would let me know. I never felt as glad of anything as that I'd been able to save in the war. I meant it for my Cliff if he came home needing help. But one thing, I'm *blessed* in them both. They have always had a strong family sense. Arthur always includes my Wanderer [*Cliff*] in thoughts of the future.

I was thankful when it was fine this afternoon. I heated a tin of tomato soup, fried bacon and eggs, and made a cornflour sweet. We were late in, and it was quickly made. We had a little rest and then my husband suggested we went to Ulverston. Suited me, although I'd only 2s 9d in my purse to do till Saturday, and knew I couldn't spend any money, however I felt tempted by bargains, but I did get a nice cabbage. My grocery order was a little more for I got a 2 lb tin of syrup and a tin of apricot jam. I'd extra milk – 3 pints – and bought 1½ dozen eggs, and the last straw was 5s 9d for some yeast tablets. Nowadays housekeeping money doesn't stand many extra demands. Our papers – just the *Express* and the local *Mail*, *Sunday Express* and *Radio Times* – mean 7½ d a week extra, and that's a small item in the general rise in everything.

Consumer prices in 1951 rose by 12.5 per cent, the highest rate of increase for any year in the early post-war period (Alec Cairncross, *The British Economy since 1945* [2nd edn, 1995], p. 61). The ream of paper that Nella bought to write on, which cost 4s 9d at the beginning of the war, now cost 10s 6d, she reported on 30 November 1951.

Wednesday, 27 June. Another day like this and I'd be starting a bit of wall climbing! Mrs Salisbury has worked for me for nine years, except for when Billy was coming and till he was nearly a year old. We have never had any trouble. I taught her how to clean things properly, how to have routine and method – and all my little 'fads' – and she never took offence at any hint or my firmness over my little ways. In fact she was only too eager to please. Lately I've seen sullenness, and she has often seemed 'short', but I put it down to her being overworked, for she has four children and two boarders as well as day places, and somehow so many people seem overstrained nowadays and the only thing one can do is not to take notice. My husband wasn't well when he rose, and when he has moods he gets cranky over nothing, argues wildly about things that don't concern him, or that he couldn't do if he was left to it. He upsets things and leaves them and tackles jobs he cannot finish, especially on Wednesday when it's worse than any other day for I try and get the bulk of real cleaning done then. He went out to the market for some leek plants after a wild search for a 'dibble'† he once made, and the last time it was used I planted the leeks. He accused me of burning it and got on his top note. I said, 'You know that ground isn't fit. You should have soaked it thoroughly. The rain we have had hasn't done any good.' Then I learned I didn't know a thing about gardening, etc. etc.

There was silence and then Mrs Salisbury sniffed loudly and said, 'Some folks think other people have no feelings'. I said, 'Mr Last's nerves are very bad, you know. We can only be patient.' She said, '*You* can please yourself. *I've* no need to put up with *anyone's* temper.' And she banged round as she added, 'I used to look forward to Wednesdays as a day out. Now I feel sometimes I don't care whether I come or not.' I felt weary. I said, 'Well Mrs Salisbury, it's entirely up to you. If you are tired of coming here, you must make different arrangements.' What would have happened I don't know, but Mrs Atkinson called over and said 'Frank Helm is dead – suddenly'. I felt shocked. They were such nice quiet neighbours, and on Monday he said, 'We are staying down at Park Drive while Cyril and Elsie have a fortnight's holiday' – Cyril's father lives with them and they are all friendly. Seems he was laughing and joking after tea, leaned back in his arm chair, lit his pipe, and died. Mrs Salisbury seemed to forget her grievances and when my husband came in upset after hearing it in the market, she was helpful – put the end of the settee down and the kettle on, and made some tea, all little grievances forgotten, and when she went out she gave her ordinary 'See you next week'.

Saturday, 30 June. The church was nearly full for Mr Helm's funeral. Freemasons, golfers, members of the Chamber of Trade and many grocers – Mr Helm had a grocer's and baker's business once – as well as fellow Magistrates, the Chief Constable and Councillors as well as relatives and people who had known and liked the genial man. Mrs Atkinson was thrilled at so many people 'come to pay their last respects'. I've always a queer shrinking from crowds at a funeral. It always seems a 'private' affair somehow. The fully choral service, hymns and music, seemed a needless torture to the relatives. The flowers were lovely in colour and variety. The curate who took the service had a rich deep voice, vaguely reminiscent of Freddie Grisewood – I thought suddenly of Freddie telling one of his own stories, about an old gardener and the Gates of Heaven. I hoped there was a garden for my genial pottering neighbour, and good sight instead of his poor, nearly blind eyes. I dislike funerals. We all have to go, but they seem so mournful, so inconsistent with the Christian belief that 'there is a happy land, far, far away'. I wonder if I'd not feel more at home at a Chinese funeral with bright colours, firecrackers and the feeling the departed really was in a 'better land' ...

The midday post brought a letter from M-O saying they were having to discontinue monthly Directives. I've read it, not quite sure whether it included diaries so put an enquiry in my envelope before posting. I'll miss it. It had woven into the pattern of my life. I've done Directives each month since soon after M-O started. Arthur was all for it, but with so much study for his Inspectorate he had to give up but asked me to keep on. [*Arthur had replied to four Directives between September and December 1943.*] I had a nap, and felt a bit better, but realise lately I'm getting desperately near the edge. Cliff's visit will be a tonic and give me time to repair the little 'tatters and torn spots'. The worst worry I have is the dullness I feel, so apathetic and tired, as if I have only bare energy for necessities, and any little extra effort is too much. It worries me too when my feet, particularly the right one, never show any improvement …

Mrs Atkinson said today, 'Have you put anything in writing about wanting to be cremated?' I said, 'No, but we told Arthur our wishes'. She said, 'That's not enough, it seems. When my brother-in-law died, though he had expressed his wishes for years, there was nothing in writing and it meant a lot of fuss and form filling – and expense.' My husband went to sit on the lawn again, and I'd seen where he had put the safe keys. I got out our two wills, steamed my envelope open and added, 'It is my express wish to be cremated, and if possible my ashes strewn on Coniston Lake', to me the most peaceful hallowed spot I know. I've often felt I'd like what remained of me to be part of that peace and beauty. I left the wills both on the table till my husband came in, and explained why I'd done it. I noticed he copied what I'd written, sealed up the envelope again, and put both in the safe. When he came back into the living room he said, 'And I don't want all the fuss of hymns and music and the crowds of today'. I thought with a little sadness, he had so shrank from life and all its contacts it wasn't likely there *would* be any.

Such a lovely summer evening. I cut off all seed pods and did a bit of weeding, conscious of the quiet garden next door, and the sound of voices, as Mr and Mrs Helm and we would have exchanged comments, and paused for a chat now and again.

Tuesday, 3 July. It was a dull heavy morning. I was surprised when the post brought a postcard from Mrs Salisbury saying she was coming this morning instead of tomorrow, as she and her mother planned a little outing to Morecambe for the day. After her attitude last week, anything could have happened, but she was quite as usual and I let it stay at that. I'd be very sorry to part with her. I baked wholemeal bread – Cliff loves it – and crispie and shortbread biscuits. My husband went out for fish and got some filleted finnan haddock. I made vegetable soup from small white beans, carrots and onions, sliced tomato and macaroni, with Bovril for stock – enough for two days – poached the fish in milk, boiled new potatoes and peas, and made a baked egg custard. I was glad to rest when my husband did, and we had an early tea and I made a salad ready for Cliff. I'd saved him some potted meat in the fridge and Jessie brought some lovely strawberries out of their garden, really 'show' ones.

I'd had a queer wonder how Cliff would look, and how he would greet us, and he strolled off the train casual as if he'd only been away for a weekend, kissed me and said, 'Well, how's my girl?', got into the car and we came home laughing and talking. He had brought a box of tinned stuff, and his tools to work, and lots of ideas for pieces of sculpture. We were amazed at the beautiful photos of pieces of carving and sculpture he had done. Soon the house looked as if the tide had just gone out, as he unpacked his bags and put things away. Quite a lot of repairs want doing at his clothes. He said, 'I'll get you to tackle them some day. I'll do something for you while you sew.' I said, 'That's alright, love, it's no trouble'. He shook his head and said, 'I've learned just

how *much* trouble things are since I've been away, and to appreci-
ate things done for me as I never did before I went away'. Doug
Hines dropped in on his way from rehearsal for the Amateurs
– they are giving *Glamorous Night* next February – and the years
rolled back as they laughed and gossiped as if Cliff had never
left. I've sent him the local paper every week and told him all the
scraps of news, so he was pretty up to date.

Nella had written about Doug Hines on 13 May 1951: 'We were surprised
to have an old friend of Cliff's call, Doug Hines. He used to be here often.
It was nice to sit and chat. He is an "old maid" type and lives alone, and his
modern semi-detached house is kept like a showplace. Of course he has
lunches out, but likes to entertain, and have his friends stay. His orderly
ways keep all dainty, but he must have to work hard as well.' Nella continued not to recognise or not to acknowledge openly (the former is more
likely) that Cliff was homosexual. Indeed, she still asserted that a marriage
to Margaret Atkinson would have been a good thing: Margaret, she wrote
on 23 December 1952, 'knows in her heart how I'd have loved Cliff and
her to "make a match"'. *Glamorous Night* (1935) was a musical play written
by Ivor Novello (Nella in fact gives the title as 'Glamorous Nights', which
we take to be an error, though this was the title of a musical from 1946–7
starring Peter Yorke).

My husband hasn't been well – it seemed to make him bright and
interested – but he quickly tired. I feel more and more worried
for him, and so very glad to have Cliff a while. I've felt so dreadfully alone sometimes lately, perhaps with not feeling well. Dr
Wayne asked me yesterday if I'd ever had a nervous breakdown.
I said, 'Yes, twice, when I'd had operations and had to keep on
with delicate children to care for, and once fifteen years ago'. He
said, 'What happened? What treatment did you have?' I said,

'Well, I had tonics and was lucky in that I could go and stay with a very peaceful old aunt in the country', and he said, 'Couldn't you have a few weeks in the country now?' I said, 'Not very well. You see my husband's health isn't good now.' But tonight I felt how things *would* be different for a while.*

Wednesday, 4 July. I got a lot of oddments of Cliff's washed and then we went down town. He got his ration book and identity card, went to the bank, and looked up a few old friends. He said, 'The Australian with whom I stayed in Whitehall, a block of flats in Regent Street [*perhaps she meant Westminster, not Whitehall*], offered to get me two or three ration books, saying it was impossible to manage on less than three, yet never eats butter, has food parcels from home every week, and has enough money to go out for all the meals he wants. I told him, "I'd like to see my mother's face if I'd handed her three ration books, and to see her remarks".' Seems the Australian said, 'Well, the offer is open till you have had a talk with her. I think you will find she will jump at the chance. I bet you a new hat you write for them.' Cliff said, 'Now's your chance for a new titfer[†]'. I said, 'No thank you. I don't need another hat. One from a man like that would only give me headaches.' ...

It was like old times to hear the phone ringing and Cliff's gay voice ring out as he joked and laughed. He went out with Jack Gorst [*a boyhood friend*], whom he looked up this morning, and we settled down by a little wood fire after I'd ironed. It turned very cold after the rain. We decided to listen to *Cavalcade* although generally my husband doesn't like to listen to anything in the

---

*'I thought', she wrote on 11 March 1951, 'of the bad nervous breakdown I had when having both of them in rages and sulks' around 1936 when Cliff had gone to work with his father in the joinery shop.

least 'stirring'. I never tire of *Cavalcade*. I've seen the picture twice, and would go again and enjoy it. In the children of the film I saw my own childhood – cambric pinafores, long black stockings, etc. I always feel it's my life on a film. I recall all the incidents, the songs, even the 'reactions' to things – all gone now.

Thursday, 5 July. I often feel such a glow of gratitude because I've such nice sons. Mrs Higham came. My husband went off to Walney to sit by the sea. Cliff sprawled on the lawn on a rug, and rather to his disgust the cats shared it cosily. He thinks they are both utterly spoiled, and prefers old Murphy's 'good old English face' to my dear Siamese, who has nearly human understanding and seems to feel a bit slighted! Old Murphy at 14 seems to have a queer youthful memory about Cliff. He has grown very stiff and old but amazed us by sitting up like a little dog and waving his paws, just like he did when he was younger – but only for Cliff! Mrs Higham and I spent a nice gossipy afternoon. I'd made feather light rolls with a little of the dough, and she and Cliff *did* enjoy them. I don't eat anything now. I don't feel too good in my tummy. There was apricot jam, bananas, cream cheese, chocolate crispies and shortbread biscuits. She said, 'I bet you never got nicer food in Australia?' Cliff said, 'I never met Dearie's equal in baking and serving food. She would have been surprised if she had known how memories of home-baked bread and cakes had travelled round the world with me.'

After tea I began to fix some of his sewing ready for machining, and then began to stitch on my white paper hat. He thinks I'm crazy not to have taken the bet and had a decent hat from his London friend, and says, 'You should "spoil the Egyptians"* you

---

*That is, to benefit from the wealth or possessions of another person.

know', but I've my own ways – and like them. He went out to meet Jack Gorst again. I felt glad he could pick up a few threads, and also thankful he seems content to drift a while before setting off. He looks tired, has lost eight pounds on the journey home, and a rest is what that Arab needs. It poured with rain – it will do a lot of good. There's no carrots to be had. Spring onions are 7d a quarter, lettuces are at a standstill, and I think of the potatoes not growing as they should be doing. We were glad of a wood fire. My husband brought some driftwood off the shore today and we burned part of it. Before Cliff went out we had an argument, but I won – he flatly refused to go visiting at first. He said, 'If I never see any of Daddy's folks again, it will be soon enough. They make a fuss of me now, but I've no pleasant memories.' I said, 'You won't get the car to drive if you don't watch out', and childish as the threat sounded, he knew I meant it. Odd how he has a respect for my top note. I was really astonished to hear my husband talking of letting him drive, though he was a much better driver than Arthur, who once smashed up a car we had. It could mean better outings, that is, if my husband doesn't suddenly change his mind.

Sunday, 8 July. We were surprised when Cliff came in about 6 o'clock. He didn't look tired at all and had enjoyed his hike. My husband decided he would like to go over Walney a while, and Cliff said he intended washing his hair. We didn't stay long. When my husband is in these nervy ways he cannot settle anywhere. He sits brooding and staring in front of him without speaking, as if something is worrying him. I could never speak as openly to Cliff as I could to Arthur, but in a roundabout way I've hinted he mustn't expect to run round in this damn car as he used to do in one of the several second-hand ones we had. He expressed surprise I'd not started driving again. We had a small Morris 8 once, 16 years ago, and I got and could drive and handle it. I said, 'If I never went in a car again, I'd not drive this one. Every scratch is noticed and mourned, and as you know Daddy was always a born back-seat driver and nagged and found fault constantly. My nerves aren't as good as they were then. I'd be slapping his ears.' I wish fervently often that my husband wasn't so heedless and would think before he opened his mouth and said such surface things he regretted as soon as said!

Monday, 9 July. I've felt a little sadness this week. I can see that Cliff has lost none of his aggressive impatience towards people and things, and being tired after his voyage tends to make him a bit touchy. He boasts he could 'never give up his freedom'. I tried to picture just what married life with him would be! Already he has grown impatient with me for what he calls my 'peace at any price' attitude, though today he has had a glimpse of how difficult it is at times. He asked, 'Just where has your tolerance and sweetness' – both words spoken a bit contemptuously – 'led you? You used to be such a fearless strong type, always gay and lively, and now I see little of that spirit.' I got cross as I reminded him how little he had seen of me these 12 years, that the war had taken a lot of people's flickering 'youth', and that these two years had been a bit hard going at times. One thing, though, for which I'm very thankful – he doesn't insist on the wireless till late, or if he sees it annoys his father. He went off to the Arts Club cinema show at the Technical School with a friend, and Mrs Howson and Leo were going. It's the Festival of Britain week. Too bad it's started off so wet and chilly.

Tuesday, 10 July. Cliff said an odd thing yesterday. He said,

'Makes you feel as if somewhere or another someone has ill wished Daddy, made a wax image, and either stuck pins in or left it where it will steadily melt'. It was not intended to be taken seriously, but it gave me food for thought as I imagined other times it would probably *have* been considered the poor man had been 'overlooked'. He hasn't felt well in his tummy either lately, and after asking for and enjoying wholemeal bread he has decided it could be that that was upsetting his digestion, so I had to bake ordinary white bread and two wholemeal raisin loaves, chiefly for Cliff. I baked a batch of shortbread biscuits too and heated a tin of beef sausage – Australian. My husband and I had steamed fish. I'd enough tomato soup, and cooked new potatoes and peas, and we finished with a cup of tea and crispie. What sausage Cliff left I put aside for tea to a salad.

I felt glad to relax when my husband rested, and then we went down town and I shopped, and then we went over Walney for a while to sit by the sea. Huge waves crashed on the shores and shingles, and the wind was high. It was amusing to see everyone collect good scraps of wood and tie them in a bundle to take home. Fire wood is so scarce and fuel of any kind so precious that no one bothers about 'what it looks like' as they would have done at one time. Men on bicycles came on their way from work and loaded up with good long planks and heavy wood, and pushed them back laden, as if a high wind and following tide was taken full advantage of.* I'd only a salad to make when we came back.

---

*The sea was sometimes the source of other valuable resources – no purchase required. On 16 June 1952, after going to Walney, Nella reported that high winds 'have brought seaweed in, so good for the compost, and everyone with a garden – and a car – likes to get it. We got two small sacks and put it in the boot of the car, and then had a long walk on the sands on the fringe of the incoming tide.'

Cliff had been on another part of the beach all afternoon and had
sunbathed in a sheltered spot. It looked a bit threatening for rain.
I felt secretly glad when Cliff saw the way my husband decided
he wouldn't risk the car getting wet. Cliff said cynically, 'Why?
Has it got a sugar top?' My husband looked so blank and then
said, 'No, but I don't want to have to wipe it down'. Cliff said, 'It
must spoil any pleasure when you have got such ideas of it being
so precious. You never bothered with any of the others, did you?'
'No' was the answer, 'but the cars today *have* to be taken great
care of'. I can plainly see, if Cliff had his way, he would be out
and about in it every day, but I can tell, too, he sees how it would
worry my husband, and he uses the bus.

Thursday, 12 July. I made a nice savoury on toast, beat an egg
into a small tin of macaroni cheese, and cooked it till thick and
put it on toast. My husband has got into a poor eating way lately,
refusing to have a cooked tea, etc. Cliff said shortly, 'You fuss too
much, Dearie. Put it on Daddy's plate. Don't ask him. You make
him think far too much of his symptoms with fussing so much'
– and my husband ate his tea with enjoyment. Cliff is strangely
sweet with his father, an attitude that makes me sigh. Cliff has
an impatience with sickness or pain, most of all if he feels illness
himself – dear knows he has conquered pain and illness in himself.
[*Cliff had sustained serious injuries in the war*.] He shares my inborn
feeling that to talk about sickness or pain or complain gives it
strength, and that it's best to ignore pain if possible, not pretend-
ing it's not there, but not letting it grow by thinking to much.

Friday, 13 July. I was looking in a shop window while waiting
for my husband when I saw Ruth, the dear sweet girl I had, for
a while, before war broke out as morning help. She has been

married ten years and has five children now, but has the sweet serene way she had at 17 when she first came to me. I was so pleased to see her. Her husband works away – Derby, and then Barnoldswich at the Rolls Royce factory – and they still haven't found a house. Ruth spends time with him, taking two of the children who don't go to school yet, and her auntie lives with her still and minds the other three ...

Cliff suggested a game of dominoes and I was glad my husband agreed to join us, but we were all a bit hazy about the proper way to play, and Mrs Howson came in and told us a few rules to be recalled, and we felt more muddled! To my great surprise my husband suggested a game of whist, and we played 12 hands. I *did* so enjoy it, especially when my husband played such a good 'clear' game and didn't seem to be at all upset or complain of his head aching. I'd like to think of him playing again – with no bad results.

Saturday, 14 July. Beyond his usual early morning symptoms, my husband didn't complain. I often think with a little sadness I'm not really good for him. Cliff ignores little pettish ways with a 'now now' and an air of 'You cannot do *that*, you know'. Little old habits are laughed at gently, and whims like 'I don't want toast with a poached egg' etc. just don't get by. When we are alone, I've either to give way to moods and whims or start an argument that gives him a nervy attack ...

We went to Coniston Lake – such a treat. I often look back with longing to the time when we used to go so often. Although there was a keen little breeze off the fells, the sun was warm enough to spread a rug and relax. Few cars passed. Peace flowed over the hills and quiet water. I was too tired to sew or read. I just relaxed thankfully – *really* relaxed, as Cliff talked to his father and I didn't have to feel I was obliged to worry about anything.

We lingered till the sun went down behind the hill. Cliff should have met Jack Myers, but he was loath to leave, and it was 8.30 by the time we reached home. It's been a very poor week for our Festival of Britain week. Cliff went off to Walney to see a show in the outdoor bathing pool, and the fireworks display. He said the latter was by far the best he had ever seen. Nothing seems to interest my husband sufficiently for him to go to anything in the evenings. There's a recital of operatic music tomorrow night. Cliff wanted us to go, but I knew it was no use. Leo and Mrs Howson are going. Cliff booked their seats when he got his own.

Thursday, 19 July. There's times when I feel so worried and down and also think of the queer frustration Arthur has. I feel there's a kind of cloud over us, but the feeling deepened this morning when a letter from Australia for Cliff from the tenant of his flat, saying he was leaving, made me wonder if Cliff was coming under the family jinx. Cliff let it to an artist friend, but he said he had misgivings soon after when people told him 'He won't stay a year. He is very changeable.' It meant a morning of letter writing – to the tenant of the flat, to Cliff's solicitor enclosing a copy of the letter as well as a copy of the answering one. Another to someone likely to hear of another tenant, one to the holder of the property who let the flat on lease – the loft, rather – from which Cliff has made a living as well as working place, at his own cost. Then an afterthought letter to two other friends in case the first one was too busy or away. My husband and I went into town to pick up some clothes from the cleaners for Cliff, and I took a hat I was tired of to be reblocked another style,* ready for autumn, and then we went to Dalton for meat...

---

*She had it steamed to a new shape, which is possible with a felt hat.

Mrs Howson came in soon after tea. I know she hoped for another game of whist – as I did – but Cliff was edgy and restless. He hadn't been out except to the post, and he went off for a 'tramp', though it looked like heavy rain, and he refused to be bothered with a mac – and came in very wet. I don't think it's really good to live alone. I feel sometimes that Cliff is fast developing into a very self-centred person, and more and more like my brother in many ways. He is *very* intolerant – he always was in small ways. While wishing he would get married, I fail utterly to visualise the woman who *would* suit him – or, I must confess, could stand his ups and downs of moods. He plans to stay in Barrow for another fortnight before going to London, but I can tell now his tiredness is passing. He is anxious to be off and away. This affair of the flat will take at least a fortnight to hear anything in the way of a reply to his letter – another source of worry.

Sunday, 22 July. Soon after tea, Margaret and Arthur Procter brought the baby [*their daughter Lynn, born in June*] in for us to see. Such a dear little mite, dark-haired and deep blue-eyed, its nose and long flexible fingers so like Arthur's. It nestled in my lap for the evening, sleeping and then waking to stare up at me. Margaret looks thin and pale, but was her gay lively self as she and Cliff joked and laughed over old times, and Arthur and Cliff had war memories of Palestine, Egypt and the desert, and we had a very pleasant evening, till they went to bath and feed the baby.

Cliff was to remain in Barrow for a few more days – and not all of them were free of tension, as far as his parents were concerned (or perhaps Cliff either).

Thursday, 26 July. Tonight Cliff was going over to Doug's so had the excuse to have to go out ... My husband looked very down. His head ached and he spoke so sadly about Cliff's impatience with so much. He shows he thinks we have grown old, narrow-minded, 'slow' – mainly because, I suspect, we cannot whip up any enthusiasm for 'modern' art. I must confess appreciation of most of it has been denied me.* My ideas of beauty and grace are old-fashioned, but it is the way of me, and no intolerant impatience would alter me or my ideas. Poor dear. I felt vexed as he spoke of children turning out so different to what one hoped. I said, 'Well dear, we no doubt affected *our* parents the same. You know my mother never liked me much.' He gazed into the wood fire without speaking and I went on, 'You know, Cliff was always a cat that walked alone. Few could understand or bear with him for long. Let's just love him and realise he *is* odd, and can only go his way. Let's look forward to when we can see our little boys, and be very thankful we haven't got to live with Cliff for always.' He nodded and then said, 'But I don't like him acting as if *you* were stupid and dull, and incapable of appreciation of all he thinks perfect'. I burst out laughing as I said, 'By the wee man,† if that lad could read my thoughts he'd get a jolt. He doesn't realise I've still got the insight of old and see that he shows a sad "inferiority" or he wouldn't want to bully anyone to make them different. He

---

*Cliff was to become a distinguished sculptor in Australia. Some of the highlights of his life's work are presented in Geoffrey Edwards, *Clifford Last Retrospective* (Melbourne: National Gallery of Victoria, 1989). In 1953 Nella judged one of Cliff's carvings (she saw a photo of it) to be '*very* odd sculpture, the kind that once, if a child had done the like, I'd have had a "Well – he's got *that* out of his system!"' (18 October 1953). Still, she accepted to an extent – even valued – both her sons' distinctive qualities. 'In rules of conduct and general behaviourism I see my teaching in my grown sons, but in wider ways they stand alone from me, with traits, strengths and achievements beyond and foreign to me' (5 January 1950).

doesn't realise that if a person of 61 hasn't come to the realisation of life and living and can see all their own follies and mistakes as well as their associates', they must be dull-witted. Cliff's opinion of me doesn't bother me one scrap. He has his own path in life. We can only wish him luck.' But I did sigh to myself as I thought how very like my self-centred bachelor brother he was – priding himself on being so tolerant yet so narrow in many of his ways and thoughts. Rain is beating against the windows and the wind is wild, giving a feeling that summer will soon be fleeting and autumn and dark days with us.

'Cliff grows more restless as he watches every post,' Nella wrote the following night, 'to hear when his Australian friend is back in London. He wants to borrow his flat for a fortnight while his friend is up in Edinburgh for the Festival.' When a phone call on 31 July left word that this London flat would be available from 12 August, Cliff made immediate plans to visit his brother's family in Belfast and 'cancelled a few engagements he had made for the coming week'. The next afternoon, Wednesday, 1 August, Cliff 'went over Walney and lazed in the sun. He *is* a sun worshipper', his mother thought, 'and has grown brown as an Indian and never feels any chill in the air. We too went over Walney for an hour, but returned to cook fish for tea, and then Cliff got packed ready, and went back to Walney till it was time for him to catch the mail train, which would enable him to catch a connection for Heysham for the Belfast boat. I'd a queer little feeling of parting. Somehow I've got so used to him at home. I'd forgotten all the years of war and the time spent in Australia, and a little chill seemed to come over me as I realised it *was* only a visit.'*

---

*'My husband had another very bad night', Nella wrote the following day. 'He has been remarkably free from very bad nightmares while Cliff has been at home' (2 August.) This was a temporary respite, and she later expressed doubts that Cliff had a benign impact on his father.

CHAPTER SEVEN

COMINGS, GOINGS AND PUBLIC AFFAIRS

September–December 1951

Friday, 7 September. I certainly couldn't complain today was dull. We both slept later than usual, and it was after 9 o'clock when we had finished breakfast. There was a letter from Paris from Cliff – from another address – and he said he would be there for a week, and forward any letter. As it was written Wednesday, and I wasn't sure how long a letter would take, I thought I'd better write by return, and enclose Cliff's letter as he asked in Arthur's letter. I decided to finish off Arthur's letter and post it today, to give him a chance to write this weekend. I dusted round and vac-ed the living room, cut fresh roses for two vases and sat down to write. My husband had been out for fish, and I prepared a simple meal of cream of chicken soup, poached cod in milk, and a raspberry blancmange to finish.

I'd been out into the garden to tell my husband lunch was almost ready – he was cutting back some brambles – and I heard a ring at the door as I came in. A sweet-faced, rather short girl stood on the step. She said, 'I'm Ruth' – I didn't catch the name clearly – 'from Australia. We were motoring down from Edinburgh and saw "Barrow-in-Furness" on a sign post and decided to come and see if Cliff was still at home.' I looked beyond her. A big light fawn car with luggage on the roof was by the gate, and a dark-haired young man at the wheel. I said, 'I'm sorry – Cliff is in

Paris – but *do* come in. You are just in time for lunch.' Although they demurred at the 'trouble', I knew they liked the idea. I said, 'Not a bit of trouble. I've only to open a tin of meat. I've lettuce and tomatoes in the fridge and can soon make a salad.' They chose corned mutton from the tins I had, and I quietly opened a tin of macédoine[†] of vegetables and added it to the icy crisp lettuce and tomatoes, and added a handful of sultanas, and I'd still some of Cliff's salad dressing. I opened a tin of strawberries to eat to the blancmange, and there was a plate of almond queen cakes and tea to finish. I *do* love to see a meal appreciated and enjoyed, and have never seen anyone enjoy a meal more.

Such nice people, both artists. She is older than she looks and has two daughters over in London, 19 and 18, and Peter, who drove her to Scotland with two other friends, is a friend of the elder girl – he looks 23 or so and he is a painter. As soon as lunch was over my husband proposed taking them to see the Shipyard where all the P & O liners are built, and as they went out of town we took them over Furness Abbey, and then called for meat. They were such nice friendly people, and I always feel I owe Australia and Australians a lot for their kindness to Cliff. I told them they would always be welcome if they liked to pay a visit – and to bring the girls, we could manage somehow. I could see they were the type who wouldn't mind sharing beds or sleeping on settees. I felt so sorry to part with them after so short a visit and I could tell my husband felt at home with them.

Saturday, 8 September. Just 15 years today since we came to this new house. I still feel the joy of the wide windows to open wide and let in sunshine and breezes. Whenever I go into my husband's room I think how our tastes have widened apart since he had his own room. If there is the least wind he closes every window

– casements and transom – and has the door shut, saying there's enough air coming in from the small grating ventilation in the wall, while as long as I've warm bed clothes, it doesn't matter if the curtains whip and billow in the wind as long as I feel I can 'breathe deeply'. He wasn't in a good mood this morning, and began to gently complain that visitors upset him, hoping no notice was taken of my 'gushing initiative for them to come again', etc. I felt edgy and tired – I don't sleep well lately – and stood up to him, not caring if I did upset him. I said, 'When I said I hoped they came again, it was *you* who mentioned Xmas. When I said I'd always plenty of tinned food so they needn't trouble about eating our rations, and that I'd plenty of fuel to make all comfortably warm, it was *you* who said, "And we can soon get plenty to drink".' So he went off on another tangent – that we were spending too much money. Again I reminded him that any small extra of mine I'd got out of my own tiny income or housekeeping, and that any cut would have to be made else-where – the car would have to go. I knew it was really more than we could afford, and I often thought so. It took the wind out of his sails completely. And when I went up to finish dressing – I'd breakfasted in my dressing gown, really because I felt it warmer than the thin dress I'd have put on – he started to vac the living room for me! ...

My husband said he would like to go to Coniston Lake to see if there were any blackberries and I suggested we go to Spark Bridge on our way home for I worry about Aunt Sarah and Joe. She writes such bright uncomplaining letters, but rarely tells me how they really are in health. (It's odd how you can see heredi-tary streaks. Cliff has exactly her reaction to personal illness – 'Don't talk about it; it's over and done with' etc. – when I used to be curious about his war injuries.) It was a glorious day for motoring. I thought wistfully of the days when we used to take long weekend trips round all our favourite places in the Lakes, both in autumn and spring, when hill and fell have their loveliest views. Everywhere tractors and lorries rolled along the roads, laden with stooks of grain – never a kern baby† left nowadays. The fields are shorn and arks of fowls or ducks wheeled on, or geese turned out, to glean every stray grain. We drew in for one large tractor had to pass on a narrow part of the road. An old man sat beside the driver, and suddenly I longed to talk to him, and to exchange reminiscences of Harvest Homes, kern babies, and dancing to a couple of fiddles. I wanted to know if he remembered all the fun, and to ask if he had ever been a Harvest King for a night and sat by the Harvest Queen and the kern baby dressed in gay ribbons. I wondered if my memories were 'general', or that old tradition had lingered longer in quiet corners of Lakeland, in old upland farms like Gran's. Yet I'd a faint memory that at all Harvest Homes where I'd been taken as a small child Irish and Scottish harvest labourers joined in with everything, as if they had the same customs.

By the look of the blackberries they will take a couple of weeks to be anything – if at all. They are wizened greenish red berries with a very rare black one where the sun has ripened them. The Lake was grey and still except for wind ripples. At last Donald Campbell has come when there was a real chance of the complete calm he needs for his trials.* I grieved to see that one little clearing by the Lake – where perhaps three cars could park – was littered with paper, tins and bottles as if untidy picnickers had swarmed in the hope of seeing the speedboat come out. I wondered what

---

*Donald Campbell strove to set world records in his jet-powered speedboat *Bluebird*. It sank a few weeks later.

kinds of minds people would have – or homes – when they left
such a place worse for their visit. We had our tea and read a while,
and then called at Spark Bridge on our way back. Such dirty tired
old people, but quite happy. They had got all their potatoes up
and carried from the little vegetable plot about 150 yards away
at the river's edge – Joe had dug them, Aunt Sarah carried them,
a half bucketful in each hand – the ground was so wet they feared
to leave them in the ground any longer ...

We were glad to light a wood fire when we got in – when the
sun went down it was so chilly. My husband was looking at next
week's *Radio Times* and gave a snort of disgust. He said, 'You're
right. Gilbert Harding *is* coming back on *Twenty Questions*.' I'm
not and never was an admirer of his particular style of 'arrogance'
in quietly – or otherwise – slapping people down. To me it was a
curious blend of arrogance that seemed a hangover of childhood
ideas. When I read his parents had been workhouse Master and
Matron I wondered if he had grown up with an ingrowing superiority complex.*

We had another by-election yesterday in a real Labour ward. I
knew this morning a Conservative had been elected, but felt very

---

*Gilbert Harding (1907–1960), a prominent radio and television personality,
was noted for his brusque and cantankerous behaviour. Early in 1952 he came
up in Nella's conversation with acquaintants. 'We talked of Gilbert Harding
and his ill bred tantrums. I said, "I'm puzzled why the BBC put up with him.
I've heard of many rudenesses. I think his boorishness is pathological rather than
temperamental." Someone said, "He was a beastly youth. I had occasion to meet
him. His parents were Master and Matron of a workhouse, and the accepted
idea was he had got his superiority complex from his youthful surroundings"' (9
January 1952). 'I wish I liked Gilbert Harding better', she added on 21 August
1952. 'If he isn't rude and discourteous he is swarmy and unctuous and gives me
the idea at times of being a bit fuddled.'

surprised to see 1,006 majority – it's not a very large ward. That makes four new Conservative candidates. With the main one and two by-elections, I wonder if it's a straw in the wind.

Wednesday, 12 September. When it was time to get up I felt like chewed string. I was so glad Mrs Salisbury was coming. She complained of feeling tired. She seems not to realise there *could* be such a thing as overwork, and this last morning's work she took had lengthened to a full day. I hinted pretty strongly this morning that if she took too much on there was the danger she wouldn't be able to please people for whom she had worked for years, and pointed out she had a lodger and one son working so couldn't say she was 'doing it for the children' for they were having to make more meals for themselves, and out of tins at that, and more bread instead of cooked vegetables. They are all going to see Morecambe Illuminations, at a cost of 6s a head, train and bus fare and 6d of chips each. She will pay for one child – 9s – and the other two not working are picking rosehips and selling them at the WVS office for 3d a pound.* I said 'You could spend that 9s on having your shoes soled' – she had said all the ones she had let in the wet – but she said, 'Oh, Mr Salisbury says he's bound to "get a coupon up" soon – it's about time he won *something* in the football pools', a remark which made me stare. It's the first heedless remark I've heard her make, for while hoping for luck, she has never banked on it.

Saturday, 15 September. After a wild night of gale and rain, there were piles of leaves and twigs to sweep up. We rose rather late, too, so with dusting and vac-ing the morning passed very quickly.

---

*Citrus fruit was still scarce, and rosehips were a good source of vitamin C.

... The sun shone very unexpectedly [*in the afternoon*]. I packed bread and butter, honey, tomatoes and cake and made two flasks of tea and we went over Walney to sit by the sea. The shore was littered with good wood – too big for putting in a car boot. People sought smallish pieces – we were amongst them – and were laughing and joking at themselves for 'beachcombing', but with fuel problems ahead, such additions were welcome. A few farm carts were further along, loading big awkward pieces. We ate tea and listened to the 6 o'clock news. I'd taken the *Express* with the lists of football teams as read by the announcer. I had seven draws and one away win, making 23 points on one 6d line, and six draws, one home win (1) and one away (2), making 21 points on the other lines. I checked as carefully as I could. I may have made a mistake and will see in the morning. Last week with 23 points each, six people divided £92, 120! My husband said, 'You take it very coolly'. I said, 'Well, there's quite a lot of draws this week. A lot are bound to have 24 never mind 23 points. I'll start getting excited *when* I see if I win much.' I don't suppose it will be much, but if my coupon *is* correct when rechecked, I'll win something, and won't have the worry of wondering it it's a lot. Cliff told me frankly he would be 'better without a lot of unearned money', but it would be a help to Arthur, and I could do so much for my husband's health if I could take him on a long carefree holiday. If it was my own money, I could insist on spending it. He wouldn't be able to nag about 'Our money won't last out if ...'

Earlier, in Cliff's presence, Nella had written of the 'help' that she and Will and their sons could get from winnings from the football pools. Cliff 'pursed up his lips, thought it over and said, "No, I don't think so. I'm sure any artist is better without security. I sometimes think it would be better if I had not even my [*Army*] pension."' Nella then admitted that this low-level gambling gave her more pleasure than she had previously allowed. 'I certainly get a lot of entertainment from the 1s, plus 2½d for a stamp, which I spend each week' (18 August 1951), and later still she wrote of doing the weekly pools as 'grand fun' (18 April 1953). As for these prospective winnings of mid-September, she discovered the next day that she had miscalculated and in fact stood to win around £2 10s 0d (16 September 1951).

Once, when Margaret Procter told Nella that her husband, Arthur, "understands football and studies hours over the different forms", I said gravely, "Oh, that's no use, Margaret. You have to have a *real* system – like me, for instance. I pick towns I've visited, places where I'd like to go, Barrow always because it's our own town, Southampton because I was so happy in the short time I lived there – Scunthorpe just for the hell of it. I think it has such a sinister ring." For some reason it struck us on our silly side and we laughed so much Mrs Atkinson came out' (21 April 1953).

Friday, 28 September. I rose feeling like a boiled owl. Aspirins always give me that effect, and my cold was so heavy, I felt I wheezed as I breathed. I felt I'd have liked to stay in bed longer, but after several cups of scalding hot tea and some bread and butter, I ate my cornflakes and milk as usual and didn't feel so bad. The morning mists rolled away and it got out a lovely September day. Suddenly my husband decided to go off, take lunch, and go as far as Bowness again. I didn't really feel thrilled for I ached all over, but I knew my husband wouldn't have settled. He would have nursed a little resentment all day, which would have shown itself in a 'hurt' manner. I made tea and put it in two thermos flasks, cut bread and butter and put it in the picnic box, and took sliced potted meat – really delicious, made from slim beef simmered tender with two tomatoes and run through the mincer. There were peeled tomatoes and tender stalks of celery, and cake and two pears to finish off.

It's going to be a real 'Woolworths almanack' of an autumn, one of those impossibly lovely, slightly garish ones. There's not many leaves falling, and already crab, wild cherry and elder trees flame pink and red on wooded hillsides, and on the fells the bracken gleams dull gold when a shaft of sunlight strikes it, and the grass gleams emerald green with the heavy rains. Streams run along roadsides; pools in low lying hollows of the roads are like 'splashes' needing fording, and down hillsides and slopes water cascades – Lake Windermere was higher than we remember. Bowness was itself serene and peaceful, everywhere gay dahlias, chrysanths and marigolds made up for the backward summer. A number of visitors were about, older people on the whole, though at least three young couples looked on their honeymoon as they passed our parked car, oblivious of everything but themselves.

Friday, 5 October. We went to Coniston. Never have I seen that quiet Lake more serene and lovely. Its glass-like surface was a phantasy of shadows of fell and hill, difficult to tell where shadow ended and substance began. Such a wonderful day for Donald Campbell – a country man answered us there had been several such days – a real worry for him and his staff when they are away fixing up yet another something or other. A lovely ageing golden retriever hovered round as we ate lunch, begging eagerly, but patiently. The country man saw me looking at his collar, but it had no name, it was just a leather strap. I said, 'I wonder who owns him. There's no house near, is there?' He shook his head sadly and said, 'I think some hard-hearted person brought him here and left him. Several men working on the road have taken him home in pity, but he hasn't stayed and has come back to this stretch of road.' I looked down at the noble-looking old dog with whitening muzzle. He looked up at me and gravely offered his paw to

shake, a detached look in his eye as if to thank me for bothering.
But he would be alright. I saw a policeman a little further on. He
had stopped for a chat at a cottage door. We stopped and I mentioned the dog – such a well bred and well trained dog – to be
'lost'. I asked if nothing could be done, and he told me of the road
men who had taken him, first to a nearby farm house, and then to
two other 'homes', but in the morning, when let out, it had gone
back to one stretch of road and wandered anxiously along it. He
said, 'It's fine weather and the bracken is dry for a bed. Two bus
conductors and several of the road men give it food – a few crusts
of bread more often than not – and there's lake water for drink-
ing. If he won't be taken to a fresh home, a nearby gamekeeper
will shoot him. Don't worry – he won't be left wretched and cold
as well as lost.' Our puzzle was – how could anyone so train a dog
in good dog manners yet be so unkind when he was growing old?
He didn't seem to have any of that wonderful homing instinct
often recorded.

'Loudspeakers boomed round the streets,' Nella wrote on 12 October,
'inviting people to a Conservative meeting in a nearby school room, the first
sign of an election except for the picture of the Conservative candidate and
his election address.' The nation had just embarked on its second general
election in less than two years, and political developments were sometimes
on her mind during the following fortnight, though probably rarely as much
as Will was.

Monday, 15 October. I was getting ready to go downstairs when
there was a ring. It was Mr Lawton, the father of our candidate.
He made a surprising jump in the Conservative vote and got into
the Council for a very strong Labour ward recently. He wanted my
husband to help take people to the polling booth, but I wouldn't

agree. I pointed out he was never well, and I wouldn't like any extra excitement. I could tell he thought excitement was hardly to be expected by taking people to vote, but I've seen enough of elections, particularly parliamentary ones, to know it wouldn't be wise after all. I have to live with him and dear only knows the difficulty sometimes when so little upsets him.

Tuesday, 16 October. We timed our shopping to include going to see a big oil tanker launched, and the lovely thing glided gracefully down the slips into the Channel, with her name *World Unity* catching a fitful gleam of sunshine. Six tugs – four from Fleetwood – nosed and pushed her gently round into the Dock, where she rode proudly, far out of the water under the big crane, ready for engines and fittings.*

Wednesday, 17 October. I put my coat on and took mats out to shake and leave on the line to air in the breeze, and Mrs Atkinson called over to tell me she had had a 'really good evening out last night' – a whist club she attends on Fridays. She had gone a few miles out of town onto the Coast Road in a motor coach, had a chicken dinner followed by a whist drive, and she had won first prize. She mentioned her brother-in-law had the same kind of bronchitis cough I had, and the doctor said it was a germ that seemed to be attacking people who were run down. My 'gossiping' only took a few minutes while I brushed the mats on the line. I was not prepared for my husband's attack when I went in. He always had a curious way of hoarding up 'slights' and 'snubs', but since he has been ill it's grown worse. His mind acts like a

---

*The launch of a large boat was seen in Barrow as a major event, and was attended by many of the men who had helped build her.

stopped up drain, slowly gathering odds and ends of tea leaves, and odd scraps of vegetables that putrefied slowly – anything and everything that would tend to block a drain. Then when it's unstopped, it's amazing what has gone to the accumulation!

I know he hates me to talk to anyone unless he is there, but his rage took the form of 'Fearing you will catch more cold – you never think of the bother you give people', etc. etc. I didn't feel too good humoured, and when I heard him talk as if he was the most neglected, abused and misunderstood creature imaginable, I let fly, especially when he raked up about me having been so lame and not able to go walking and he 'Always had to trail about by himself if we went over Walney', and I knew how he hated going for walks on the sands by himself. It takes me quite a while to really get on my top note, but by Gad when I do so, fur and feathers fly. I was the only one to quell that Arab of a Cliff and pull him together, and I was really nasty. I told him he was so spoilt and pampered and so full of self-pity he was his own worst enemy. I couldn't but recall how I'd had to crawl down last winter when I had flu, or I'd have soon been unable to do so. Weak half cold tea, half warmed soup and milk brought with an offended offhand manner, and knowing he was boiling up for one of his 'dos' wasn't any inducement to stay in bed. I couldn't but recall either, when shaky and ill, I got down to the fire, and he went off in one of his nervy fits and I told him if he persisted in having hysterics I'd throw cold water over him. He pulled himself quickly together *and* has never had an attack since.

Mrs Salisbury was upstairs. It was just as well I heard her coming down, or once started I knew I'd have said things I'd have regretted. Then he turned his attention to Mrs Salisbury and picked and found fault with her work till she began to look thunderous. I gave her an old shirt and some old socks as a little reward for taking things as well as she did, not liking either her pity or advice to 'Land him one. *I* would if *my* husband went on like that.' I could only hope with a sigh he had got it out of his system, and he ate a good lunch as usual, while I felt what I did ate nearly choked me.

Occasionally Nella was satisfied with something Will did. The previous week, on 9 October, 'I was delighted to find my husband had cleaned my wine-coloured court shoes – when I had them soled and heeled they had been handled with dirty hands, and I've never got them as nice.'

Saturday, 20 October. We had two lots of canvassers. My husband's pious attitude has always made me chuckle. For years he has said the same 'I'm a businessman and it's not policy to state my views'. As I pointed out he might just as well do so. As one who has done a lot of canvassing in years gone by, I'd have known enough to put the 'opposition's' mark against his name. I knew the two men who came for the Conservatives and asked, 'How do things look?' He rubbed his ear reflectively and said, 'I'm blest if I can tell you. We've had no startling results, either from meetings – rowdier than ever I've known – or house to house talks. Perhaps things will warm up after the weekend.'

Monday, 22 October. After my husband had his rest we went out a while and round the Coast Road to Ulverston. Across Morecambe Bay the Yorkshire hills could be seen covered well down with snow, though the Lake hills were only white-capped. In the bright cold sunshine, ploughing, potato lifting – and mangels too – hedging, and gravel spraying along a long stretch of road, and sheep were being brought down to fold, ready for lambing. Their feeding troughs had turnips and kale, but I noticed they preferred and could find grass to nibble … We were only out an hour. Some coal had been delivered just before we went − 3 cwt at 4s 7½d a cwt. I didn't think it looked up to much, but put a few pieces on the fire, and when we came in it had put the fire out! Before it had done so, the coal had been scorched white, just like chalk. What beats me is what they did with all this rubbish before the war. We exported more, and coal moved ships before oil was used, yet every coal cart had at least three grades of coal and at the colliery shops you were bewildered with choice and variety … Even with a good fire of coal and wood, there seemed no heat in the room. The coal man spoke of empty coal boxes everywhere. He said, 'That trip to Wembley is having to be paid for by many silly folks. No coal taken when they could have put it by, money even being paid off and vacs paid for that were sold straight away. You know I'm sure folks get dafter. It's no wonder children get to the problem stage when they have no lead from parents.'

Tuesday, 23 October. Heavy frost covered the lawn like a light fall of snow this morning. The herbaceous border looked odd with its bright bank of flowers. I'd an appointment with my hairdresser and we went down town early so I could go to the grocer's and the greengrocer's. The grocer's wife served me. She is rather a grumbler, and I've noticed the shelves keep a bit too well stocked − tinned ham in small tins, crayfish, chicken from 3s 6d to 24s, the latter 'guaranteed to contain a whole fowl'. This morning she was so gloomy as she complained, 'Things have never picked up since we had such bad trade when the town went mad to get to Wembley'. I thought, 'Well, I didn't go, but my money shrinks. I'd love to buy a lot of things I see but I dodge up something tasty, as even in the war we did, but with cheaper food on the whole.' Women complained of it being cold, but added, 'One thing, there will be no power cuts till after Thursday and women have voted'. It seems the general opinion that women will sway the votes. I suppose they won't want to irritate anyone! I see by the notice in the local *Mail* every district in Furness as well as Barrow are 'charted' for different days. Our bad day will be Tuesday, so I can plan a plain meal of soups to heat and perhaps fish to cook, or bacon. Even a four-hour cut ends at noon, so men from the Yard can have a quickly prepared meal.

Wednesday, 24 October. I finished Edith's letter, and put my bet in for Arthur about the election. He takes rather a gloomy view. 'Conservatives in by 25 or 30 majority'. [*This was Nella's prediction*.] He has the quite popular view 'It's a pity the Labour Government isn't returned – to clear up the mess they have got into', forgetting the old adage 'While the grass is growing the horse may starve', and not taking into account how near the edge we are and only wise statesmanship, especially a good Foreign Minister, will gain us respect again in the world. The very *look* of [Herbert] Morrison [*successor to Ernest Bevin as Foreign Secretary*] makes me think 'Here we are again' of a circus clown. He cannot help his features but he could get his hair cut differently and use hair oil to make him look less irresponsible!

Thursday, 25 October. A perfect autumn day. The sun would have been warm in early September. We went to vote on our way to Ulverston, and things were very quiet about 10 o'clock. We went through Dalton and didn't see one sign of voting – not even a car or house with colours showing, not even children in processions as often. I got 2s 2d of undercut, and 1s 9d of rather poor mutton 'best end of the neck' to make a one-pot meal, some very good soup bones, only 3d, and a bit of lights for the cats. As we left Dalton we saw the first signs of election day. From the upstairs window of a small terraced cottage flaunted a big blue table-cloth tied on to a prop! Not another sign till we neared Ulverston and saw a blue-edged card 'Vote for Fraser' in a window. Ulverston was busy – not election, but a rather bigger cattle sale had brought people in from the countryside. I went into a very old established draper to get a buckle to match Peter's buttons. One of the partners served me, a pleasant man of about 40, and we got talking of bygone elections when they had bought blue and yellow ribbon in different widths in thousands of yards, when part-time sewing women made rosettes from sizes taking a yard of ribbon to huge ones taking up ten yards, to put each side of horses' blinkers, when *everyone* sported a rosette, yards of ribbon decorated horses, pony chaises and carriages of all description, as well as the décor of house and shop windows. I said with a little sigh, 'So much enthusiasm is passing. We don't seem to have those clear-cut convictions.' He said, 'No, more's the pity. It's not good to let toleration grow into apathy. That's what is wrong with our foreign policy, in my opinion – and who benefits? *We* don't *or* the half-baked agitators whose undeveloped minds have been dominated by underground Communism.' All Ulverston people are said to be 'local preachers' and 'debaters'. I felt I could have settled on that high old-fashioned stool and talked and talked …

It grew dusk rapidly in spite of the lovely day. [*Summer time had just ended.*] At least no one can say the weather kept them from voting.

Friday, 26 October. Few were optimistic enough to expect to return our Conservative candidate – about 12,000 majority [*for Labour*] last time. [*The Labour majority in 1950 was only c.9,500.*]

I thought it showed the trend of thought in Barrow when that majority was down to 6,000 odd. We went to Ulverston after shopping in Barrow, only because it was such a nice morning, and I left vegetable soup simmering and prepared potatoes and sprouts. I was glad we had gone out, for a bitter wind blew up, and heavy clouds made it a gloomy afternoon, and I'd been longing to sit and listen to the election results. I worked busily at Peter's coat – tailored garments want much inside work if they have to look at all well on little boys. We got so thrilled and excited, and our spirits began to droop a little when, after climbing to a majority of about 40, we began to drop. I was tickled, though, at the faith my husband had in my forecast of 25 to 30 majority [*for the Conservatives*]. If it hadn't been for that faith he would have been downcast.

Gradually a feeling of security stole over me, difficult to explain except a feeling that competent people would soon be in command. Mr Churchill has a place in our hearts no other mortal could have had, but it's not just his leadership that is needed, but the decisions of wise experienced men. No ground-nuts scheme, Gambia eggs and so on with Government money.* If big business want to launch out, well, let 'em, if they use their own money. They won't waste it or pay big overhead wages for 'supervision' and doodling round, with their coats on. Not that I've great hopes of much betterment in the near future. Without undue pessimism, clouds seem to be rolling up rather than dispersing, but always there will be confidence in knowing men of

---

*These were projects in the late 1940s concerning colonial food production and economic development, both of which were seen as failures. The attempt to grow peanuts in Tanganyika became notorious as a waste (however well intended) of public funds.

experience will be at the helm. I was amazed at the light-hearted feeling that came over me. Dear knows I'd nothing really to make me suddenly feel more cheerful about the future …

When on the 9 o'clock news it was announced that now we had 25 of a majority, my husband looked thoughtful and then said so mournfully I burst out laughing, 'To think of you wasting a hunch on an election result when you could have used it when filling up your football pool!'* Last week the treble chance prize was £7,800 or so. I would like to win that amount better than ten times the amount. A quarter of it would mean Arthur had no worry about buying a house – he earns enough for everything else. Cliff's share wouldn't overwhelm him, and our shares would be riches. I'd book a passage on a cargo ship going a long voyage – round the world if possible. No frills, just ordinary comfort, just to sail away somewhere warm and interesting in the dear hope it would give my husband that interest he so needs, and so utterly lacks.

Saturday, 27 October. Mrs Howson was so annoyed. They were none of them pleased at the WVS office at the remarks of two newcomers. They seemed to have moved round the country a lot with their 'Vickers' Metropole' husbands, always making for a WVS office as a means of fresh contacts. They are both only young – under 25 – and had rather cruelly 'taken off' the people in various WVS offices, but somehow given the impression that

---

*Will was not alone in this judgement. 'I'd a good laugh over Arthur's letter,' Nella wrote three days later, on 29 October, 'as he demanded why I wasted a perfectly good "hunch on an election forecast. Why not keep it for your football coupon or the winner of the Derby?"' Although the Conservatives won the election, the Labour Party actually got more votes.

this one in Barrow beat the lot! I bet it would too. Mrs Newall, the part-time paid secretary, has a lovely gay and generous personality, but looks like a tinker's wife. She wears no corsets on her spreading figure and as she says as she looks down on it, so fat and shapeless, 'I cannot get anything ready made to fit, but handkerchiefs and hats', which she rarely wears on her badly cut and kept 'urchin cut' hair. Her lovely melodious voice can string more weird cuss words than any but a bargee, and her cigarette ash seems everywhere.* Mrs Diss, in spite of her money and lovely house, always makes us squirm when offcome† visitors come so trim and neat, for her shoes always look run down and dirty, her permed hair always looks as if it needs a trip to the hairdresser's, and she is so erratic in her manner and leaves far too much to Miss Willan, a retired school mistress who finds a queer satisfaction in wearing the shabbiest WVS uniform I've seen outside London and Manchester, where uniforms got so much hard wear in the war. Miss Willan took a cottage in the country, and she and her sister never came to Barrow if there was any danger of a raid, and never slept in Barrow. She was always a little power-crazy when at school, and tries to run every effort in her own personal way. Miss Mawson belongs to that queer school of thought when any kind of trade, even that of a wealthy jeweller like Mr Diss has, was outcast. Her family were solicitors, and a few of them, if not exactly shady, were on that road, and in addition plain to ugliness. She is no exception.

---

*Mrs Newall had been invited to take tea at Nella's home on 17 March 1950, and though she 'ate a good meal, she was depressed and down as she spoke of her lonely life, and of her husband's preference for Dorothy Crosbie, who, "though she could earn £500 a year as a librarian, is content to steal my husband and live off him".' Mrs Newall's marital woes are detailed several times in *Nella Last's Peace* (pp. 65–6, 69–70, 74, 269–72, and 284).

I'm always wildly amused by both her and Miss Willan's attitude to me. As the wife of a businessman, I'd be amongst the untouchables, but for the fact my mother's people were 'the proud Rawlinsons'. The fact they were as poor as jack turkey – and Granny must have worked like two farm servants rolled in one to raise her family when she was left so young a widow – doesn't seem to count! She spends most of her time when she and Mrs Howson are not busy on clothing, reckoning up whether to class people as sheep or goats, and no one could class Mrs Howson as more than a little eccentric, always clinging to home and her mother, condemning every action of more venturesome women, anyone who has saved money or anyone with a different point of view of any kind.

I listened to all Mrs Howson had to say and felt a little chuckle as I wondered if I was in the bunch of 'funnies'. I must have some kind of affinity with the feather-brained little thing or she wouldn't seek my company as often. Tonight my husband complained she wearied him and said when she went, 'You know, that bunch at the WVS office *are* odd'. I didn't want any offcomers to point out that fact.

Tuesday, 30 October. We set off and got to Ambleside, taking rests, first to eat lunch by Windermere Lake, and then to stroll round Bowness in the sunshine and the serenity of an off-season day, so lovely and peaceful. The shops were as usual so well stocked, every kind of luxury from good fur coats, Shetland woollies and tweeds, handmade toys, antiques – just *everything* if you had money. Taste was all round. There never seems anything trashy in country shopping centres. The sun was warmer than it often was in July or August. We strolled by the Lake at Ambleside, the water so smooth that when swans sailed majestically across in hope we had bread for them, their wake was like a crack on its surface. All the rowing boats were washed and stacked in sheds, while boatmen dismantled large craft and washed seats etc. in the Lake. The trees were a glory of gold, yellow, russet and red. Holly trees were covered with scarlet berries, yet sheltered gardens still had lovely roses and marigolds as well as chrysanths. Such a lovely colourful day, such a treat to be out in the warm sunshine. We were back home before 4 o'clock. I made a fire and fed the disgruntled cats. They hadn't liked the fire going out evidently.

Thursday, 1 November. We went down town and I called in the Library. Last Thursday I was talking to one of the girls and the under-Librarian and gave my bet for the election. I'd forgotten today and wasn't prepared for the welcome I got from them, the girl especially. I don't know her very well. She is just one of the very nice pleasant girls in the Library, but today I might have been a dear friend as she came up to the table where I was turning the books over. She said, 'Are you psychic in some way? Do you often have "hunches"?' I laughed at her earnest expression, but when she went on to say, 'I wish you would join with me in doing a football coupon every week', I burst out laughing as I said, 'I do two lines of treble chance every week, and I never have any luck', and thought to myself, '*Well*, who would have thought a girl like you would have gone in for pools'. She said wistfully, 'I *do* want a lot of money', and I said, 'Why?' She said, 'To get married. I'm not really a business-minded person. I want to be married and have children and a home of my own, and my boy and I say however we save it will be three years before we could have even a reasonable sum for deposit on a house, and the minimum of furniture.' Poor dear. I wondered how many of the sixpences and shillings of the pools are made up from people like her.

Saturday, 3 November. Mrs Woods called to see if I'd heard a disquieting rumour that was going round town – that Mrs Diss's son's wife, Sheila, had polio. [*She was also pregnant, as was later learned.*] She was on a visit to her people near Birmingham and had complained of feeling queer and ill in the train, and had looked so ill they got the doctor. Mrs Howson came in before Mrs Woods left and said it was true, but only one leg was badly affected, and the doctors said she 'will be alright'. As Mrs Howson had got the news from the WVS office and Mrs Diss had left it there, we felt relieved. Sheila is such a charming vital girl, so capable, so keen to dance, swim, motor and play tennis. The thought of her even being a little crippled is saddening.* It's a very queer thing that the man who died from polio the other week only lived a few doors from the young Disses. It's very noticeable that any cases I've heard of or seen should be of the best types from a health view. It seems to leave a weakling in a family to attack the strongest.

Tuesday, 6 November. Cliff said last night he had a huge pile of washing. He scorned the idea, though, that he needed help.** He is the handiest and most thorough doer of odd jobs. He had

---

*Nella, who did not hesitate in her diary to render harsh judgements about others, had written almost rhapsodically about Sheila just prior to her marriage. 'Sheila is such a charming, well educated and well bred girl. Her family are all the same – love for each other and happiness in their parents – and the same friendly approach to Geoff's people made us think what a treasure of a wife he would get.' Nella went on to praise 'the warmth and depth of Sheila's nature, all her breadth of outlook, her dainty, charming ways and desire to be admitted into his family' (11 July 1950).

**On 4 November, Cliff returned to Barrow after travelling for a couple of months, including a stay in Paris and journeys in Spain.

seven shirts, bathing togs and towels, ten pair of socks as well as a week's change of underwear, and no woman could have washed them better or with less upset. It was a lovely morning, too fine to wear out the day, and he was a bit late getting them out, but mangled well. They did blow sweet and fresh before it began to rain ...

A letter from the art master of the studio where he attended before he left England wrote and offered him a corner of the studio and use of any models, and Cliff said it was a 'Good chance, and anything I do can go back to Melbourne when I go, to form the nucleus of another exhibition', but it means going back this Saturday. I said, 'I thought you would have liked to go to Ken's wedding [*the son of Will's brother, to be married on 17 November*]. I know an invite will come when they know you are here.' He gave me to understand his relations didn't interest him much and 'that lot especially'. I laughingly said, 'Family ties don't mean much to you, do they?' He scowled as he said, 'I remember when we were small that we were frightened when we saw you cry – you so seldom did – and Arthur and I always say that the rare times you did cry was trouble of some kind with Daddy's family. How could they "mean anything" when we crall† so much!'

Thursday, 8 November. Mrs Higham came. She had grave news about Sheila Diss. Mrs Howson so lightly discussed the subject, saying, 'Oh, she'll be alright. Only one leg is affected.' Cliff heard last night that the crisis would be today. Mrs Diss had told Mrs Higham, 'Sheila is helpless, both legs in plaster, unable to lift one arm and hand, and also so helpless she cannot hold anything or lift it as far as her face. She lies staring helplessly up at the ceiling and at the weekend was so depressed they let her parents and husband stay for several hours.' We were puzzled, thinking it was so very infectious. Two more children have gone down with polio, but no child is really ill. It's adults who have fared the worse …

The previous day Nella had read in the paper that a cousin of her husband (William Herbert Forrester), 'a clever civil engineer' and 'one of the men in charge of the building of the new power station, had died of infantile paralysis, leaving a wife and four tiny children. He was only 30, an only son – only child – and his mother is a widow. I thought sadly how difficult it is to understand why strong youth should go, and old people like Mother seem to grow stronger and more difficult every day.' Polio was particularly prevalent in the early 1950s.

Friday, 9 November. I got a dollie finished off to let Cliff see it finished. I made a baby dollie, with golden hair, and bought a mask for its face. It has woollen vest and booties, a nappy, long pale pink slip under long puff-sleeved nightdress with blue ribbon threaded through a lace slot in front for a sash, a scrap of blue ribbon round one wrist and a small handkerchief tucked in, and a Mother Hubbard bonnet and cloak, tied at the neck with blue ribbon. With a cellophane wrapping to keep it clean, it looks tempting for some little girl's stocking, and the money is badly needed at St Paul's.* I made a salad to the rest of the tinned beef and there was bread and butter, fruit bread, gingerbread and crispie. It's such a delight to see Cliff so enjoy his food – well

---

*There was a strong demand for these dressed dollies. 'I've made dresses and matching bonnets, pyjamas and dressing gowns, aprons by the dozens, afternoon tea clothes, and napkins – *anything* the good little scraps of material will cut, yet still they clamour for more', Nella wrote on 16 November. 'Mrs Higham says frankly, "The stall holders say they are going to queue before the rush starts". Seems no little girls are taught to make their own dollies' clothes nowadays and mothers are often too busy.'

chosen food like salads and vegetables. Arthur enjoys his food, but eats far too much starch and fat – he so likes cakes and things like chips. We sat talking. I made a list of any oddments Cliff will yet need in his bag ...*

John Myers came up – Cliff should have gone out with him tonight. He scorned the idea that Cliff will be able to travel – on Monday, never mind in the morning – knowing that self-willed Arab. I reserve judgement! Jack works in a bank and, like Arthur, takes a keen interest in the economic side of things as a whole. He affirms, 'If Labour *had* got in, England *would* have been sunk – every way'. He holds a fairly prevalent opinion that Attlee never wanted to rule any more – he was badly frightened and that was why he had so sudden an election. We talked of future hardships, of how much better it would have been to face things firmly and not let the American loans go to bolster up a false sense of security of employment, etc. He is far from a pessimist, but tonight he was really fearful in his gloomy outlook for the next year. I wondered as he spoke of 'less and less coal' how Mrs Howson's mother would fare. Their coalman has never been for over two months, and the agent said civilly, 'Oh, you will get all your back coal'. I've kept urging her to go to the fuel office and report that the monthly ration hasn't been delivered, telling her what my coalman said about 'A wagon load comes in and gets bagged and delivered to as many as possible who are next on the list. When that's done, no more can be done. There's NO stock of coal in town, except a small one at the Co-op yard, and a growing pile of fire bricks made like small coconuts.'

---

*Cliff was preparing to leave Barrow for London, although he had injured his back working in the garden and was in considerable pain (and did in fact have to delay his departure).

Saturday, 10 November. Today an Army cadet spotted me and said, 'Have a poppy, Mrs Last?' I said, 'I'd like three for this, Jim' and showed him I was putting in a silver coin and not a penny each. He grinned as he said, 'I'll make you a little posy for that', and I passed one to Cliff and one to his father, as I'd heard them say they had no small change. My husband got well away with his complaints of 'The way Dearie throws money away sometimes, you would think we were living on a good income and not out of capital' etc., but he had his match today as Cliff pointed out I 'could cook like a chef' – he had 'never tasted plain food with such flavour', 'had been amazed at her thrift in every way', and 'I know that half crown won't come out of anything you should have had', till his father decided to change the subject. I'd left soup simmering – *such* good bone stock with a sliced kidney added to the mixed vegetables. I fried bacon and eggs for them. I'd an apple fried, and we had bread to it. Cliff insisted on a double helping of cold cabbage being fried up for him. Together we could eat our way through a well kept plot of garden!

It got out a lovely afternoon, like an early January day when the sun has crossed the line. My husband relaxed a while, and to my surprise I heard them discussing going to Bowness. Cliff insisted he felt well enough and took three cushions to pack behind his back. I felt it was folly, really, but he so longed to see the Lake and hills in their autumn tints, saying it would be his last chance. It was one of those dream days for the Lakes, so beloved and well described by Walpole. Fells and hills, small islands on Windermere seemed to float in the soft crystal air. The Lake was like grey metal, fringed by shadows of trees and hills, a golden day for enough colour lingered in the bracken and in many of the trees to catch every gleam of sun. I bought some Windermere toffee and some little sugar mice wrapped in silver paper for my little boys.

This year happy gay little Christopher can suck a sugar mouse. We were back just before 5 o'clock, just as dusk fell swiftly. I made up the fire. Cliff lay on the settee with a grimace of pain, still protesting he was nearly alright but thought he wouldn't go back till Monday …

Mrs Howson came in. I sat and plaited crepe paper to make little baskets and put sweets in. Her news of Sheila Diss was distressing. She lies helpless, cannot turn her head. Only her hands have a little power, but at that she cannot raise them to her poor face. There has been a lot of talk about the two adult deaths from polio in Barrow recently. People are saying, 'If they had been in Birmingham they would have had a chance', inferring our town's doctors haven't the skill or knowledge of those in Birmingham, but Mrs Diss was told it depends where the infection is. Two more children have been taken to the Isolation Hospital. When the first adult died, the undertaker told of a by-law which prohibited bodies taken into church who had died of polio. Yet Sheila Diss still has her husband by her bedside, and her parents come and go, trying in every way to move her from the depths of depression from which the poor girl suffers, so there must also be degrees of infection.

Thursday, 15 November. I never saw anyone quite so averse to 'touching capital' as my husband. As I sat finishing off the two monkeys, with scarlet fez and little felt banana in white and yellow, I couldn't but think of good chances he had thrown aside just because of 'Never touch capital'. Once I had a plot of land offered. A friend had bought twice as much as she needed to put up two semi-detached houses for herself and sister. Although I'd enough money of my own and badly wanted to 'speculate', he nearly went mad – *literally* so – as he shouted and rolled his eyes and stuttered in rage. I gave way for peace. The one who bought the land for £130 sold it six months later for £200, and all he would say was, 'I couldn't have stood the worry of knowing I wasn't getting interest and mightn't have sold it at all'. Useless to point out it was my money and that my father had made his money with just such speculations rather than be niggardly saving.

Saturday, 17 November. I felt glad of my bits and pieces all matching and good as I got ready [*for the wedding*]. The cultured pearls Cliff brought from Spain are the best I've seen and link up with my good pearl earrings and filigree gold and pearl spray brooch, and were perfect with my leaf-green two-piece, but my Texan lamb coat *did* look 'utility' amongst the lovely fur coats. I've never seen so high a percentage in a comparatively small gathering – both mothers had new ones. Nellie is inclined to be jealous of Roma's mother and to copy all she has, but it will always be a copy. There's too wide a gulf between Nellie, so narrow-minded, so fond of making trouble and laying down the law, and pleasant, busy Mrs Harper, who teaches and runs a home, except for making a midday meal as well or better than Nellie herself. Roma looked like a fairy princess in stiff white brocade. She brought her dress from London and sent the bridesmaids' dress material to be made up, a lovely wine-red silk with faint 'shot' effect of gold. They fit so very badly, as if the maker had bought the pattern and made it up exactly, with no thought to little individual differences. They looked like Mrs Howson used to do before I convinced her that *all* clothes needed a bit of fitting. It poured with rain, but there was no waiting about. A motor coach took a full load and taxis and private cars the rest. The hotel, on Morecambe Bay at Rampside, had big wood fires in the two comfortable lounges and in the big dining room, and a really pre-war spread was laid, looking as if restrictions were quite unknown. The ham, served with the tender chicken, would be tinned no doubt, but the small crisp lettuces in the salad and quite half a new laid egg, hard boiled, *was* a treat. Butter, with the unmistakable freshly churned taste, a huge blob of fresh whipped cream on the delicious small trifle, seemed too good to be true! I felt vexed that Cliff had forgotten to send a wire when a handful were read out. His memory is really deplorable for his age.

Saturday, 24 November. At the hospital Dr Wadsworth drew me aside and said, 'I feel concern for your husband's deterioration in health since he was last here. Can you account for it in any way?' I said I couldn't, but in my mind I'd a great sadness as I realised how Cliff had innocently upset him so often. Little arguments, chance remarks and opinions as to how he should 'try and snap out of things', far from helping his father, were like tiny thorns that worked deep, later to fester. Even after 40 years of married life together I still get little amazements when such trifles can so affect my husband. Times I long for money to take him to a psychoanalyst or the like – and then wonder how deep he would have to dig. If I can keep control and courage to pick every rose leaf of worry from his path, always keep cheerful and gay, never let him see I feel ill, worried or depressed, I can manage to help him. If things get past my guard, it sets up a quick and devastating reaction and seems to knock him off his feet. I can tell his going to the wedding brought old worries and upsets back into his mind …

My husband finds pleasure when he is not well by watching me make things. I generally work on a belt system – hats all made, pants, collared shirts, etc., and then assemble them. Tonight when he was impatient to see a whole cowboy, I made one. Always does it puzzle me that my dollies look so different when their faces are embroidered off the same pattern, and their clothes cut more or less alike. It's as if a few stitches put differently or a different material makes a totally different individual. I was frowning at the happy-faced little cowboy who suddenly came alive to me as his felt two-gallon hat was firmly fixed by a few stitches on his fur wig and said, 'What should we call the little man?' My husband considered a while and then said, 'Andrew – he has such a "Merry Andrew" look'. So my wee man got his name tag on. I've often been so amused when people as well as children keep to the original names I give them. The baby doll I sent up for the sale of work I called Susan Mary – she looked both demure as well as gay. Mrs Higham has referred to it several times and never as the 'dollie' but always as 'Susan Mary'. My mind *would* swing backward tonight as my little doll child seemed to smile up at me. I wondered how many I *had* made, where they had all gone – little Ann still has Dear Ruthie, a now dirty-looking shabby crinoline dollie in felt poke bonnet whose skirt has been washed and replaced many times in three years, but as Mrs Atkinson says, 'Never a stitch needed in repair'. My own little boys keep and love their animal toys. It *is* a nice hobby to have.

Months later, on 7 August 1952, Nella 'suddenly thought how lucky I was to be able to sew, and to lose myself in seeing something take shape in my fingers'.

Sunday, 25 November. What a DAY! I'd a rest and wrote two letters before I rose at about 11 o'clock, feeling a bit disgruntled at the coolness of the water as I bathed. I'd just got out, feeling it wasn't warm enough to linger, when I heard my husband dash upstairs, then down, and then up again clanking a bucket and the step ladder. He called, 'If you are out of the bath, for goodness sake come here'. Snatching my dressing gown, feeling a vest and one stocking, poor 'fighting gear' whatever it was, I dashed into the back bedroom and gasped as I saw water pouring out of the top of the cistern over the hot water tank and splashing on the floor. I ran for all the towels in the bathroom to mop up, wringing them into a bucket. My husband said, 'I'll go for Charlie Atkinson. He might know what to do.' For a 'practical' man, my husband knows less of the other fellow's job than most men. I took it for granted he would have turned off the stopcock† on the kitchen-ette to cut off the water from upstairs. He hadn't thought to do it. When Mr Atkinson did, it lessened the cascade of water, and running all the taps lessened it again. I took all the sopping wet clothes out of the airing cupboard shelves and got dressed. My husband took the car and went to search for a plumber who lived on the premises. When he did locate one, his wife said, 'That's odd. He has had to go to two other similar jobs.' He came and turned the stopcock with a spanner, for a trickle of water still ran. I've feared for the living room ceiling all day, wondering where a spate of water could drain without coming to the corner of the ceiling …

What made me vexed was that we had warning there was something amiss some months ago when, for some reason, the outlet pipe threw water out like a fountain, splashing all the living room window and frightening Mrs Helm at the time. I thought we should have had a plumber but my husband said it wasn't necessary, but it seems as if the joint on the ball arm that was found broken could have been going.

Friday, 30 November. Mrs Howson and I talked of Sheila Diss, wondering how long she would be in plaster. Looking back to last Xmas when that vital glowing girl made such a spread for Mrs Diss's big house party, nothing was a trouble or worry for Sheila. She loved to use her Domestic Science training in any way, from arranging lovely flower displays to boning a turkey and folding it round a chunk of ham before cooking – and was ready to go playing golf or dancing half the night with her adoring young husband. I thought with a sadness that was half relief, 'It's a good thing we *don't* know what lies ahead of us'. Mrs Howson said, 'They hope Sheila will walk again', as if there was doubt. The only bright spot is that there's unlimited money as well as all the love and care the whole Diss family, as well as her own, pour on her, and dear little Michael.

Tuesday, 4 December. I wasn't out of the hairdresser's till just before the Shipyard came out so knew I'd have to walk two stages before I could hope to get on a bus, when the men started getting off. When I got in I felt concerned to see my husband looking so upset. He said he had had a little upset while he was in the barber's – a young woman 'just fell flat' by the door. She had been ill and was out with her mother for the first time and they had been to the doctor's. They phoned to the surgery and the doctor said he would 'be along', but it was a while before he came and the patient lay without the slightest movement, and the barber, a first aid man, couldn't feel the slightest pulse in her wrist. The doctor got the ambulance, but my husband said he was sure she was dead. [*He was right.*] I wished to goodness I'd not suggested – insisted – on him going to get his hair cut.

I scrambled an egg for him and made toast. I'd toasted cheese and there was apricot jam, bread and butter and crispie. We had settled down by the fire. I was finishing Edith's letter when there was a ring, and to my great amazement it was my husband's brother, Harry, and his wife. They had come to see my 'Wonderful hospital dollies. Our Ken [*a doctor*] had been at Dr Ronald's to call for him and his wife to go dancing on Friday night and had seen a loved, battered gollywog you had made in the war. It had been loved by both their own boys and got out for a child visitor. Dr Ronald *did* rave about all the pleasure you had given the children, and said you had done it for, he thought, 30 years.' I got a real surprise to think of my huge ragbag family. I used to make two to three dozen dollies and animals every year. Then there were all the ones I made in the war to sell and raffle, as well as those for my own children and little friends. My brain reeled as I heard her say, 'You must have made *hundreds*!' They loved the monkeys and the felt Dutch dollie, but as Harry said when he picked up a cowboy clothed from such small oddments, 'It's easy enough to make nice things from whole cloth. It's chaps like these, though, that have the individuality.'

Thursday, 6 December. I'd a little rest after I'd dusted round and then went to the committee meeting at Mrs Diss's house. Although I've known so well she has wanted to resign – and now with her having her little grandson and her son when he isn't at Birmingham where his wife still lies in plaster after polio – it shouldn't have been the shock that it was to all of us when she said she had at last convinced Headquarters that her resignation *must* be accepted. We all sat dumb after the breath like a hiss had died away, as if we were too surprised to have anything to say. Then I began to get pokes and nudges and several said, '*You* get up and say something. If I do I'll only burst out crying.' I did, feeling what I said was the outpouring of all the years of endeavour, friendship and loyalties. I noticed tears running down many faces and was surprised I too was crying. Mrs Diss said, 'If that's how people have thought of me my dear, I feel I can only say thank *you* – all of you', and Miss Willan, that odd old schoolmistress, said, 'Thank you for saying everything I'd have liked to say. It was the most heartfelt speech I've ever heard', which left me wondering as I sat down what exactly I had said. It was just a little fleeting inspired moment.

CHAPTER EIGHT

TIMES CHANGE

January–July 1952

While most of the public events that Nella mentioned were local, a few were national, including the death of King George VI on 6 February. 'My pity and concern went in a rush of sympathy to Princess Elizabeth,' Nella remarked that day, 'whose youth dies at 26.' Other occurrences that she wrote of were personal or at least rooted in community: the imminent move of Arthur and his family from Northern Ireland to London, and their plans to buy a house (to do so, they borrowed £500 from Will and Nella); the illnesses and deaths of several people she knew; her usual frustrations and spats with her husband. 'I had such a passionate longing to set off on the bus to Ambleside', she wrote on 29 February. 'To have done so would have created a situation of hurt such that living it down in the next few days would have taken away any benefit a flight would have been.' The weather was sometimes severe, especially in January, which tended to keep her at home: on the evening of 17 January 'the howl of the gale wind and the rattle of hail made the cosy fire seem even warmer'. And there was the usual wear and tear of everyday life. 'I feel I've been whirled round in a lift shaft today' (4 February); one day in the Barrow market 'I had the dim feeling of always rigid economy ahead, and it didn't help to see women eagerly snapping up the very bargains I'd have liked' (29 February). Some of Nella's most striking observations – in addition to descriptions of natural surroundings – concerned changes in entertainment and popular culture, taste, material provisions, and household and family arrangements, all of which figure frequently in her diary for the first half of 1952.

Saturday, 12 January. We went by the Coast Road to Ulverston. The tide was high. The last one had evidently been higher and tossed sea wrack† and sand on to the edge of the road. Every 50 or 60 yards or so people strolled along, keeping a keen eye on scraps of wood. Gone are the days when no one bothered. It's a recognised walk to go to Walney or Morecambe Bay shores, gleaning the smallest pieces. The sun shone so warm and bright. The ewes folded in sheltered fields, and climbed slopes to nibble grass on the sunniest part of fields. Thousands of plovers and sea birds made huge carpets as they waited anxiously on the shingle for the sea to leave the sands – they could begin to get the cockles before they sank too deep in the wet sand.

Ulverston was as thronged as on a busy Thursday market day – perhaps with last Thursday's snow and sleet making Lakeland roads impassable. I heard an odd remark in Woolworths. Two middle-aged women, both with heavy shopping bags, were discussing some 'quick-working' rice in packets – 1s 3d a pound. One said, 'I got two packets today and two last Saturday. I'm storing up all I can – Kellogg's Cornflakes, packets of oats and cornflour – anything unrationed'.* I had such a longing to know if she had been to a Civil Defence exhibition and got a 'C.D. slant' on things. They all – the organisers – have a 'when' as against 'if' war comes!

I got some elastic I needed to finish off my underwear, but this week and next I have to be so very careful. I had nothing in my purse against coal and the electricity bill, with it being Xmas and Cliff here. It's the first year I've felt I begrudged the tips to trades people I felt were so much better off than myself. I begrudge the money spent on the coal I got – 4 cwt were £1 1s 6d and it's the

---

*Food rationing was not finally abolished until mid-1954.

kind only to be burnt with the help of wood, which we cannot get. In all the years and through two wars we could get small log wood – in Lakeland it looks as if the long line of woodsmen who cut coppice woods in rotation every 5–7 years will follow the equally long line of charcoal burners. Even when Arthur was small there were plenty of them, spending lonely hours in small rude huts on the hillsides.

I got so out of patience with my husband as I walked round. I asked him if he was going to take Gilbert Harding as a model, adding, 'You may find yourself alone more if you do', and wondering if part of his mood could be due to the knowledge I will be out every Tuesday afternoon for six weeks at the Civil Defence canteen class, an idea rather confirmed when I saw his reaction to another C.D. notice saying First Aid classes were starting Wednesday evening – would I attend? – if not, stating an evening I could. It was said WVS would take over 'Canteen and Welfare', and not be full-time Civil Defence. No Civil Defence women seem to be bothering about any of our training, which we did all the war years.

Saturday, 19 January. It was a bright cold morning. We would have gone out, but with having the appointment with Dr Wadsworth at 1.45, it would have been a rush to have lunch and be out again by then … I *do* feel these visits do more harm than good now. My husband is the very last person to whom a doctor should say, 'I've never yet come across a case like yours, Mr Last'. Poor dear. He cherishes every symptom as unique but takes comfort always from hearing of worse cases that have responded to treatment of some kind. I've felt for some little time now that no psychiatry is any use, that it is some physical decline or lack. Looking back over the years, he always had symptoms of this breakdown, little traits and behaviourisms that made them say in the family, 'Our Will and Flo take after Mother'. She was always a law unto herself. Born very late in life to parents brought up on a remote Cumberland fell, she never seemed to fit in with any kind of town life or any difference in thought, customs, etc. Added to that she had a – for them – very good little income of £4 a week when her aged parents died and it helped to give her that 'I'll do as I like' attitude. Her odd ways were first put down to those facts. When she grew really away from life, at between 50 and 60, her ways were talked of rather as a spoilt and somewhat subnormal child. She was old at 60, as she is today at 83, when her mind went and her body gained strength. I pondered on both mother and my husband, striving to find any suggestion that a psychiatrist could have reached something that was never there. I *do* feel glands could be the root of the trouble, though Dr Miller pooh-poohs such a suggestion.

Today when my husband came out of the doctor's consulting room, I'd a great sadness as I realised his visit had really done him harm. He had asked Dr Wadsworth if there was *no* treatment, tonic, diet, etc. likely to benefit him, and been told flatly 'I'm afraid not, Mr Last'. I could have rushed back into that room and told Dr Wadsworth a few things. I felt, 'To *hell* with your so modern notions. I'm utterly ignorant of "isms" and what not, but I've enough natural wit to realise the result of such a remark on so obviously a sick man. Why couldn't you have given him some simple cheap tonic, told him he needed a long holiday in the country on a farm, asked, "Couldn't you have a sea voyage?" etc. – I've heard of such "treatments".' I could have wept aloud in pity for the poor dear, and a lot of help *that* would have been!

We sat a while in the car till he had stopped his nervous trembling. I asked, 'Like to go home and relax, love, or do you feel like

going on the Coast Road in this blessed sunshine?' He decided
we would go. The glittering sunshine was deceptive. The sands
froze as the water left them, and the thousands of birds, sensing
this, paddled and fluttered in the shallow edge, seizing cockles
or small sea creatures. Morecambe is the only place I know where
hordes of rooks and crows compete with plovers and every kind
of sea bird, though, each kind of bird keeping to their kind, from
the air they must look like big rugs and carpets in their close
masses. My tired mind wondered how many uncounted genera-
tions of them had stood in the same spot.

Tuesday, 29 January. All was snow-covered and where people had
cleared sidewalks and pavements were sheet ice, as it thawed and
then froze in the night. I was doing my hair and looking out of
the window on to the snowing street when a baker's van lurched
to a standstill over the frozen ruts and drifts. The roundsman[†]
alighted and wiped the back of his hand across his nose, slapped
his arms round his body in the cabby's way of bringing back circulation, breathed heavily into his cupped hands, fumbled with
a gate latch, gave it a violent wrench and push with his hands,
took hold of a knocker and knocked, and then walked back to the
van, opened the door, stacked three loaves on his coat sleeve and
clutched some rolls in one hand and what looked like shortbread
in the other, and walked back to deliver them to the waiting
woman. I felt my stomach turn over. I've often noticed assistants
coughing and sneezing into handkerchiefs, put them back into
their pockets and reach for cakes, and felt that what I couldn't
bake I'd do without. I was once told in Canteen I had a 'neuro-
sis' – he was a smarty college conchie and he was referring to my
firm refusal to let the boys on 'lamp' or heavy oil fatigue take
sandwiches or cake into their filthy hands. We wrapped a wee

piece of paper on one side to hold them by. This morning I really felt *sick*, yet realised there were much more unhygienic tricks we never saw ...

Mrs Higham picked Mrs Howson and I up, to go to the Civil Defence meeting ... Today we were shown the use of food containers and the layout of a field kitchen. Somehow those two huge double skinned, cork insulated carriers – the square one, with three flat-lidded containers, each to hold enough to feed 26 people with solid food like porridge, mashed vegetable or pudding, and the big one, rather like those for ice cream – brought home to 'simple' minded housewives the utter senseless futility of 'having to be prepared' and stockpiling generally [*in case of war*]. We seemed to see the tens of thousands of such carriers at a time when essentials were going to be cut and goods get more scarce and dear. Civil Defence classes *do* depress me. I think it's that fact that makes women hang back from attending, but someone will have to do it. Mrs Higham said as we were coming home, 'Penny for them, Lasty', and I said, 'Just a formless montage, impossible to describe – fears, broken hopes, a tired body and mind and somehow a faith and courage that does burn low'. She nodded and as I got out she said, 'Worry won't help us, ducks. If the worst ever happens, we will be the lucky ones again. Remember those of us who worked busily the last time and had a purpose in life that did bring us peace of mind enough to carry on.' I thought with a sadness, 'Yes, but my lad had a strong young body then, not a damaged one and as I often think a little "kink" in his mental make-up, *and* my husband had strength and health that didn't weaken with every passing week.'

He had a good fire and had been reading, and it wasn't 4 o'clock, so he hadn't been alone long. I wrote Cliff's letter, sitting up to the fire to get warm, and made tea early. There was cress and cheese, bread and butter and jam, cake and shortbread biscuits, and not a bad wireless programme. I've often been amazed at the number of TV sets bought. Mrs Higham said the other day, 'We must be freaks. No one believes me when I say I haven't the faintest longing for one.'

Friday, 1 February. Mrs Howson came in before I'd cleared the tea away. My goodness, she was in a paddy†. There's been a lot of talk of *much* higher fees for evening and afternoon classes. They have always kept the same quite ridiculous figure of pre-war in spite of rising cost – 5s for two winter classes, and 4s 6d for two summer ones. The new fees were posted on the board in the hall last night – £1 for *one* winter class a week, 15s for one summer one, or £1 10s od if the whole year is paid for in advance. I pointed out that they must have been almost charity for some time; that the lucky few who almost fought their way in queues at the beginning of each session were heavily subsidised by people who couldn't go or were not interested; and as for country dancing, I thought if people were interested enough to go, they should be interested enough to pay the salary of a teacher. She 'hopes *no* one goes, and that all interest in hard or soft furnishing dies'. She *was* cross!

We talked of Sheila Diss. Her baby will be born at the beginning of July, and her general health has been so low the Hospital authorities are relaxing the rule of 'no child visitors under 12' and little Michael is to be taken to see his mother. He will stay for a fortnight with his other grandparents and visit every day. Mrs Diss is very down. They cannot get the muscles going in her legs, which have shrunk to sticks like President Roosevelt's. No massage, exercise or electric treatment does any good. Mrs Howson said, 'It's really a pity she didn't die, like Mr Last's cousin's boy, Whinray, the accountant'. I said, 'Her task isn't finished.

We may see a little of the Pattern – unborn child may carry the Torch, and Sheila herself rise above things and find happiness where none is apparent now.' She never struck me as a shallow person, in spite of her gaiety and love of good times.

Saturday, 9 February. After a quick tidy round and dust, we went down town, taking Jessie and little Kath to hear the Proclamation [*of the accession of Queen Elizabeth II*] from the steps of the Town Hall. It's years since I've seen such a crowd in Barrow. The wide road before the Town Hall and the square were packed solid, and fanned out each side, where little could be seen. Most people seemed to have children and were anxious *they* should see if they themselves couldn't, and everywhere quite big children as well as small ones were hoisted onto shoulders. Kath has one of those vivid intense faces. Her small mouth was pressed tightly, her brows knit in concentration and her hands were clasped together as she perched on Cliff's shoulders and got a really good view. As she slid down afterwards she said, 'I'll 'member it all to tell my Daddy when he comes home'.*

Monday, 11 February. A sadness beyond description hung over me, not lightened when my poor man said wistfully, 'I'll not see Cliff again'.** I could only say 'We're all in God's Pocket, and we must let Cliff go off cheerfully – we went our way, remember', but realised he had never done so, for he never slept away from home till he was 18 and went on a holiday with his father, and then never again till we went on our honeymoon at 21 and 23.

---

*Around 1,000 people were in attendance, and the Shipyard Band played the national anthem.
**Cliff was about to sail to Sweden, to start his return voyage to Australia.

He worked in the business at the back of the house, only getting very small pocket money till he was 21 – money for clothes and board at home were given to his mother. On reflection, I can well understand what a disrupting element I must have been in the family! ...

I picked up the *Express*. The sight of poor old Queen Mary's ravaged grief-stricken face made me feel how little, after all, were my worries and grief. She has had sorrow and loss all her life from girlhood, when the man she loved died and the then Duke of York succeeded and made her his Queen, and to lose two loved sons by death – and one in what to a proud woman would be worse than death, as he laid aside all duty, not, as I often suspect, at the bidding of an over-ambitious woman, but because he felt himself unable to go on – and to live on herself. 'We go when our task is ended', no sooner, no later.

I made good vegetable soup from the stock of the one-pot meal, fried up sliced cold potatoes with tomatoes and made custard. There was enough cold meat. I felt I couldn't drive myself further and sat down after washing up. I'd letters to write and hopefully did my football pool. For four weeks I took advice from the sports forecast in the *Daily* and *Sunday Express* – and didn't have one draw in my two columns. Last week I went back to guessing and had four in one column, three in the other – looks as if it's a real gamble.

Saturday, 16 February. Mrs Atkinson called in, really I could see out of curiosity. [*Redecorating was under way at 9 Ilkley Road.*] She sat and talked, and I said, 'While we have used the front room for meals, I've been surprised to see several obvious boarders coming in for lunch'. Our little estate of three short roads and two crescents have never had boarders in the nearly 16 years we have lived here, except relatives, or in one case a widow 'took someone for company' when she found she couldn't live alone. Mrs Atkinson said, 'Mrs Stewart across the road has got two in who share a room. She told me they paid a lot for the house. The two girls at the Grammar School cost more and more for clothes etc. and prices rise and rise for food, and her husband's salary doesn't, so she just *had* to do something.' I often wish my husband would let me have a boarder, from a nearby, very highly priced place. Men who come to work for a while in the Yard often seek more reasonable and homely accommodation. He gets so wild at the thought of anyone [*boarding*] and points out that even Cliff coming in when he had 'got nicely settled off' spoiled his night's rest, but on the other hand I do feel strongly the 'interest' would counterbalance that.

Saturday, 23 February. It was a lovely February day [*en route to Spark Bridge*]. I always think if you look round you notice as much beauty in the country as any muralist. The tracery of bare twigs and branches seems to take on a waiting look, like a happy woman who knows she is going to have a baby, although there's no sign to other eyes. Wheeling gulls hovering or swooping on straight swathes of newly ploughed earth; beauty and purpose in the chugging turtle-like tractor; the cut-back hedges and piles of useless trimmings whose smoke, like that of the swale fires on hill sides and fells, today went up slowly in a spiral, into the blue and white of a spring-like sky; snow on all the hills, and snow of drifts and tussocks of age-old snowdrop patches, left to grow and 'make' unmolested in orchards and grassy verges in old gardens. I thought of the wee handfuls picked – 6d and 8d in florists' shops – as I kept seeing them in increasing patches as we got away from the sea.

Aunt Sarah looked like a bundle of old-fashioned clothes. She had been for wood to the hut and began to peel off an ulster coat[†] of unknown vintage, a woolly wrap, and a weird balaclava helmet which left her fluffy grey hair in a bush round her little withered face with its snapping sparkling dark eyes. She welcomed us with a flow of local gossip, all she had read about the King's death and funeral, world affairs, rising prices, etc. My husband said enviously, 'I wish I had a fraction of her memory and interest in things'.

Tuesday, 11 March. The bridge had been up for half an hour while ships, delayed through the fog, came in on the rising tide. Hordes of nervy women, too laden with heavy shopping bags and baskets to walk home, queued at every bus stop. My husband had cleaned the back windows when I returned. I felt so glad, more for the fact he had made the effort even than the clean windows. My face and ear had ached badly in the night, and I'd had very little sleep. After our lunch of soup, cold meat and watercress, bread and butter, cake and a cup of tea, my husband went to rest and I relaxed on the settee for nearly an hour. Mrs Howson came across to tell me we have got a new WVS organiser, a comparative new-comer to Barrow who spent most of the war in Newcastle and did WVS work, driving mostly. She has a big house in lovely gardens. Mrs Howson and I couldn't help wishing she would do as Mrs Diss always did and let us have a garden party every summer, not only to be a grand meeting place for every branch of WVS and to interest new members, but it's our only source of income for charitable subscriptions and little expenses generally.

I made a cup of tea and we sat talking till it was time for her to make her sister's tea. Someone told her she had put on weight the three weeks she had been away and she had been horrified to

find when she was weighed she had — near 4 lbs. Her father was
a fat stockily built man, though her mother is only slender and
it's the fear of both Mrs Howson and her sister they will put on
weight. My husband pottered in the garden and Shan We frisked
busily around. I had the feeling of thankfulness that soon the
garden will be 'compelling' and need odds and ends of digging,
etc. I did cheese on toast for tea, and there was shortbread and
chocolate cripsies.

We listened to the Budget with rather a sinking feeling. While
family allowances and OAP *should* be raised, we felt it was people
like ourselves who would feel the rising prices most. We really
cannot afford to run the car now, but I'm always very firm — we
will do as long as my husband can drive. I'd never hoard anything
we have, feeling with simple care and our OAP we could manage
as long as we live. I pooh-poohed all his little nervous 'wonders'
away, saying, 'We *will* keep the car. Rising cost of living, petrol,
etc. won't make us pinch. *I'll* economise and make do. We have
plenty of clothes, bedding, linen, etc., and I'll manage.' But I felt
slight dismay. It's not just food, it's coal, soon electricity too, and
every tiny item that seems dearer. [*Consumers were to be squeezed in
order to finance Britain's rearmament programme.*] No wonder people
go in for pools. I'm staggered, literally speaking, as the most
unlikely people seem to go in more and more. My modest 1 shilling is one of the only interests I seem to have, causing endless
trains of thought, of what 'I would do', but under the interest
there's the growing hope too, not to win a huge sum like, say,
£75,000 but, say, £10,000, which split into four would be useful
rather than damaging, giving Arthur and Cliff that little extra,
and making our lives 'roses all the way' with our simple tastes.

We listened to the *Tommy Handley Story*. I felt myself transported
back to a queer jumbled life when sirens, happy companionship,

grim 'keeping on', feeling in some way I helped my Cliff when I tried to help other lads, and through all the worry and tiredness beyond relief at times ran a thread of purest gold, difficult to put into words, a mixture of courage and faith in tomorrow as much as the determination 'to be a soldier as long as my dear lad is'. Of all the great ones of the war, I felt our loved King, Tommy Handley and Winston Churchill would be the very spirit of those times. Only Churchill could be described as gifted or clever, and even in him it was the 'Saw his duty as a dead sure thing – and did it, then and there' that made him great to ordinary people like myself.

Tommy Handley's death in January 1949 had caused almost universal shock and outpourings of appreciation, not least from Nella. She likened him to 'an old puckish friend who you knew would poke fun at little everyday things. Somehow he always seemed like one of my own saucy little boys. Yet how good had God been to our Tommy, who never saw people tire of him, never grew bitter and disillusioned – he was no "laugh clown laugh".* He loved life and laughter and his sense of fun bubbled out of him' (9 January 1949). On New Year's Day 1951 Nella recalled *ITMA* (*It's That Man Again*), in which Handley starred, very fondly. 'I listened to *Memories of ITMA* as I would have done to one of Churchill's broadcasts – the two are entwined in my memory somehow. The laughter had such a hearty "gusty" sound – a joyous sound. There will never be another to take his place. He was like home-baked bread – his humour was never cruel, dirty or suggestive, often verging on age-old slapstick, often subtle and witty, and *no* artist ever had grander support. My mind was a montage of Canteen, boys who put *ITMA* catch-phrases into the language for all time – boys who went gaily off, never to return, with some bit of *ITMA* nonsense. I hope Tommy has met them

*See the note for 26 January 1950.

now.' She was full of praise for 'the value of his nonsense – those silly bits of nonsense that were woven into life and living in the dark days of war, when laughter ranked so high as a "pick-up"' (10 March 1953).

Wednesday, 12 March. It's been a real bright March day. Mrs Salisbury came and we worked busily. I've two ends of Army blanket folded in a clothes basket for the cats' bed. They need a windy day today to dry thoroughly. I decided to wash them today. I heard Mrs Salisbury laughing, and talking to Shan We. She came in and said, 'He is sitting on top of the coal box, watching his blanket flap in the wind and "fretting away to himself", and sure enough, when I went out, he lifted a puzzled face as if to ask what his blanket was doing up the line. Mrs Salisbury – a *very* keen Labour woman – was so elated at the Budget. She will get the extra child allowance for two of her children and 'Overtime will be worth working now and the Yard is going to be very busy soon, and everyone will have a lot of overtime'.

Saturday, 22 March. I could have nearly finished my coat but felt too restless. I said, 'As you are going to be in bed all afternoon, I think I'll go down town and get a buckle for Peter and *might* decide to go and see *Streetcar Named Desire*.* His face was a study but I didn't say anything else. I had to pay 1s 3d for a buckle with a prong – I'd have been surprised to pay more than 6d before the war. Sewing at home comes dear nowadays. I saw a nice donkey brown coat, about the shade of the one I'm making, but the price, £12 5s 0d, made me glad my own had turned out well.

By cutting out another film and only showing a news film, the cinema got in another show. I went in at 3.30, just as the newsreel

---

*The film of Tennessee Williams's, directed by Elia Kazan, was released in 1951.

started, and was surprised to find the place more than half full, when my eyes got accustomed to the dark. I'd only seen Vivien Leigh in *Gone with the Wind*, a picture I've often longed to see again. Through it I sat enthralled, swept into another epoch, as if I'd stepped into a story book. I sat fascinated by this one – horribly so. Marlon Brando's acting of brutishness matched the soul and spirit degradation of Vivien Leigh. Every character, however small, was polished perfection. Yet with a sadness I thought how unnecessary the picture was, giving nothing, no memory to treasure, not the tiniest candle flame of hope, help or guidance, no lovely line to recall and remember, nothing but a feeling of pity for the lot of the sub-humans that helped make up the crowd, and a vague feeling that was a feeling of indecency at seeing a woman's mind, mixed with regret so much talent had been so misspent. I saw several women leaving, murmurs of 'I don't know why I wanted – or you wanted – to come'. As I walked to the bus with my mixed feelings I puzzled as often – with so much that is lovely and gracious from which to choose, films and books did so little to help people. No use saying people *like* horror, false values, decadence. It's an exploded fallacy that pigs prefer dirt when anyone who has lived on a farm knows they are a clean nice animal with more intelligence than cows or sheep, and if given clean surroundings and let alone in fields, chose hedges and grassy dells. They wallowed in dirt and filth if they didn't have any other alternative.

Wednesday, 26 March. It was a lovely, though very cold, spring day. Mats and cushions aired on the line all day. Everywhere round the sounds of carpet cleaning and lawns being mown told of people taking advantage of the day. When I was shaking a big rug and dragging it over the lawn to help remove dust, Mrs Atkinson drew my attention to the many new TV aerials that had gone up. She knows an assistant in one of the chief TV distributing shops and said, 'There's a long waiting list at Kelly's – plenty of sets but aerials are a bit slow'. Till she pointed out the fact, I'd not realised we could count over 20 from our gardens. My biggest surprise was when we cut through a region of small terrace houses on our way to the Library, mostly occupied – and owned – by steelworkers; there's a larger average of TVs than in 'residential' areas.

Saturday, 29 March. Geoff Diss is turning RC, resigning from the Freemasons and his position of Secretary for St George's Dinner. Whenever I've seen Mrs Diss these past months I've been struck by the ageing look she has had, but dismissed the thought as I know how worried she must be about her daughter-in-law having polio, and on top of it, that she was having a baby. It was a great grievance that Geoff fell in love with his sister's friend, who was of a very old R.C. family, and her attitude was a bit puzzling when as a family they never went to church. Mr Diss was C. of E. by family tradition, but Mrs Diss, born and bred in Keswick, was more nonconformist with all the narrow outlook of a person reared in a small shut-off community and with the fixed idea a bank manager [*her father's occupation*] was definitely better class. Her mother was Matron of a big London hospital and in turn had quite a lot of bigotry of her own, charming woman though she was when old and came to Barrow. Mrs Diss's oblique references to Papists, priests and confession showed how bitter were her views, and now not only will priests constantly visit the invalid Sheila, but Geoff has 'gone over'. It's bad – and sad – when wide differences of outlook separate families. It's best that Geoff and Sheila can have the same way, but sad for the Diss family. I thought to myself, 'Edith being Irish could have been easily RC', and wondered if there would have been any greater barrier than the fierce bigotry of the Ulster Orangemen, though a lot of the prickles seem lessened after life with easygoing, tolerant Arthur, who seemed happier when he had persuaded her to smoke, go to the cinema, dance and take an odd cocktail or glass of sherry, in spite of her mother's outraged feelings that Edith was on the road to hell!

Tuesday, 8 April. Mrs Diss was telling us that Sheila has a self-propelling chair, and that 'Her courage is like a flame'. She 'never whines or whimpers', and never gives way unless she feels she is being too much of a burden to people. Mrs Diss seems to have gained in what could be termed a jolly tolerance, as she told of all the upset of workmen turning her lovely big house into two, the smaller half for Julia, her daughter, getting married soon, and of little Michael's 'old fashioned ways', but his dear delight at Sheila's homecoming. I felt a God bless for the way she had taken polio, a semi-crippled daughter-in-law, another grandchild, which, I can tell, she wonders if it will be strong and healthy, and the latest 'blow' that Geoff is turning R.C. In spite of – or could be now because of? – all her worries, she has gained a grandeur she never had.

With the renewed concern in the early 1950s for Civil Defence, memories of the recent war were apt to come to mind. In late April there was actually a 'gas test', in a van, involving gas masks.

Wednesday, 30 April. Mrs Higham said yesterday, 'Don't you bother about the gas test if you aren't up to it', but I knew it would be best to kill the bogey I've had about gas, since Mrs Diss and I got such a fright once in the war when the gas 'rolled back' in a big test with Home Guard, Civil Defence and the Army. We saw something was out of hand by the scurrying round, warning off anyone without their gas mask – people had been told to wear one or keep off the streets. If it hadn't been for our mobile {*canteen*} we might have run away, but we turned our backs and held each other's hands tightly, knowing each other's fear. Tonight we had no inconvenience at all. Mrs Higham said, 'Killed your bogey?' I said, 'Yes, though when I was going up the steps of the van I felt my heart pounding as madly as if I was going into action'. She said such a nice thing. She slipped her arm through mine and said, 'Never worry, Lasty, whether you would be able to work hard if trouble came. *I'll* do your share if you're only there. You've got something that would help more than being able to rush round. You don't get rattled.' Then she started to laugh and laugh and added, 'But gosh, if we *are* ever in a tight corner I hope you remember your old wartime swears. Your "Hell's blue light" went round George's office long after you had got another oath.'*

Thursday, 1 May. What curious things minds are. I went to bed last night feeling quite happy about the gas test, and felt myself drifting off to sleep earlier than these last few nights. I wakened with a sound of bitter, bitter weeping. Half awake, I felt that strange stirring of nerves up the back of my neck and head that gives rise to the 'hair stood on end' theory. Age-old sorrow seemed to fill the room, more bitter than shrill keening† in its dull hopelessness. Then I realised it was myself who was so distressed. For a split second I felt there were two of us, and one, a stronger and more serene person, overruled the desperate frightened creature before we merged into one again. I shook with nerves. Sobs

---

*George was Mrs Higham's husband, who worked at Vickers-Armstrongs.

seemed to choke me before I could control them. No wonder I used to frighten my husband so in the beginning of the war when I often had a 'crying jag'.† If I'd been given a golden apple I couldn't have told anyone why I cried so bitterly. I lay spent till my shaking hands could unscrew the top of the thermos of hot water and take a drink. Still feeling badly shaken, I took a codeine tablet and slept fitfully till it was light.

Monday, 5 May. I was walking up the Dalton Road [*to the WVS club meeting*]. It was busy with shoppers and some very exotic-looking people who looked like pros from one of the Revues in Barrow this week. A couple were attracting much attention. He was a huge, nearly black man. She was a dainty brown slip of a thing on high spike heels and an expensive suit and handbag – and a startling 'poodle cut' – and as she wore no hat and her face was rather narrow and wistful, it made the resemblance to a French poodle a bit startling! I had my WVS overcoat and beret on. I thought as they passed they stared very hard, and I'd the feeling the smile on the man's face was personal as he looked at me. They seemed to make up their minds about something and turned back. The man, in a velvety voice, said, 'I beg your pardon, Madam. Didn't you serve in a Forces' Canteen in the war?' I said, 'Yes. Don't you come from Jamaica?', for I recalled a huge black naval man who dwarfed the other sailors. Such nice people. We walked slowly up the road, and the girl said, 'My husband was delighted when he heard the show was coming to Barrow. He said he didn't think Barrow people even noticed his colour!' I said, 'Well, for a small place, we get a lot of different people, all colours, all races, but when they are nice friendly folk, and mix, they seem to fit in.' I asked them to come in the club for a few minutes, knowing Marjorie Fletcher, Mrs Whittam and

Mrs Howson would have arrived and be pleased to meet an old Canteen friend – and they were. Until I saw the man standing amongst us I'd not realised how huge he was. He sings calypso songs and she accompanies him, it seems.

It was a nice meeting and a good speaker – a rambling talk on what she called 'Bluestockings' – gave thumbnail sketches of clever women from the middle of the 18th century.

Sunday, 18 May. Never have we been by the Lake [*Coniston Water*] on a more perfect day. In fact, we couldn't recall its equal. We had a little stroll before lunch. I'd made a salad in a little bowl and cut the cold meat before we left home. We sat down by the water's edge on the rug and enjoyed our lunch. Few people arrived before two o'clock, which meant over two hours of the quiet peace, with little sound beyond the lap of the water on the stones. I washed my hands and started back at the icy chill of the sunlit water. There must have been very heavy thunder showers, for the little streams and rills[†] were full as they drained off the fells and high ground. The day flew past. We had another little walk, and found some old acquaintances parked near when we came back, and we sat and talked – of Singapore, where their son has a super job as an executive in a big airline, and of Civil Defence preparations. The husband was a warden and very keen but pointed out, 'When you get to 60 you don't want to begin again. Let the younger ones have a go. Goodness knows *we* did our share in the last war.'

A dreadfully overweight corgi panted up and collapsed. We didn't know to whom it belonged. I thought of Shan We's love for a rub with a wet duster. I took a picnic napkin and soaked it in the Lake and wiped its poor hot face and ears, and we got it a drink in a tin someone had left. Mr Hetherington lifted it in the shade but the poor thing crawled back to lie by us. They were only pausing to have tea. I began to wonder if I was going to be left with what looked like a dying dog. A voice with an Irish accent sounded, calling 'Tonky', or a name like that. I stood up and saw one of the loveliest, if overweight, women of round about 37 – if her daughter's appearance was a guide. She looked like a poster advertisement for strawberries and cream or the like. She was so excitable and picked up the dog like a baby and talked baby talk. Her husband came up and to hear them slop over that dog was comic when I thought it didn't go so far as to look after the poor thing. They were in a huge car with an Antrim number and were going to tour a week, so what that dog would be like I don't know. I almost said, 'He is far too fat', but looking at its owner I realised it would be tactless, to say the least of it!

We didn't reach home till 8.30. It was so perfect motoring home. I was washing up and saw the blue of the sky disappear and suddenly sea fog rolled in shore, though the weather forecast is good.

Monday, 19 May. I felt it my turn to half wash up [*after the WVS meeting*]. I'd got some bananas to send to Margaret and some leeks and tomatoes and some carpet thread to try and repair the tubing round the car door – this car was a poor job in several ways. The long meeting made me forget how times passed, and we knew we would run into the Shipyard rush if we went into the Town Hall, so we walked through town, knowing we could get on when at each stage workmen would get off. Mrs Howson and Miss Willan decided to walk home. I got off the bus and strolled the five minutes home, enjoying and savouring the loveliness of flowering trees and shrubs in the gardens. The lilac has rarely done as well, the golden laburnum giving me a sadness as I thought of my lovely golden tree which my husband cut so ruthlessly. There's only a few tufts of growth. It will never recover in my lifetime and be so lovely.

Will had committed this offence on 20 September 1951. 'My husband had said he was going to do a bit of gardening and said, "I'm going to thin that laburnum tree well and cut some off the top. It's getting far too big for a small garden." I agreed, and offered to hold the ladder, but he said he could manage. I never looked out of the window, for my back was turned to that side of the garden. When I did look out I couldn't speak. I think I'd have screamed with annoyance – rage – if I'd opened my mouth. He had sawn it off by the top of the trellis. I *loved* that tree more than anything else in the garden.' Some days later Flo, Will's sister, was visiting and looking around the garden. 'She came in with a shocked look and said, "Why ever have you had that lovely, lovely laburnum tree cut off? It will never grow as nice again, and be several years before it flowers by the look of it." I didn't speak. My husband said brightly, "*I* did it. I cut a bit more off than I intended." Flo said, "I should think you did. Looks as if you had a spite against the poor lovely thing – and I know that Dearie and Cliff loved it so"' (2 October 1951). The tree had been a gift from Cliff to his mother.

There was tension in the air when Nella returned home after this WVS meeting.

I was in that quite happy peaceful frame of mind, idly going over the afternoon's plans and discussions. And not prepared to see the half frantic man at the gate, too upset to even tell me what had made him shake so, and robbed him of colour as well as speech. I felt something dreadful must have happened as I half led, half carried him in, put him on the settee and got brandy. After my fright I felt I could have slapped him soundly when he began to reproach me for not telling him how late I'd be! He had been across to see if Mrs Howson had got home, and Mary hadn't told him she had seen me waiting for the bus when she had passed on her cycle. What upset me most was to realise in my heart how he worsened. He cannot bear me out of his sight for long. He never has had friends or liked company, not even of his brothers and sisters.* I'd a little feeling of real terror. No one should so cling or rely on another person, and my ever constant prayer rose to my lips – that I could live longer than he does, that he will never be left lonely and desolate. For a little while I felt such a sense of responsibility it crushed me. It's easy to tell me, 'You should be firm. You have a duty to yourself. You must keep contact with outside.' I made tea – strong, sweet and hot – tea's a great comfort. I couldn't swallow any food, and when I saw my husband didn't eat the piece of thin bread and butter he took on his plate, my worry grew. Mrs Howson came in, in a half laughing manner, saying, 'I feel I'm a little to blame, for Mrs Last washed up instead of me doing it.' She didn't stay long when she saw him lying on the settee, but long enough to prevent him listening to *P.C. 49*, a real grievance! I relaxed in the big chair by the window and mended some socks, but was thankful when I could come to bed.

Sunday, 25 May. Mrs Wilkinson [*recently returned to Barrow*] was here by 3.30. She has put on weight but looks less than her age – about 67. She was as jolly and lively as 32 years ago, when I first knew her. She made us both laugh as she said as she looked me up and down, 'Just as elegant as ever. I bet that dress cost next to nothing and it looks a model.' She was always a bit dumpy, with a poor taste in clothes, with a longing to look well dressed that

---

*A few days later Nella wrote of Will's attachment to his car: 'after myself, it's his chief anchor to life and living' (28 May 1952).

she described as 'looking elegant'. Her life is like a story book romance. She met her Southern Rhodesian husband on a chance visit to Morecambe. He had brought his two daughters to school. She married at 34 and went to a totally different life some miles from Bulawayo, to a country store that sold everything to settlers, learned to ride and love horses, and had a happy life till her husband died having an operation. Depression by then hung over Rhodesia. What property and plots of land there was was divided between her and her two stepdaughters and her share only valued at £2,000. Now it's worth £40,000. She decided to close with a big syndicate and cabled her lawyer to sell half the property. Now Bulawayo has so grown, in a place where large eleven-storeyed flats are being erected. She told of her house boy, a 12-year-old 'pican' who cleaned and polished, washed and ironed, washed and exercised the dog, 'kept the windows like crystal' and had a passion for washing curtains – for £3 a month. Her part-time gardener, shared with three friends, costs about £4 a week and she has every kind of vegetables and fruit, a perfect lawn and stone garden with a collection of English rock plants. Their food consists of mealies,[†] 'lots of steak' and the vegetables grown. She is shocked at most food prices and our shortages and says she could never stand the cold dampness of our winter. She had a good knowledge of South African policy and of racial 'differences', saying, 'In Bulawayo there's no nonsense about blacks being as good as whites'. There's an accepted difference and a feeling of understanding, with, as she says, 'not as yet that urge to leap centuries that have made non-coloured people as they are. They are more inclined to leave burdens, responsibilities and judgements to anyone in authority.'

Wednesday, 28 May. I've had a good if rather rueful laugh at myself today. I didn't feel so well – a bit breathless again – so planned

jobs where I'd not have to bend. Mrs Salisbury is always so understanding if she sees my lips a bit blue. I washed some socks and
stockings through and used Dreft. As I put the packet back on
the shelf I thought idly – that competition [*for purchasers of Dreft*]
must be decided by now. I wonder who was the lucky winner. I
went to hang them on the line and heard the bell chime, and as I
came in Mrs Salisbury said, 'There's a gentleman at the door who
wants to see you'. As I went down the hall I saw a well dressed,
rather city looking man, handsome in rather a Jewish way, who
raised his hat and said, 'Mrs Last? I've called ...' – I felt a tingle
run right through me, and talk about hearing birdies sing!!! –
but heard the rest of the sentence, 'to see if you have any scrap
gold, old watches, brooches, tie pins', etc. It's a good approach to
glance at the name on the gate I suppose. I didn't exactly think he
was the 'Hedley Group' man. I suppose it was with the competition's running through my mind.

   I turned out my oddment drawer in the dressing table, where
I keep cosmetic oddments, beads and jewellery, toilet oddments,
etc. There was half a bottle of Chypre[†] perfume, which ranks with
garlic in my faddy[†] nostrils. I'd put some shabby handkerchiefs,
ditto felt buttonholes and a comb I didn't want, to give to Mrs
Salisbury for her girl of 12. Holding up the perfume I said doubt-
fully, 'Would you like this scent?' The look of rapture on her face
was startling, and she said, 'Would you *really* give it to me? I've
never had a bottle of scent and I do love it.' In her delight she
sang the rest of the morning – a fearsome noise, she is tone deaf.

Thursday, 5 June. Margaret came in with the baby, and the wee
thing romped and rolled with Shan We. It often surprises me how
he adores babies and small children. There was a hoot outside and
Margaret hurried off. They were going to the Fair, and later we

saw them there. Last year two long rows of luxury motor trailers and caravans had palmists' and clairvoyants', crystal gazers' and phrenologists' signs, and I didn't see a single person having their fortune told. This year only five fortune tellers – and no one in the least interested! My husband was quite huffy last year when I firmly refused to have my hand read. It was always my custom before the war to do so, when I went to Blackpool. There was a Madame Curl in Olympia who was uncannily good. It's 16 years ago since she rather shook me with what she said, as she told me of my removal, dark shadows and bitter tears which I would shed with many others (the war), and, 'Just when things look brightest for you, when the shadows have passed, deeper trouble – you will be a widow, and for signs, when your two children cross water to live'. Today when my husband kept teasing me to go, saying he would pay, if that was stopping me, I pointed out if he was all that keen, he should go!

My memory of Whitsuntide Fairs at Ulverston goes back as long as I remember and it fascinates me to see the changes the two wars have brought. From gypsy booths and music, and 'freak' shows, horse-drawn caravans, wrestling, log splitting for 'silver shillings', soft-voiced, dark-eyed half clad children whose glisten-ing teeth and shining curls were the admiration and envy of so many, steam roundabouts to electricity, when a different type of people took over, to the well dressed business type of today, with a very small coterie of real gypsies, who I noticed kept aloof. Bal-loons and comic hats were the chief lines at small stalls. People were buying 'fairings'† to take home in Woolworths and [*there were*] two big furniture vans with loudly 'spieling' Manchester Jews, selling towels and pillowslips, pairs of sheets 'all direct from the mills'. That the standing crowds made traffic jams was a detail. It was *Fair* day, when no one bothered about much – they rarely do anyway in that quiet market town – when, if the powers that be suddenly take the notion that cars must *not* be parked on each side of the road and in every side street, busy farmers, in for a brief market day, blandly refuse to take notice. Not one side show, no wrestling booth, no 'freaks', like bearded ladies or 'the fattest girl on earth'.

We laughed again at a family yarn. One of my father's brothers was a restless, nosy child, as Cliff was when small. He had been to the Fair, which then came to Barrow, and seen all the sights. The one that took his fancy was 'a lovely mermaid with a real tail'. The next day he had gone with a friend, snooping round the tents and caravans, and a voice had called from an open caravan door and a lady with yellow hair had asked him to go for some musk cachous[†] for her. When they came back with the sweets, she was busy sewing, and to poor Walter's horror, she was stitching sequins on her tail! It shook that 8-year-old's faith in things. His mother, a gentle sweet soul, used to say sorrowfully, 'Our Walter has never been the same little lad since'.

We had a cup of tea, and I met several old friends from the country, including a cousin I'd not seen since the beginning of the war. It was a really happy afternoon. My husband wasn't at all cranky at me gossiping. I made toast and scrambled eggs for tea. It was nearly 6 o'clock when we got in. I felt tired and sat sewing, after writing to Arthur. Comparisons are supposed to always be odious. Every Thursday evening I think of the old *ITMA* days – Ted Ray's show falls very far behind it – or else, like other features of the war years, they have a kind of halo, never again to be recaptured.

Saturday, 7 June. Mrs Howson called on her way to town to say we had better go before 1.30 to the church to see Julia Diss's wedding, as there was 200 invited guests and she knew most of the WVS she had met wanted to go into church. Mrs Atkinson, who always rushes off at the last minute wherever she goes, set off with Margaret at 1.45 – 'plenty of time' – but had to stand outside. It was one of the most fashionable weddings in Barrow since the war – men in morning dress and grey top hats, the women in model gowns. But I had a good laugh to myself, and shared it with a few WVS friends afterwards. THE best and smartest dressed woman amongst the crowd, made up largely of Julia's young friends, was a school friend of mine, so she must be about my age. She is very slender and looked more so in a straight and narrow-skirted dress in fine black woollen material, black court shoes and almost transparent black nylons. She had a string of pearls and earrings to match, a short 'full' coat the colour of made mustard, with wide sleeves, showing black chamois ruffled on her thin wrists, and a shallow-crowned, wide-brimmed black straw hat. She stood out like a rare hot house flower amongst cottagey flowers, models or not; and knowing Brownie of old, I knew her outfit would have been made by herself.

Mrs Diss is a kind person; so that poor Sheila should not feel out of it, the reception was held in a big marquee on the lawn. A leading hotel did all the catering – rare for them to do outside functions when they have large beautifully equipped rooms and every convenience at hand. It kept fine but I thought of those short-sleeved dresses with a shudder. I'd a thin woollen dress and my new woollen coat on and still felt chilly. I didn't get in until after 3.30. There seemed so many people I knew. My husband had been to bed and had a sleep and felt a bit better, but looked ghastly and made no mention he would like to go out. I sat and told him all the news of the wedding, though he didn't seem very interested. I made a salad to cheese. The tomatoes are almost as nice as local grown. There was bread and butter, honey and cakes.

I'd half expected Mrs Howson to be in, but she didn't come in till nearly 7 o'clock, and, I was very much relieved to see, in a much less prickly humour. She has such a snob complex. She wouldn't join Margaret and Mrs Atkinson as we came out of church, saying plaintively, 'I know it's snobbish of me, but I don't like to walk down the road with people like Mrs Atkinson', and she glanced down at her really lovely jacquard suit in soft blue, with gloves and shoes the exact shade. I chuckled spitefully as I thought if it had fit better and hadn't had the absurd modern bustle effect at the front where she already had one of her own, she would have looked nicer. I wonder if her spitefulness springs from the knowledge she has nothing behind her. She has always spent everything she could get hold of, in a kind of gesture. It's not as if she has been used to anything when young, and her insistence on perfection doesn't extend to her 'underneaths' – she even buys the cheapest girdle or corset. She gazed at the lovely dresses, the really gorgeous summer fur or soft evening fur capes of some of the older women, at make-ups and what she calls 'hair dos', really in covetous admiration, but on the surface with contempt. *Nothing* fitted. Nothing was 'suitable for her age', or height, weight, colouring, etc. A pawky† Scotswoman, whose dry humour has enlivened many a dull committee meeting and who stood rather behind Mrs Howson, looked very critically at the too wide armholes that gave a baggy instead of smooth fit across the back of the lovely blue suit, and glanced at me with an 'As others see us' look. She scoffed at the men in morning dress as, with a toss of her head, she said, 'Catch me letting Steve make himself look so ridiculous. I bet they are hired anyway.' I pointed out if that *had* been the case, they would have been more immaculate and not looking so well worn. Why she puts up with my company is always a puzzle. I rarely agree, and often, not very tactfully, infer she is jealous.

I longed to hear her say this afternoon that she couldn't come in this evening, feeling I'd had my ration of catty remarks today, but she was quite different. What remarks *were* passed were, if not exactly complimentary, at least only critical and not so utterly destructive, and we laughed in rueful sympathy at two near enemies who both had the same on, not only the same dresses in deep blue and white, but exactly the same hats, gloves and wide reversible scarves. I doubt if they could see each other in church. We know them both and pictured their feelings when they met.

Saturday, 14 June. We went down town. In the market I saw a wide choice of lovely, slightly flawed 'export' remnants, and I could have lengths of from 3 to 4½ yards, at prices ranging from 17s 6d to 25s. I'd have liked two glazed chintz lengths to make Edith and I dresses, priced at 5 and 6½ guineas in the shops, costing less than 30s to make. I've read articles from time to time about American comics and the like, thinking of the day when my two little boys loved 'Tiger Tim' and the like. I was looking at a big magazine stall, hoping to buy a couple of light novels for my husband to read, knowing none of Arthur's books would interest him.* I saw rows of *Life in the Future*, *Tales of Thrills and Horror*, *True Love Stories*, etc. I've often said lightly 'My breath nearly stopped', but felt it true this morning. I never imagined such sexy, pornographic pictures and captions, such sadistic, grim torture, such 'Might is right' type of trash. How they got past the censors who ban books is a mystery.

---

*Nella and Will were soon to travel to London to stay for a fortnight with Arthur and his family.

I watched two 'half baked' working lads of 13–15. They had that uncertain look of slack mouth, gaping open, pimples and 'oooh-er' manner that 'half baked' fits so aptly, and which seems to affect a type of boy at the age. One being over a magazine I'd leafed through, where a woman crook of peculiar build, mostly long shapely legs, sensuous bust, rolling eyes and a mane of untidy blonde hair, seemed to solve the remarkable situation she got into by showing her legs from heel to buttocks, or jabbing a revolver into people with the tense remark, 'If *you* don't talk, my gat† does, big boy'. I felt slightly sick to see his tongue licking his loose lips and hear his little snicker. I could see the page of the magazine the other boy was looking at – Japs torturing American G.I.s, twisting wire round their necks till their eyes bulged, or round their wrists till blood spurted from each finger tip.* He seemed to quiver slightly, shifting his weight from one foot to the other. The stall holder came up and snarled, 'How often have I told you two not to touch those books. If you want one, buy it, and be off.' They sidled round the corner, evidently knowing the man would soon be going to the other end of the long stall. When I think of the so-called 'French' novels he used to sell so furtively – I saw one of Godfrey Winn's 'Oh So Sweet' novels with a lurid paperback – I marvelled again at the stacks of American 'fifth column' to youth being brought into the country – bought, too, with dollars.**

---

*These villainous images were almost certainly intended to be of Chinese (or possibly North Korean) figures.

**Nella seems to be saying that these imported products of American popular culture were both betraying the youth of Britain and a drag on its fragile economy (because they would have had to be paid for with scarce dollars).

Later that month Nella and Will left Barrow for London – it was their first train trip together for years.

Monday, 23 June. I don't feel I am the traveller I used to be. I felt wearied by the train journey, even more, apparently, than my husband felt. Arthur and Peter were at Euston and we got a taxi to New Southgate. We were agreeably surprised by the really lovely house Arthur bought, and Blake Road all seems to have owner occupiers, which shows in well tended front gardens. Built only 26 years ago, it's on a 'modern' plan, with nice-sized rooms, and a French window leads to a long, rather wild but pleasant strip of garden, quite cultivated enough for where two small lively boys need to play. They *are* little loves. Christopher at 18 months promises to be as 'old-fashioned' as Peter. They seem little people with ideas and views, pursuits and occupations to busy them. We sat and listened to the wireless before going to bed fairly early. Peter slept with me, my husband in his small bed in the smallest room.*

Thursday, 26 June. We went out, taking a trolley bus as far as Holborn. All transport seems so easy, but there's a lot of walking to be done. I set off with a swelling ankle and foot and when I rose in Lyons felt I'd have to be a bit easier on it if I hadn't to crock up.† We went to Greenwich by boat – a lovely trip as we met a cool breeze – and then sat on the pier, watching river traffic, feeling we *were* on holiday. Every oddment I've read of the Thames' history seemed to flow through my mind, whirling in a montage of peoples of every nationality and colour, American

---

*The younger Lasts' home was at 64 Blake Road, N11; the nearest Tube station was and still is Bounds Green on the Piccadilly line, about half a mile away.

and German – or Swiss in leather shorts – docks, cargo ships, and the hundreds of school children in parties being taken by steamer. In one huge party I heard at least four names of schools through the megaphone – the proportion of half caste children, or at least with a very strong trace of colour in their parentage – and so widely different. It's amazing the lack of difference in school age and adolescents there is between South and North – just the different accent. We were in Woolworths about the lunch hour, and the things they chose! I only hoped they got a decent meal when they got home. I'd have awarded top place for oddity, though, to a gentle old world type of man who could have been a country parson or doctor. In Lyons he had a glass of lemonade with ice cream dropped in, and a double portion of ice cream, with four wafers, and by his look enjoyed his odd lunch. I wrote my diary and a letter to Cliff as I sat on the pier. My husband went for a walk. The cool breeze seemed to lessen the swelling on my foot, taking a little of the worried feeling I had, and we had a simple tea at a café on Greenwich Pier before setting off for Westminster again ...

As we walked down the hill to the Tube this morning my husband was full of wild plans to sell up as soon as we got home, and buy a house down here. Because he feels lifted out of himself so much, he feels a London suburb would cure him of every ill, not realising we so live in ourselves. I pointed out he hadn't the energy to take advantage of all the little functions at home – wouldn't visit, go to a show, etc. He maintains it would be different if he lived in London. My remark was that New Southgate was not 'London', that going up the river would always mean a journey as far as Lakeside – *and* home again. I made him pout and he became so moody as I said NO. I've not altered my view always held – London means a 2d ride, or higher now of course with fare increases, to Kensington, Forest Gate, Chelsea or the like, not even Hampstead, Chiswick or Putney a second choice, and housing problems *terrible*. In his present mood he 'will make a change as soon as we go back – I *want* to get out of Barrow'. As I've always maintained, it was what we should have done at first when we knew he would have to retire, but reminded him how much more money we were spending in Barrow. Any move would have to be down scale, not where we would need twice as much if we were not to be more restricted than at present. I began to feel glad it was my own house as I listened. I'd a growing conviction he would have gone a bit haywire otherwise.

Saturday, 28 June. Arthur had off work this morning and we went down to Kensington, really to go and see Derry and Tom's roof garden. A bad day, really, for we didn't have time to look round much and have our lunch before the shops closed. Still, I'd talked of the lovely 'unexpected' place so much to my husband and he was satisfied, though we would have liked to spend more time. We got a really good, well cooked lunch, at just under 6s a head – cream of vegetable soup, two *huge* portions of fillet of plaice and more chips than could be eaten, and a strawberry ice and coffee – and Arthur and his father had a light ale and Edith cider. The two little boys had a 'special' – there was a good choice of children's meals. Peter was good, but to see Christopher in his high chair, blue eyes blazing and golden curly hair drying in the draught after the heat of his hat, seize his fork and begin was a joy. He had his fish cut up, but refused to have any long chips touched, even if they did need spearing on the fork with his fingers. His look of ecstasy at his strawberry ice in the goblet, with the biscuit still in, amused the waitress and manageress who was near ...

I love Kensington, and was astonished to see so many large

maisonette type of houses for sale, and so many dirty, neglected ones as if owned and just shut up. I'd like a good small flat over-looking the gardens, though my first choice would be a small house in one of the unexpected quiet streets off Kensington Church Street. The types, colours and languages which swirled round were a joy. I'd have liked to linger, but Edith wanted to come home and wash! – such a *huge* pile. We had tea. I'd been on my aching right foot and ankle too much to go strolling round the neighbourhood with my husband, and knew I'd better finish Edith's sun dress. She looked so nice today – a new navy moiré silk dress, small white hat and gloves – pity she hadn't a pin in her hat; it blew up an escalator and was only rescued when it had got nearly to the top – and she didn't bother to change to wash till I tactfully told her my sleeved overall would perhaps fit and she could have it. After 10 o'clock I helped her hang all on the line. I'd washed my dress earlier and ironed it. I'd a sneaking wonder what the neighbours thought of our garden of washing on Saturday night – they seem very conventional.*

Monday, 30 June. It's a real heatwave. I think longingly of sea breezes in the rattle and noise of the Tube.** We would have been content to sit in the garden this morning, but the little boys were cross and screamed. Christopher was tired for he had been

---

*Early the next morning, 'I looked down at the untidy line of washing, and crept down in my dressing gown and brought all in, smiling to myself at my deep conventional streak which made me feel so horrified at the sight.'
**Will was not always sensitive to the protocols for using the escalators in Tube stations. 'My husband has been unpopular a few times', Nella wrote on 1 July. 'In spite of my warnings – and given by Cliff – to keep always to the right, he will use the left, and has been bumped as well as told curtly "keep to the right".' (Nella mistakenly writes 'left' instead of 'right' in quoting this admonition.)

up before 6 o'clock. I thought of children in flats and closed-in streets. We went down by Tube, already feeling hot, men in shirts and pants and girls in topless sun suits, ladies waving little paper fans, looking as if the two last lots *could* have been going to the Sales; breaths of coolth and sweetness at Covent Garden station when boys brought huge bundles of green forms, presumably for fish shops, and women and men had even bigger sheaves of gorgeous flowers. We had a light snack of tea and a sandwich at Lyons and got on a boat to Kew – in blistering heat, when to rest arms or back unexpectedly on the rail was to jump suddenly. We had a nice Australian sitting by us – we met him first the other day. He lives in the 'back blocks' 100 miles from Melbourne. When he goes on to his verandah he can 'see two lights and likes it that way'. I felt I understood. The masses of perspiring people and the cross children around and the 'breathed' air everywhere stifled me. I'm constantly amazed at my husband's seemingly inexhaustible fund of 'go' and think of Dr Miller's 'out of patience' with his complaints of 'no strength' and 'going all to pieces' and saying that most nervous illness was no physical illness – it could be thrown off.

We had a very nice tray lunch at Kew – good salad with ham, a roll and butter and a fresh salad of pineapple, orange, cherries and sweet apple with a little wedge of ice cream. The shade of the trees drew people, the lovely flowers and hot houses only being noticed by parties of people who seemed to have come by motor coach, and dozens of children, with harassed-looking teachers seeming bent on telling them everything. A huge though shapely figure moved majestically along alone, a negress *really* black as coal, in the hottest most shrieking shade of zinnia purple. Our eyes met and she smiled in so friendly a fashion as she seemed to flow down the path. Such interesting people you see – the lovely flower-like

Eastern women in filmy saris, beautiful as houris, fascinate me, as I wonder if they are on holiday, knowing their mothers would have been strictly purdah†, making me realise as nothing else the mass movement to 'freedom' of today.

Monday, 7 July. We had the most enjoyable day of our holiday and at the last place I'd have imagined – the Food Fair at Olympia! I knew the right bus to take from Piccadilly for Cliff – I used to use a No. 9 or 73 to go Richmond way and passed Olympia. I'd never seen a big Food Fair, but used to like the travelling Exhibition that came to Barrow. We were in at 11 o'clock and didn't leave till 4.30. Being Monday, there was no crush, and till mid-afternoon not many people at all. We had lunch at the best place of Lyons yet – quite good soup, roll and butter, and good choice of sweet, with a salad extra, made up at the counter … I *love* gadgets and new ways with food. I use 'Serocream' and watched new ways of icing and piping, and a kind of 'baba' made out of a piece of cake, small block of ice cream 'insulated' with a thick layer of the whipped cream, and scorched rather than baked in a very hot oven. But I pointed out to the two nice young fellows that they hadn't anything as nice as the 'butterfly' cream bun I make, or the sandwich with raspberry jam and thick cream between – 'Ordinary no doubt, but after all, ain't we all?'

It grew hot. We rested frequently in comfortable chairs, watching the ebb and flow around. Even since my last visits, six years ago, there seem a more cosmopolitan crowd, and India and her peoples, with South Americans, make the biggest difference. I dearly love perfume, and nowadays there's no 'lasting' fragrance, even in simple things like lavender, when once handfuls strewn in linen kept it fragrant till lavender time came round again. Some of the expensively dressed, dark-skinned ladies in saris have the most beautiful clear oil perfume. I coveted a big bottle. I bought wee oddments of 3d jars of jam, crisps and biscuits for the little boys, and three small 9d jars of Brand's meat paste, for Edith and I will make sandwiches of one to eat on our way home. We sat in Kensington Gardens till the rush had gone in bus and tubes.

The next day they were exposed to a different slice of London life. 'We went down to Euston to book two seats on the train, seeing our first real "working" part of London. I realised the hopelessness of behaviour and decency of many evacuees was the result of such drab places, where ordinary standards of cleanliness were impossible in the smoke and squalor of railways and big concerns which made smoke and soot.' Then, on Wednesday the 9th, they were back in Barrow, and 'I was surprised to find our house seem so small after Arthur's'.

There were, of course, some local happenings to catch up on. Mrs Higham 'told me Sheila Diss had a lovely baby boy after an oddly easy confinement. The doctors say it's usual in polio cases. Poor girl – she has been dreadfully depressed since Julia was married and spent her honeymoon in Paris. At 24, it's hard to feel she will be more or less crippled for the rest of her life' (10 July). Mrs Salisbury, at her first Wednesday visit to Nella's house, had alarming news to report about one of her boarders, 'a very odd type' whose 'great hobby was model airplanes. He always seemed to have young boys of 14 and 15 around, but they were all interested in model making, and he always seemed busy developing photos'. One day 'Mrs Salisbury was turning out his room and saw some of the photos and to use her own words "I felt I could have died of shock". They sounded not only beastly but dangerous. The naked boys in acts of perversion and masturbation were plainly recognised from the group he went about with. Mrs Salisbury was the most shocked by photos of a 15-year-old Grammar school boy, a member of the Scouts and choir and one of the two sons of a widow Mrs Salisbury knew. After thinking things over, she took the photos to her, saying, "I'd have been glad if anyone had let me know about the dangerous friendship if it had been one of my boys". There was a big row. The widow wasn't without the advice of sensible friends, and a condition of not going to the police was that he had never to be seen in boys' company – and the photos are retained by the one who gave the advice as "guarantee"' (16 July).

Saturday, 19 July. If joyous days should be called red letter days, today is a black one. My little Shan We died suddenly, apparently of a heart attack. He ate his usual good breakfast, went to play on the lawn and ran in hurriedly when it began to rain suddenly, and sat on my husband's lap for the rest of the morning. I'd tidied up, and machined[†] for an hour. There was good beef soup, cold brisket beef and salad, cornflour sweet and stewed raspberries. Shan We coaxed a meaty bit of gristle and ate it, and then sat on the rug till I'd finished lunch and then jumped on my lap as usual, his paws on my chest, his clear blue eyes lovingly on my face. I remembered again how much more loving – if that was possible – he had been since he came home [*from the boarding kennel*]. I rose soon saying, 'I'm going to wash up, and then you can relax till 2 o'clock' – we had an appointment at the Hospital with Dr Wadsworth, the visiting psychiatrist. I'd lifted Shan We down on to the rug, and my husband passed back and forward clearing the table. It couldn't have been more than five minutes when he said, 'Come quickly, Dearie'. I saw my little cat lying on his side, his tongue hanging out, his head lolled helplessly as I put my hands under him and raised him. I'd once brought him out of a similar attack when he was only a few weeks old, with whisky and holding him pressed to my warm body till I got a fire going, but today half a teaspoon of neat brandy poured into his open mouth was no use, or warmth and massaging his heart, which had ceased to beat before I lifted him. The light died in his jewel-blue eyes.

I felt stunned – and so terribly worried at the way my husband took it. I never saw him so distraught. I wanted to phone to the Hospital and say he couldn't come, but he roused himself a little and we went. Dr Wadsworth was shocked at his appearance, till he knew about our little friend, and then was so understanding. I've always found Ulstermen to be insensitive. We came home. I'd laid my pet in his bed and covered him warmly in the forlorn hope a miracle *might* happen. I could not believe he would never rush to meet us again. My husband dug his grave in the flower border, and we made a soft cushion of lawn grass clippings and laid him on – he looked peacefully sleeping. As we covered him with more grass I murmured, 'Goodbye, little cat. Thank you for your love and affection. It's been grand knowing you.' And I wondered how many people were buried so sadly.*

I made tea, but beyond several cups of tea and a little bread and butter we couldn't eat. I had a lost feeling when no eager little blue-eyed cat jumped on my lap. The moment I'd finished I looked at my husband's face and shaking hands and thought of Dr Wadsworth's advice 'It would be as well to get another Siamese as soon as possible. I don't like *any* upset for Mr Last.' I asked him if he would like another, but he said simply, 'No, it would never be Shan We'. I said coaxingly, 'Wouldn't you like a little dog? You could take him out.' Nothing could rouse him. I felt I pushed my own grief deeper and deeper till I was choking, Kipling was right – you should 'never give your heart to a dog to tear'. I felt I hadn't to keep anything I loved. I looked at poor

---

*'You carried flowers for Shan We as if he was a person', Will later remarked (20 July).

old Murphy with near loathing as I thought, 'Oh *why* couldn't it have been you? At turned 15, you are past much sweetness of life.' My dear Shan We was only 6, loving life and living, radiating love and affection. With Cliff buying him and the trouble he was to rear, he never seemed 'just an animal'. I'd a feeling I'd lost a real link with Cliff.

I coaxed my husband to take two codeine tablets and gave him some brandy and water, feeling really afraid he would collapse altogether, wondering what I should do. Often he has said half-jokingly to Shan We, 'I wish you were a little dog and could come for a walk'. I felt wearily I didn't want to face training a puppy. I like cats best, but realising how on the edge my poor man is feeling I'd undertake to train a hippo if it made him happy or gave him an interest. We went for a little walk. I suddenly thought of my hairdresser – she bought a Cairn puppy some time ago, an adorable beastie. My husband saw it and wondered 'if Shan We would agree with a puppy if we got one'. I rang her up for a chat. She lost a much loved dog at about seven years old and said 'A friend advised us to get another one straight away'. I asked her if she thought there were any puppies at the breeding kennels where she got hers, and she said, 'Ring up and see. The number is in the phone book – a place near Carnforth.' When my husband came in, looking wild-eyed and nervy, I said, 'Now if you *would* like a puppy, I know where I might get one'. He didn't speak. He didn't seem to hear properly. I thought wildly 'If I could go tonight and get one I'd gladly go – *anything* to take that lost expression off your face'. I felt my constant prayer rise to my lips – that I could live longer than him. I felt little bargains in a montage of wild pleas. *Whatever* happened to me, I'd never complain if only I *could* live longer, to always look after him.

AFTERWORD

Following their adventures in London, Nella and Will resumed their (mostly) quiet lives in Barrow-in-Furness. There were changes in their household, one of which was the acquisition of a dog to replace Shan We. Nella had mixed feelings about dogs, and clearly preferred cats. Still, a dog it was to be, and on 21 July 1952, after inspecting a litter of seven puppies, Nella wrote that 'I'd not have known where to choose, but one little fellow was determined to be chosen – he made such a fuss over my husband. I was delighted. The colour came back into his cheeks. There was no doubt from the first.' The puppy was named Garry; he and Will hit it off reasonably well and in due course regularly went out together for walks. Nella, an exponent of firm discipline, thought Will over-indulgent with Garry. In January 1953, 9 Ilkley Road became a cat-free household when old Murphy, aged 15½ and seriously ill, was put down.

Passing scenes of daily life continued to attract Nella's attention.* On 14 January 1953 she remarked on how 'Fog or not, the gypsy people keep to their routine', which involved visits to houses in Barrow in January. 'A *lovely* girl rang this afternoon, and the coloured woollen raincoat and hood of deep cherry made her look like a magazine cover. She had a very smart case, specially made to contain toilet articles and perfumes etc., and there were

---

*The following appendix presents selections from the one significant facet of public life in 1953 that she wrote about at length – the mobilisation in Barrow in February of help for flood victims in other parts of the country.

Red Rose nylons – America's best, "no shoddy English ones", as she explained. I didn't want anything but "for luck" bought some talc powder. She offered to tell my fortune. I thanked her and said I'd rather not, and felt taken a little aback when she said, "Well, perhaps not, it's one of the bad roads you're travelling just now, lady".' A few weeks later Mrs Salisbury saw some gypsies going door to door in a nearby street, and 'she was very disappointed when they didn't call. She had sixpence ready to "cross the palm" to have her fortune told. I said, "They wanted me to give two half crowns the other week. The sixpenny days are gone for good"' (18 March 1953).

From time to time Nella thought about moving out of Barrow, and while this did not happen, she did have a clear sense of the sort of bungalow – 'with one room in the roof' – that would suit her. 'It would have a long sunshine room, one end to be used as a dining room in a big bay and with a radiator, the big open fireplace heating the living end. A good kitchen place, with an Esse† for cooking and heating water, two fair-sized bedrooms, bathroom and lavatory, with the room in the roof sparsely furnished for my families' visits, wood block or the new concrete floors. NO fitted carpets – rugs everywhere. Fixture wardrobes made between bedrooms, with sliding doors, window seats with cushions, divan beds with bed head fixtures instead of bedside table, and not one unnecessary article of any kind' (15 August 1953). Hers, clearly, was a very spare, streamlined and functional vision of household comfort.

Occasionally she and Will had a memorably cheerful outing. One Saturday in early summer she persuaded him to attend a garden party at Aldingham, and 'he enjoyed every minute. The lawns overlooking Morecambe Bay were bathed in golden hot sunshine, and the big trees' shade was more than welcome. The vicar had written a little pageant based on the history of the Norman church, the little brief life of Lady Jane Grey – who was arrested while seeking shelter at the old Aldingham Hall – and bringing in brief items of interest. *Very* well acted by villagers, members of the choir and school children.' This was an upbeat event. 'Everyone seemed so gay and happy in the sun and sea air – really the most wonderful day for such a function. I met so many folk I knew. I felt it was like a party of my own, without the work and worry entailed' (27 June 1953).

Nella was sensitive to the passage of time, and she occasionally thought about the momentous changes that civilisation – notably her civilisation – was experiencing, which gave rise in her mind to big questions. Modern technologies certainly produced vastly more power – but to what purpose? On 7 September 1952 she was wondering if 'there's already a sign of a "brave new world" after all, not in our time – *or* in our children – but perhaps when they have harnessed atomic power to something useful, and then turned to put all the resources that split the atom to simple, necessary things, like food growing, irrigating useless deserts, and finding cures for things like polio.' On another occasion she commented on talk that she had heard of the possibility that one H-bomb might destroy the whole world. 'No wonder there's such a "live for today", "grab while you can" philosophy today' (17 November 1952). One evening that autumn she thought about humans in space. 'When I came to bed I leaned against the casement, looking at the so bright stars, wondering afresh how man could be so presumptuous as to think none but our Earth has inhabitants, and idly wondering if man would ever land on the moon and other planets, glimpsing in a very small remote way that we are indeed entering on a new era' (16 October 1952).

This new era left Nella with mixed feelings, partly because

she detected a decline of mutual trust. She heard of (and perhaps observed the results of) some vandalism of the decorations and floral displays in Barrow for the Queen's Coronation, and this led her to a gloomy reflection. 'Times change, but in some ways I *do* feel the old ways of responsibility towards others and their possessions were good. I never knew fear – of lonely places, roads, living alone and the like – but today's "attacks" and disregard of other people's property makes for fear. No country person even would go out and leave a key under the mat. I feel in many ways our young Queen belongs to *my* girlhood, when there was right and wrong, kindness or cruelty, clear-cut ways of thought, and when "spiv" action was yet to be universal' (2 June 1953).

Other changes that she thought about were more mundane. On Sunday 25 January 1953, after an outing to Grange-over-Sands, she thought about 'how shortages and circumstances are changing people's habits', notably Sabbath observance. 'I never saw as many big washings blowing in the sun and wind on a Sunday and in gardens of houses whose owners wouldn't under *any* circumstances put washing out on a Sunday – Saturday even! Farmers worked normal too, not actually doing field work, but busy tidying, carting turnips from pies† in nearby fields to be cut in barns, clearing out shippens† and pigsties, and carting away the dung and straw.' When Will and Nella later arrived home they 'saw another changed [*Sunday*] habit – two big farmers' carts coming slowly down our road – and at the top could see loads of farmyard manure dumped on the sidewalk. We wondered how it would be possible to clear it into the gardens before it was dark. Bad enough having it delivered on a Sunday morning, but hopeless late afternoon this time of the year. We wondered too, knowing the habits of one neighbour, if they would be in till much later in the evening.'

Then there were the thoughts of the might-have-beens in Nella's life, and the roads not taken. One day, when reviewing her personal past, she wrote of some decisions made when she and Will were young parents. 'We were down in Southampton [*in 1919*], Cliff a baby of a few months. My husband had such good prospects. A man – he was in the Navy – wanted him to go in partnership, building as well as shop fitting. His wife and I were very good friends and she adored my two little boys. My father, who had always said he would retire to St Austell in Cornwall, decided to come down to me when he retired. In every way the future looked good – and free from worry of narrow-minded in-laws who thought a son in the business and a slave at his father's command were one and the same. With my husband's fear of change of any kind, he decided to come back to Barrow, and I came back to a deeper bondage, till when Father died and I had a little income all my own. I refused to be answerable for every gesture, every deed, years of ill health and operations, aggravated by rheumatism keeping my husband off work for months at a time. I often feel we took the wrong road when we chose to come back to Barrow' (3 May 1953). Later she disclosed her more general feeling on the subject of regret. 'It's what you *haven't* done when you get to my age, not what you *have* done, that saddens you' (19 July 1953).

Nella was in a ruminative mood at the end of 1952, and she wrote of the way Will thought of her. 'My poor dear talked as if I was a cross between an angel, Mrs Beeton* and a kind a Pollyanna, which combined to make some kind of anchor in his mind.' She was deeply aware of the tension between the image that others had of her, as a strong, cheerful, confident, even serene

---

*Author of the famous *Book of Household Management* (1861).

person, and how she felt inside, which was so often weak and tired – 'I feel sometimes like a hollow shell' (31 December 1952). Life was wearing her down. 'I often feel of late,' she wrote on 2 June 1953 (the day of the Queen's coronation), 'I'm a goldfish in a bowl, never achieving anything in my round of days, the bowl a little wall that shuts out every outside interest or dims and distorts' (M-O Coronation Directive, June 1953). Will's mental fragility was a continual concern (on 9 March 1953 she spoke of the strings of his mind loosening); constantly trying to soothe him and buoy him up was a strain; she often felt drained and 'tired beyond words'; and ill health darkened many of her days. Nella, in fact, predeceased her husband. She died in June 1968, in her 79th year; Will outlived her by eleven months.*

'I'd a note from M-O this morning', Nella wrote on 14 October 1952. 'It rather set my mind at rest. At best I could never see any value in my scribblings but nowadays nothing seems to happen. My life is so narrow. Arthur said "Don't give up your diary. It must be of some interest in some way." Odd a nice little "Thank you" note should come soon after he said it.' Nella's self-assessment was not inaccurate – her life had narrowed, and, as a rule, there was much less going on to stimulate her pen. The best of her writing was over. Still, this vigorous diary writing, which began in August 1939, had been sustained for more than a dozen years – she continued to write for M-O until February 1966 – and has now yielded three books. During the years up to the early 1950s Nella Last was, at her best, an astute observer of English

---

*Their sons died at younger ages. Arthur, whose health had been poor through much of his adulthood – his mother worried a lot about him – died in 1979 in his mid-sixties; Cliff died in 1991.

life, and often of herself and her relations with others. She wrote colourfully about her family and neighbours and community, her daily movements in and around Barrow, her household affairs, her visiting and meetings with others, the sights and sounds of nature – and also about what she and others said to each other, in both private and public spaces. Sometimes, too, she pondered deeper questions of war and peace, civic duty and individual responsibility, pleasure and prudence, freedom and self-control. Her diary, indeed, stands out as something of a triumph of dedication, discipline and self-taught sensibility. It also stands as a tribute to Mass-Observation, the organisation that both gave Nella Last the incentive and encouragement to write and, by archiving her writing, assured it an unanticipated permanence, to the benefit and for the pleasure of later generations.

FEBRUARY 1953: HELPING THE VICTIMS OF FLOODS

On the night of 31 January–1 February 1953 there were monster storms in parts of the British Isles (and elsewhere, especially the Netherlands). A car ferry went down off the coast of Northern Ireland and 128 people lost their lives; there were also over 300 other deaths as a result of the massive floods that night, almost all of them in settlements in, on or near the Thames Estuary and in coastal areas of East Anglia (Essex and Norfolk were very hard hit). 'Thousands were rendered homeless,' according to the *Illustrated London News* of 7 February (p. 193), 'and from every quarter of the flooded districts poignant stories were recorded. Some were drowned in cars on the roads, dead were found on roofs or caught in trees, and families were marooned in flooded houses, crouching in lofts and upper storeys in their night attire. Public services were disrupted and fear of epidemics was an added anxiety.' Some 32,000 people were flooded out of their homes.*

This was a major disaster, and it summoned up the sort of relief efforts that Britain had witnessed a dozen years earlier. 'It is "like the war all over again"', wrote Tom Driberg in the *New Statesman* (7 February, p. 141), 'not only because of the troops, but because of the spirit of comradeship and hospitality among the thousands of voluntary workers who have "mucked in" – the hotel-keepers and yachtsmen at Burnham-on-Crouch who have looked after evacuees from Foulness and cooked meals day and night,

---

*A succinct account of these floods is presented in David Kynaston, *Family Britain, 1951–57* (London: Bloomsbury, 2009), pp. 257–9. At Barrow's WVS Club meeting on 2 February 1953 'quite a number wondered if "H and atom bomb trials could possibly be the cause of the high tides"' that had inundated some coastal areas.

the boat-builders who have crossed to the islands dozens of times every twenty-four hours bringing off boat-loads of the homeless, the ladies who have made the Royal Corinthian Yacht Club a model rest-centre.' Help also came from more distant places, including Barrow-in-Furness; women there threw themselves into work that was highly reminiscent of some of the wartime efforts of the Women's Voluntary Services. Nella's diary for the first half of February testifies to the aid organised in Barrow for the unfortunate victims elsewhere.

Tuesday, 3 February. I didn't feel so well and my face ached badly. The thought of all the homeless cold people in the flood areas haunted me. I packed a pair of shoes I can do without, some shirts Cliff once sent, two old but well mended vests of my own and two of my husband's, some underpants with worn knees – I cut and machined a hem and made them into shorts – and packed a little cretonne bag I made with a drawstring with a few sylkos, cotton, darning wool and the necessary needles. I'd the good heart to pack up nine-tenths of my clothes, but they will have to do me much service yet, before I can part with them. I'll send 5s to the Mayor's Fund, and more if I can scrounge it out of my housekeeping. I can never interest my husband in giving anything away. He wouldn't have parted from his old underwear if I'd asked him … [*Later*] Mrs Atkinson came in and said, 'I've a big pile of things if you will pack and send them off for the flood victims'. I said I would, and stared at the two big armfuls she brought, costumes, coats, overcoats and suits that had belonged to a brother of Mr Atkinson's who died last year, and shoes of her own and Norah's.

Wednesday, 4 February. A ring brought me to the door, where a strange young woman stood smiling. She said, 'Will you put these children's rubber boots and clothes in your parcel? Someone told me you would be sure to be sending something for the flood victims or would take them to the WVS office.' Then for the rest of the morning phone calls to ask if parcels could be brought or if I'd pack things and send them, and rings at the door with parcels, till before lunch my front sitting room looked like a second-hand shop! I'd soup, and stewed rabbit enough, and cooked sprouts and potatoes, and we finished with a cup of tea. I planned to relax a while when my husband went to lie down, but there was no rest for either of us – more knocks, rings and phone calls. I wondered wildly wherever I'd get paper and string to pack all, and thought of the sugar sacks I once bought off my grocer, and rang him to see if he would let me have some – they are doled out sparingly to people on a list usually, and he isn't a really pleasant man. I felt it just another part of my odd day when he *gushed*, '*Certainly*, Mrs Last. How many will you have? It will be a pleasure to send you as many as you want. Would you like some today?' I said, 'Well, I think I could get them in four of those small sacks or three of the larger ones'. He said, 'I'll send what I have and you must let me know later if you want more'. I went over all, and stitched all buttons on even if they were not a perfect match, and did little repairs.

My husband came down and when he saw what I was doing he offered to clean and polish all the shoes, and we will get some laces to replace worn ones. I asked everyone to spare odd bits of flannel and toilet soap, needles, cotton and mending wool, and packed them in little bags, if only paper ones. We were both tired by the time I made a late tea. There was a notice in the local *Mail* tonight saying the [*WVS*] office would be open every day this week for gifts, so perhaps people will send them there. Mrs Higham has a lot of oddments left at her house. There was toast and cream cheese, Turog[†] bread and butter and cake for tea, and it was nearly 7 o'clock before I rose to clear the table and wash up. I felt a bit tired, but unravelled two good home-knitted sock legs and two big balls of darning wool. Mrs Higham said she had a huge pile of goodish socks if they were darned.

Thursday, 5 February. Another hectic day. I got four sacks packed neatly, folding and packing tightly all garments in an effort to avoid crumpling, if not creasing. I decided that any more things could go down to the WVS office, for big sacks have been provided from Regional. We went to Dalton for the meat. I left a note pinned on the curtain to say, 'Back about 11 o'clock. Parcels of clothing for WVS can be left in garden or at no. 7.' ... We went into town when we returned from Dalton, the back of the car piled high with some quite good car rugs, a big old blanket that could be torn into babies' blankets, nappies tied up in a bundle, little woolly coats, little boys' clothes and some elderly women's clothes that had a note pinned on to say 'Call in later if these are suitable – have lots more of mother's clothes' and the name of a neighbour in the road behind whose mother died recently. The scene at the office was a surprise, even though I'd expected a good response – looked as if there would be a van load when packed. We stayed. I'd have stayed over lunch time, but said Mrs Higham and I were coming down with a car load of things she had collected and took back an armful of pants, feeling really scornful of a woman's mentality who would send pants without buttons enough for decency, never mind use. I pictured a distraught man who felt hopeless and lost being handed pants with one button on the flies, and felt a 'Bad end to you' to the thoughtless person who sent them.

Friday, 6 February. We took parcels of clothes to the WVS. I

longed to join the busy workers, sorting and packing. There's
such a different atmosphere since merry capable little Mrs Woods
took over, and she has nice helpers. Never was there so friendly
a feeling. When old Mrs Manson and Mrs Howson were Clothing Officer and Deputy someone was always offending one or the
other. Such good garments have been sent in, two quite wearable
fur coats amongst the pile on the counter. Miss Willan asked
if Mrs Higham and I could collect one night next week at the
Odeon – most of the picture houses are having a Relief Fund collection. She asked in my husband's hearing and he said, 'Of course
you must go'. So I took him at his word! …

I'd more buttons to sew on, and more clothes came in. They
have had such a wonderful response at the [WVS] office they are
keeping open till 8.30 each evening. It's such a small place to
work in. The Railway van calls each day. Everyone is so eager to
help. Collections at rugby and soccer matches tomorrow, dances,
collections at others and efforts in every direction. The Round
Table are canvassing for money if no clothes are available. In
Barrow we won't have much coal for a few weeks. Householders
are asked in an article in the *Mail* to 'use other available fuel,
including nutty slack', as our supplies will be diverted to the
East Coast. I scrambled eggs and made toast and there was Turog
bread and butter and greengage jam and cake. I kept wishing I
could have been at the WVS office helping. When I looked at
them working so cheerily my mind went back to wartime, when,
whatever our worries and anxiety, there was 'always tomorrow'
… I thought wistfully as I sat sewing I'd have liked to recapture,
however slightly, that comradeship.

There was a ring and Mrs Higham's voice said, 'I'm down at
the office. Mrs Woods is off to London tomorrow to help with
clothing. Will you lend her your [WVS] overcoat?' I couldn't

refuse, and she is a very dainty person, but I *don't* like wearing anything of anyone else's, and that goes for my own that anyone else has worn. She will be away four days at least. I'll have it cleaned when she returns it, and wear my WVS suit for collecting at the Odeon. I felt mean to have that 'shrinking', but it's one of those things that, if you have it, it's as much a part of you as the colour of your hair. Mrs Woods came just after 9 o'clock. I'm only about 5 feet 1½ inches* – in my shoes – and she is nearly half a head less! Still, shoulders and sleeves were all right. She said, 'Never mind it being too long. It will be warmer for travelling. Thank you *so* much, and I've already borrowed Miss Willan's dress. It's good of you both to lend them. I'm so fussy. You are the only two WVS I'd have liked to wear anything belonging to.' I felt I chuckled as I realised there were others as odd as myself! She is a merry little thing and laughed as she told of her rush to get ready. I said, 'Your husband doesn't mind you going, then?' She said, 'Dear me, why should he? I'm only going for a few days, and he knows enough to look after himself if all is in the house. He's not a child.' I didn't glance across at my husband, knowing darn well the fight I'd have had to put up, and if I'd insisted on going, the reproaches and recriminations, the feeling of guilt that spoiled enjoyment. I felt she didn't realise how lucky she was.

The next day she and Will drove to Spark Bridge to pick up some clothes that Aunt Sarah had collected. Her 'bundle was a bit old-fashioned, but there was a good thick cape with a hood, and a grey homespun suit of Joe's I've remembered for years. All had a sweet musty smell. Wood smoke, lavender and smoke of tobacco struggled with the sweetish smell of stored

---

*Will, for a man, was even slighter than Nella: he was 5 feet 3 inches in height and weighed 8 stone 8 pounds (8 June 1951).

apples, for Aunt Sarah has all her boxes and oddments in the attic. In two black bodices she had stitched white frills in the necks, crisp and freshly starched and ironed. I wondered if there were any old dear who *would* wear them – women like herself who had stayed still as regards fashions.'

Sunday, 8 February. A ring took my husband to the door as I was dressing. I heard an oddly pitched voice saying something about 'Looking for a little WVS lady who lives hereabouts', and felt a bit surprised to hear my husband asking him in. When I went into the living room a huge young fellow rose and said, 'Good morning, ma'am. I'd like your advice about some clothes I have for the flood folks.' We began to talk. He is in one of the small flats made from several of the big houses on the main road into which our small road runs. I'd have said he was an American with his slow drawl, but he is a Canadian, working just now in the Yard. I said I'd gladly take charge of them, thinking, 'I'll ring up Miss Willan and get her to send up for what I have if she wants all down before we get the car back.' He went and then I heard a car, and looking out saw a huge low-slung grey car with two young men in. The boot was opened and a very large parcel lugged out. The one who had called said, 'These are mostly boots, ma'am, but wrapped in a heavy coat to keep them together'. Before I could say 'Thank you – leave it in the hall there', his companion appeared from the open car door with his arms full of rugs, coats, suits and bright plaid hip-blouse† things Canadians wear. When they had finished I felt a bit dazed as I looked at the huge pile, women's clothes amongst them. I said, 'How *generous* of you to spare all these marvellously warm garments', but the friend in a curious 'Hush your mouf' honeyed tones gave me to understand it was a relief to be rid of them. They had brought all as a matter of course and realised they 'would be a real "noosense" and expensive to store or tote round', and left me with the impression *I* was doing them a favour! ...

I had a rest on the settee after my husband went to lie down and then mended socks and put some elastic in two good pairs of corsets. I felt they would be better than with an ordinary lace, giving a wider fit. They are both made to measure corsets, only needing a bit of repair, but I wouldn't have insulted anyone by offering them before I soaked and scrubbed them. When I think of the giver I marvel – so beautifully turned out whatever she wears. I've heard her boast she can '*Never* use any other than Elizabeth Arden toilet requisites' and 'I *never* buy anything off the peg. I am so particular about fit and cut.' Yet I lightly touched them as I poked the sleazy greasy things into hot Tide suds!

The next day, 'Shoes and scarves and some good little pants and shirts came in a parcel from my brother – none needed any attention – but I made some garters from oddments of elastic in the parcel ... When I was talking to Miss Willan over the phone, she said 327 huge cigarette cartons and parcels nearly as large had just gone. The Railway man had been "staggered" and had had to make several trips.'* On Tuesday the 10th 'I packed the last of the oddments ready to go to the WVS office, and then had a rest on the settee after taking a codeine.' By end of the week the rush was over for Nella and the other ladies of the WVS, who had been kept uncommonly busy for nearly a fortnight, re-experiencing some of the solidarities of wartime.

---

*British Railways and the Post Office were delivering relief parcels free of charge.

GLOSSARY

Allenburys Diet	a fortified, dry, milk-based nutritional supplement
Arab	someone wandering, unsettled (referring to Cliff)
backened	retarded, put back
bank	to build up a fire with a tightly packed fuel so that it burns slowly
basque	continuation of a bodice slightly below the waist
cachous	lozenges to sweeten the breath
Chypre perfume	heavy perfume made partly from sandalwood
conchie	slang for 'conscientious objector'
cornflour shape	a blancmange, or milk pudding, mould
counterpane	bedspread
crall	to behave obsequiously or abjectly
crock up	break down
crying jag	intense period of crying
cut	hundredweight (112 lb)
diamanté	given a sparkling effect by means of artificial gems
dibble	a pointed instrument for making holes in the ground for bulbs, etc.
Disprin	painkiller, sedative
Directive	questionnaire sent by M O to its volunteer Observers
dollies	stuffed dolls made from scraps of fabric

embrocation	liniment
Esse	range cooker
faddy	concerned with trifles, fussy
fairings	presents bought at a fair
Fynnon	brand of salts, for rheumatism
gat	firearm
gertcha	expression of disbelief
gormless	slow witted, lacking sense
hip-blouse	shirt designed to hang out
inaffectedly	without artifice
ITMA	*It's That Man Again*, a very popular radio comedy programme, starring Tommy Handley
jankers	punished with confinement/ imprisonment
kapok	silky fibre used to stuff cushions, etc.
keening	lamenting
kern baby	doll/image decorated with grain, flowers, etc. at harvest time
machine	to work on a sewing machine
macédoine	mixture, medley
Mail	*North-Western Daily Mail*
marrons glacés	chestnuts coated in sugar or syrup
Marshall Aid (Plan)	American financial assistance to Europe announced in 1947, implemented from 1948
marshmallow	shrubby herb with pink flowers
mealies	corncobs
mugs	fools, gullible people
nowty	moody, sullen
offcome/offcomer	outsider

paddy	fit of temper
pawky	artful, shrewd
petersham	heavy ribbed cotton or silk used for strengthening
Phyllosan (tablets)	a vitamin and iron supplement; it 'fortifies the over-forties', it claimed
pies	heap (of turnips) covered with earth and/or straw for protection
proud	overgrown
purdah	women screened from men by a veil or curtain
rills	rivulets, small temporary channels formed after heavy rains
Rogue Herries	a central character in the historical fiction of Hugh Walpole (1884–1941) which was set in Cumberland
roundsman	man who makes deliveries and takes orders from customers
Sanatogen	restorative tonic
scrattling	making difficult progress
screw (noun)	small quantity wrapped in a twisted piece of paper
Serocream	a synthetic whipped cream
shippens	cattle sheds
simnel	rich fruitcake made partly with marzipan; usually eaten at Easter
slack	inferior coal
spiv	someone shady, unscrupulous
stopcock	valve for regulating the flow through a pipe of a liquid or gas
suited	made agreeable

swale	shady place
Sylko	sewing thread
titfer	hat
Turog bread	wholemeal bread ubiquitous in the North of England
ulster coat	long loose overcoat of rough cloth
union suit	single undergarment for the trunk and limbs
wee man	fairy, spirit
whims and whamseys	fanciful, capricious ideas
whin	gorse bush
wrack	wreckage, flotsam
WVS	Women's Voluntary Services
Yard	Vickers-Armstrongs shipyard in Barrow

MONEY AND ITS VALUE

In the early 1950s, British currency was calculated in the following manner:

   12 pence = 1 shilling

   20 shillings = £1

   One shilling was written as 'is', a penny as 'id'. A farthing was a quarter of a penny. A sum of, say, two pounds and four shillings was usually written at that time as £2–4-0 or £2/4/0; such an amount is presented in this book as £2 4s 0d.

Efforts to propose modern monetary equivalents are rarely helpful. Rather, it is more useful to keep in mind that Nella's housekeeping budget at this time for one week was £4 10s 0d, and from this sum she had to pay for such sundry items as medications, periodicals and bus fares as well as make her purchases of meat, fish and fresh and processed food, not to mention the shilling a week that she bet on the football pools. Her husband seems to have been responsible for maintaining the car. Nella's household had little leeway for luxuries, especially with Will now retired. They rarely (for example) ate out in the early 1950s, except on food they brought from home.

CHRONOLOGY

The diversity of English life in the early 1950s is richly portrayed in two books by David Kynaston, both of which have impressively panoramic perspectives: *Austerity Britain, 1945–51* (London: Bloomsbury, 2007), especially Part 3 of 'Smoke in the Valley', which is now available as a separate paperback; and the first third of *Family Britain, 1951–57* (London: Bloomsbury, 2009). For a concise and informative survey of the eight or nine years after 1945, see Andrew Marr, *A History of Modern Britain* (London: Macmillan, 2007), Part 1 and the first thirty pages of Part 2.

1950

January	UK recognises Communist China
	Soviet Union boycotts UN Security Council (until mid-summer)
February	Narrow Labour victory in general election; Clement Attlee continues as Prime Minister
May	Petrol rationing ends
June	North Korea invades South Korea
July	United States acts through the United Nations to resist North Korean military advances
	Churchill warns of a third world war
	Soap rationing ends
August	Major increases in UK defence estimates
September	US/UN counter-attacks in South Korea, forcing North Korea to retreat
	British troops fight in Korea

	National Service extended to two years
October	UN and South Korean forces cross the 38th parallel, the boundary between North and South Korea, and capture Pyongyang, the North Korean capital
November	George Bernard Shaw dies
	UN forces move further north
	Chinese troops enter the Korean War, pushing UN forces southward
December	Talk of the possible use by the US of atomic bombs in Korea (continues into 1951)
	Marshall Aid suspended
	Chinese troops cross the 38th parallel

1951

January	Attlee announces major increase in military spending over three years; reservists called up
	Meat ration reduced
January–May	Fighting continues in Korea around the 38th parallel
February	Iron and steel industries nationalised
April	US General Matthew Ridgway replaces US General Douglas MacArthur as commander of UN forces in Korea
	Ernest Bevin, post-war Labour Foreign Secretary, dies
May	US tests components for a hydrogen (fusion) bomb
May–Sept	Festival of Britain
July	Negotiations begin to end the war in Korea
October	Conservatives win general election; Winston Churchill becomes Prime Minister

1952

February	George VI dies; his successor is Elizabeth II
April	Sir Stafford Cripps, prominent Labour politician and post-war Chancellor of the Exchequer, dies
May	De Havilland Comet, the world's first jet airliner, enters commercial service
October	Tea rationing ends
	Test explosion of Britain's first atomic bomb
November	US tests world's first hydrogen (fusion) bomb
	Dwight D. Eisenhower elected President of the United States
December	Great London smog; some 4,000 people die from respiratory problems

1953

February	Over 300 people die in floods in Eastern England
March	Joseph Stalin, Soviet dictator, dies
	Iron and steel industry denationalised
April	Road transport denationalised
	Structure of DNA disclosed by researchers at Cambridge
May	Ascent of Mount Everest by Edmund Hillary and Tenzing Norgay
June	Coronation of Elizabeth II
July	Korean armistice signed
September	Sugar rationing ends

EDITING NELLA LAST'S DIARY

While the main task for editors of Nella Last's manuscript diary is to select what to publish and to shape these selections into chapters, there are several other ways in which we have exercised judgement and revised what she wrote. The following are the most important of these editorial interventions. (1) Since Nella did not use paragraphs, wherever they now exist they are our creations. (2) Her punctuation was casual, often whimsical. (Mis-punctuation is a common feature of MO diaries, indeed, of most diaries whose authors lacked the time or incentive to revisit what they had written.) We have routinely re-punctuated her writing to make it as clear and smooth-flowing as possible. (3) Obvious errors – she almost certainly wrote in haste, and usually at night – have been silently corrected. These include misspellings and phrases that lack a necessary word, such as a preposition, article or conjunction. (4) Very occasionally an additional word is needed to convey the meaning of a sentence. In these rare cases we have silently supplied a suitable candidate. (5) We have standardised the usage of particular words in order to ensure, for example, that a word is always spelt the same, or that it is consistently capitalised or not capitalised, and that the prices of goods and services and other numerals are presented in a consistent form. (6) Nella was much given to underlining words for emphasis and to putting a great many words and phrases in inverted commas. We have eliminated these practices except in cases where they are helpful or even essential to grasping her full meaning, such as when she is reporting words actually spoken by others or when she had chosen language that was regarded as colloquial or not

Housewife
60?
24/2/80

Mrs Nella Last
9. Ilkley Rd - 6 MAR 1950
Barrow - in - Furness
Friday night

It was so cold & wild this morning. We learned
that Labour had got in for Barrow - as was expected - & that the Liberal candidate had forfeited his
deposit. I felt I hoped more had done, but was
not prepared for the large number who did! My Arthur
& son came in & discuss the election. Neither of us felt
like Friday morning & our busy round! In fact I did
very little. When I'd dusted & vac-ed. I machined a
big patch on a sheet. I'd previously fixed & then
made lunch. Good soup with shredded onion & raw
parsley today. Chops, turnip & potatoes, custard & dates.
I are felt so irritable about my pantry slopped up
lavatory through Mrs Salisbury dropping soap powders,
& in spite of many buckets of strong soda water,
& the 'nosey parker' wine. I couldn't clean it. &
in spite of the rain I said I was going down town
to get some caustic soda. My husband said he

yet in common usage. (7) Three dots are used to indicate omissions in a day's entry *other than* those made before a selection starts and after it concludes. Omissions at the start and the end of what she wrote on a given day are more the norm than the exception, for her first and last sentences are generally less interesting than what comes in between. Many entire days of her writing – and she wrote almost every day during these years – have been omitted altogether.

This may seem like a rather long list of editorial interventions. The need to make them stems in part from the fact that Nella had no reason to think that she should edit her own work, to polish or perhaps even to re-read what she had written. So her writing, while frequently rich and robust, tends to be raw. The photograph on the previous page shows a page from her handwritten diary from Friday 24 February 1950 and gives a sense of the decisions that any editors would routinely have to make in converting her handwritten diary into pages suitable for a book.

MASS OBSERVATION

Mass Observation,* which was set up in 1937, was created to meet a perceived need – to overcome Britons' ignorance about themselves in their everyday lives. MO aimed to lay the foundations for a social anthropology of contemporary Britain. Given that so many basic facts of social life were then unknown – opinion polling was in its infancy, social surveys and field studies had just begun (with a few exceptions, such as those of London by Charles Booth in the late nineteenth century) – how, it was asked, could the nation's citizens adequately understand themselves? This lack of knowledge was thought to be especially pronounced with regard to the beliefs and behaviour of the majority of Britons: that is, those who lacked social prominence, and who had little political or intellectual influence.

It was vital, according to MO's founders, to focus on norms, customs, routines and commonalities. The goal was to help bring about a 'science of ourselves', rooted in closely observed facts, methodically and (sometimes) laboriously collected. And in order to pursue this science of society, MO recruited hundreds of volunteer 'Observers', who were asked to describe, to pose questions to others, to record sights and sounds, and sometimes to count. Their efforts at observing were likened to those of an anthropologist working in the field. One of the early publications that drew upon these findings was a Penguin Special from early 1939

---

*Mass-Observation dropped the hyphen from its name in 2006, thus becoming Mass Observation. We have chosen in this appendix consistently to adopt the current usage, except when the hyphen is used in book titles.

written by MO's two leading lights, Charles Madge and Tom Harrisson, *Britain, by Mass-Observation*, which attracted lots of attention at the time.

Volunteers were crucial to MO. Without them it would not have been possible to acquire the facts on which a proper social science would have to be based. And it came to be accepted by MO's leaders that these Observers would not only be data-collectors; they could also function as 'subjective cameras' that captured their own experiences, feelings and attitudes, and circumstances of living. This acceptance of the legitimacy of subjectivity in MO's enquiries was a major reason why diary-keeping came to be promoted as a promising vehicle of both social and self-observation. A diary was one way of recording; and it was a way that inevitably tapped into the individuality and inner life of one personality. MO's striving for a better social science, then, facilitated the production of a particularly personal form of writing; and from late August 1939, with another great war imminent, some people responded to MO's invitation to keep a diary and post their writing regularly (usually weekly, fortnightly or monthly) to MO's headquarters. Nella Last was one of the dozens – eventually hundreds – who responded to this initiative. She was, though, one of the few who wrote regularly during the war and continued to write regularly after 1945 – and her diary entries were unusually detailed.

These diaries – some 480 of them – have been held since the 1970s in the Mass Observation Archive at the University of Sussex. Numerous books have drawn upon these riches. Sandra Koa Wing (ed.), *Our Longest Days: A People's History of the Second World War, By the Writers of Mass Observation* (London: Profile Books, 2008), is an excellent anthology of extracts from MO's wartime diaries. Dorothy Sheridan's edited volume *Wartime*

Women: An Anthology of Women's Wartime Writing for Mass Observation (London: Heinemann, 1990) includes extracts from numerous diaries. Simon Garfield has edited three collections drawn from the MO Archive, all published by Ebury Press: *Our Hidden Lives: The Everyday Diaries of a Forgotten Britain, 1945–1948* (2004); *We Are at War: The Diaries of Five Ordinary People in Extraordinary Times* (2005); and *Private Battles: How the War Almost Defeated Us – Our Intimate Diaries* (2007).

Nella Last's wartime MO diary was the first to appear on its own as a book, in 1981, and others followed, including Dorothy Sheridan's edited *Among You Taking Notes ...: The Wartime Diary of Naomi Mitchison, 1939–1945* (London: Victor Gollancz, 1985). Several other MO diarists have recently been published in volumes of their own. These include *Wartime Norfolk: The Diary of Rachel Dhonau 1941–1942*, edited by Robert Malcolmson and Peter Searby (Norfolk Record Society, 2004); *Love and War in London: A Woman's Diary, 1939–1942*, by Olivia Cockett, edited by Robert Malcolmson (Waterloo, Ontario: Wilfred Laurier University Press, 2005; 2nd edn, Stroud, Gloucestershire: The History Press, 2008); and three volumes edited by Patricia and Robert Malcolmson – *A Woman in Wartime London: The Diary of Kathleen Tipper, 1941–1945* (London Record Society, 2006); *A Soldier in Bedfordshire, 1941–1942: The Diary of Private Denis Argent, Royal Engineers* (Bedfordshire Historical Record Society, 2009); and *Dorset in Wartime: The Diary of Phyllis Walther, 1941–1942* (Dorset Record Society, 2009). James Hinton, who is preparing a history of Mass Observation, has recently published a stimulating account of some of MO's most interesting diarists: *Nine Wartime Lives: Mass-Observation and the Making of the Modern Self* (Oxford: Oxford University Press, 2010).

The Mass Observation collection is open to the public and is visited by people from around the world. In 2005 it was given Designated Status as one of the UK's Outstanding Collections by the Museums, Libraries and Archives Council. Much helpful information, including details of the Friends scheme that helps to finance the Archive, which is a charitable trust, is available on its website: www.massobs.org.uk.

ACKNOWLEDGEMENTS

Since this edition of Nella Last's writing builds on the work that we did in preparing *Nella Last's Peace*, almost all the debts we acknowledged there still apply, since advice and support provided up to 2008 has continued to be helpful as we moved editorially beyond the 1940s. Erin O'Neill of the BBC Written Archives has helped us on a number of matters, and we are very grateful for her well-informed advice. *Nella Last in the 1950s* has also benefited from suggestions and information kindly given by Peter Last, Joanna and Oliver Murphy, Kate Pearson of the Cumbria Record Office and Local Studies Library in Barrow, and Karen Watson, Jessica Scantlebury and Fiona Courage at the Mass Observation Archive. We are especially grateful to Catrina Hey at the University of Sussex for her excellent work in providing us with copies of Nella's voluminous writings; without her help our work could not have continued. We are also glad to acknowledge the support of Camilla Hornby, formerly of Curtis Brown, and Matthew Taylor, our copy-editor, who saved us from numerous errors and suggested several improvements, almost all of which we adopted.

Much of the praise given to the Mass Observation Archive is also praise for the work of Dorothy Sheridan, who headed it for many years and bears a major responsibility for its successes and the high regard in which it is held, and we are grateful for the assistance that she has given us, in various respects, during the past decade. Our editors at Profile Books, Daniel Crewe and Lisa Owens, have aided and advised us in all sorts of ways. We very much value their helpful comments on our work, their

suggestions for changes, and their enthusiasm for the richness of
the Mass Observation collection.

Cobourg, Ontario
June 2010

LIST OF ILLUSTRATIONS

(1) Nella and Will Last, and their dog Garry. Courtesy of Peter Last.

(2) The Lasts' elder son, Arthur, with his wife Edith and their sons, Peter and Christopher, around late 1952. Courtesy of Peter Last.

(3) The Lasts' younger son, Cliff, a sculptor in Australia. Courtesy of Peter Last.

(4) End of a shift at 'the Yard' © North-West Evening Mail.

(5) The exodus © North-West Evening Mail.

(6) The WVS in Barrow, February 1953 © North-West Evening Mail.

(7) Flooding on the Coast Road © North-West Evening Mail.

(8) Nella Last, Christmas 1958. Courtesy of the Mass Observation Archive.